SEE SAW

FINDING BALANCE THROUGH LIFE'S UPS AND DOWNS

A MEMOIR

By
Patricia Solaimanian

Published by
Hybrid Global Publishing
301 E 57th Street
4th Floor
New York, NY 10022

Manufactured in the United States of America, or in the United
Kingdom when distributed elsewhere.

Solaimanian, Patricia.
See Saw: Finding Balance Through Life's Ups and Downs: A Memoir
     ISBN: 978-1-957013-06-0
     eBook: 978-1-957013-07-7
     LCCN: 2021922971

Cover design by: Jonathan Pleska
Copyediting by: Wendie Pecharsky
Interior design by: Suba Murugan
Author photo by: Stephen Beal

To Iden

*And in memory of my parents, Gloria and Joe,
my first teachers of love and courage.*

See Saw

Each step taken
Brings a new day –
Ups and downs uncertain
But either way
I will be near.

When soaring high
I will catch you
When crashing low
I will pick you up

When too tired,
Sad, angry, or weak
And not wanting to speak –
I will listen,
And feel your love,

Take hold of my hand
Through each ride
Never alone—
Forever loved.

CONTENTS

Playgrounds have always held a mystery and magic for me. As a young girl I spent many joyful days at the 85th street Park in Jackson Heights, NY. There, I would play with my two older brothers, Mark and Ron, for hours. Some days the monkey bars were a jungle, where we would climb tall mountains, racing to the top. We would soar up on the swings to touch the clouds. My brothers took turns pushing me so I too could reach the sky.

Playing in the sandbox was my favorite place to be while at the playground. For it was there, inside the fenced-in box of sand, that I made castles and I was the princess living inside. My brothers preferred to walk along the top of the wrought iron fence, pretending to be the royal guards. And, oh yes, the seesaw! It was my nemesis on the playground.

My brothers enjoyed suspending me in midair and bringing me crashing down. I still can remember that sick feeling inside my stomach when the seesaw came banging down on the ground. When they felt like being nice to me, they would take turns balancing the two sides, finding that perfect place to balance. There was a tremendous sense of peace in not moving, just being. I knew that at any moment with just one little move, I could disturb the balance and be sent flying up in the air or come soaring down.

Anxiety took hold of me at a very young age. I realized at that moment that I would not be one seeking thrills and taking risks, but rather I would be perfectly happy living a life that was steady and in control. Little did I know that years down the road, I would

Iden, 2021 ©

be struggling to maintain balance and control in my life and in the lives of my family.

My story is about living with someone with bipolar disorder. It is not written to inform readers about the disorder, but rather to help those living with someone with the disorder. This is to let them know that they are not alone, and that the journey to practice self-care to remain well is difficult but necessary and possible.

Iden, Patricia, Claudia, and Elizabeth ©

CHAPTER ONE

CHANGES

"The secret of change is to focus all of your energy, not on fighting the old, but on building the new."

—Socrates

Waking up to cloudy skies and the start of another school year did not make me feel like getting up after a restless night of thoughts had kept me up until dawn. My youngest daughter, Claudia, ever present on my mind, kept me awake. At 23, she still behaved like a young teenager, unable to figure out her next move without constant guidance.

My oldest daughter, Lizzy, was currently living in Boston and about to make a move back to New York City. She needed emotional support to search for a new apartment and a new job.

Iden, my ex-husband, was a threat to any long-term happiness I might have had because of his mental imbalance due to his bipolar disorder.

First days in a new school year always brought on some jitters, no matter how many years I had been teaching, but I felt an overwhelming sense of anxiety and was having trouble catching my breath. I needed to get up and walk around my small studio apartment to settle my thoughts. Going through my morning routine of yoga and meditating didn't help to quell my nerves.

Besides my family's issues troubling me, Stephen, my boyfriend of almost five years, was also presenting a problem. I was unable to say what I truly felt without creating an argument if he disagreed. I was approaching a crossroads of change, one that had been coming on for a long time, but it finally crept up on me like the darkness on an early-winter night.

After trying to shake off the troubling thoughts, I made coffee to fuel myself through a powerhouse day. First priority was walking my much-loved dog, Mimi. Mimi is my 15-year-old Shih Tzu-Maltese mix who follows me around and gives me loving looks. She even laughs when she knows I need her to, and she knew today was one of those days.

Next on the agenda was to head into work. I had just retired from teaching after 30 years. During a long summer vacation, I realized that the stability of work was important in keeping me grounded, so I decided to work a few days a week as a substitute teacher. I wanted to try working in a different field, but I wasn't ready yet to make the change with so many other things going on. The need for something familiar was important.

I had been married to Iden for almost 30 years and separated for five years when I finally filed papers for divorce. I was no longer a wife or a daughter since both my parents had recently passed away. My relationship with my daughters had also changed over the years, and I missed the closeness we once had together. The one constant relationship I had was with my Mimi, and her love was steadfast.

I was in a committed relationship with Stephen whom I loved, but unfortunately, he wanted more than I was capable of giving at that time. I was in limbo as to who I was, what I wanted to be, and what I thought I should be. My conversations to myself were wearing me down. For now, I knew I didn't want to live with anyone, and living alone was an adjustment, but one that I slowly accepted and felt good about. I now had quiet nights with Mimi lying next to me snoring while I read, which settled me into a peaceful sleep. I was transforming a life of doing for everyone into doing more for myself, which was a very difficult change. I was learning to accept the change, and it was beginning to feel good, even if it brought some feelings of guilt.

Though the last few years were difficult, I was able to keep myself together on the outside, although I was a complete mess on the inside. There were days I felt as if I had it all together and days when I didn't. I felt moments of happiness when I could clearly see my future and I felt committed to those plans. On those rare days I felt everything was in divine order. How wonderful it would be if I could feel that way more than just once in a while.

The last few years had been troublesome due to my parents aging and ill health. My mother, Gloria, who I loved very much and was at the center of my strength, fell and broke her hip, then soon after suffered a massive stroke. The stroke left her in a vegetative state for a few months and watching her life slowly leaving her body a little every day was very painful to witness. Each day after work I would visit her in a hospice in Jamaica.

My dad, age 93, was also experiencing health issues due to heart problems. Mom passed away in May 2015, and Dad's heart stopped beating four months later. It was a very sad time indeed, and not having parental love present as a source of constant support and love was tough.

After the deaths of my parents, I took time off work, but soon returned to my much-needed routine. The smiling faces of the young students I taught lifted my sadness and gave me a reprieve from my thoughts. Teaching was the powerful glue that kept me together.

I still grieved the loss of my husband, even though he was still alive. He was my best friend and I still loved him very much. Our friendship started in college and blossomed into a love affair that lasted decades. As the years went by, his mental illness created space, distance, and dysfunction that I could no longer tolerate and, therefore, I had to walk away from our marriage.

After a sleepless night I was not sure I had the energy to get through a day of teaching, but I had already committed to working and I did not want to disappoint the teacher for whom I was subbing. As I walked to the subway, I called Stephen to exchange our morning hellos. I always needed a morning talk, a connection to validate that I was loved. I almost always felt lonely, especially since the passing of my mom.

"Hey," I said.

He asked where I was, and I said I was heading into school to sub for the week for a teacher who was out sick.

Stephen listened and then he said, "I thought you weren't going to be teaching anymore."

He agreed I should work, but he insisted that I should look for work someplace else, namely Metuchen, New Jersey, where he lived. I heard those words and my stomach tightened. He wanted me to move in with him and had often said if I truly wanted to, I would have found a way.

My grief needed to be healed and I needed to make peace with my past to enjoy living in the present. I needed space to do that.

"Do you want to be a Queens girl forever?" he asked.

I had thought of moving into Manhattan, but rents were very expensive. I had lived in Queens most of my life, and Forest Hills was a very comfortable, familiar place that I needed at this time. It was tiring trying to convince him of my need to stay put.

As I eased into a new life without parents, as a retiree, and living alone, it was important for me to be surrounded by familiarity, not strangeness. I didn't want any more changes. Trying to tell Stephen that was difficult because I knew he wanted to start a life together that was more than what we already had: weekends and a few vacation weeks.

I longed for days of waking up, walking Mimi, working out or going for a run, then returning home, making a pot of coffee, and typing away on my book.

Now that I was retired, it was my plan to finish a book that I had started many years ago. I did not want more have-to's in my life. Being selfish about what I wanted to spend my time doing was beginning to finally happen. It gave me a chance to start a new episode in my life that I happily embraced.

Stephen had all the qualities I needed and wanted in a man and he always professed his love by writing songs and playing them for me on his guitar. We had many things in common. We enjoy running and working out in the gym, reading, music, and travelling. Since we had been together, we had travelled to Europe and to many islands in the Caribbean. We constantly talked about other places we wanted to visit together in the future.

For the first time I had a partner I enjoyed having a physical relationship with. Sometimes I thought that the physical aspect is was what held our relationship together because it gave me the feeling of being loved. I loved Stephen, but I needed a life with myself right now more than a life with him. I understood those words were difficult for him to hear and were at the root of many of our arguments.

After the death of my parents, I moved a few times and finally settled into a lovely studio on a tree-lined block in Forest Hills. I sat with all my boxes and thought back to the time I had moved into my house with Iden and the girls.

Over the course of eight years, I went from a four-bedroom house to a two-bedroom apartment, and now to a studio apartment. I am a bit nostalgic but I feel I have arrived in a place where I can make a new beginning.

The apartment had many windows, which allowed both the morning and afternoon light to enter. I was excited to locate the right spot for my desk. It had to be near a window so I could have good natural light, and to see the trees and life outside as I finally continued writing my story. It was a story that needed to be written, not for anyone else necessarily, but one that needed to come out of me.

I once read that everyone has creative energy, thoughts, and ideas that come into our being, and they need to be acted upon and released. It is giving birth to ideas and beauty for no one other than oneself. This story is that need for me to tell, so I began putting, one word after another, my thoughts and feelings down on paper.

While I rode the train into work that day I thought of my conversation with Stephen. He had the ability to give me confidence to face my day and to say just enough to let me know he missed me and desired me. I walked to school, the same way I had for almost 30 years, but the walk on this particular day felt different.

I no longer had to be such a perfect teacher with detailed lesson plans, nor did I have any fears of having a lesson be observed unexpectedly by an administrator, which had become the new daily norm in schools.

The new school year brought about all the familiar smells and sights: the freshly painted walls, shiny waxed floors, and cleared bulletin boards on which another promising year of students' work will be displayed.

Today, instead of going straight home after work, I headed into the city to meet my brother, Ron, at a restaurant for our biannual lunch and catch-up. I loved walking the streets of New York City. The city made me feel alive with all its sights, sounds, and smells.

As I entered the restaurant, Ron greeted me from his usual table. The waiter immediately came and opened a bottle of champagne that my brother had requested. The attention and luxury immediately lifted my spirits. We looked at the menu, and I allowed Ron to order because he frequented the restaurant often. As we started on our appetizers, we chatted about my daughters and about Iden and Stephen.

When Dad passed away, I had stayed at his home in Florida, and when I returned to New York, I took some things with me that I thought my brothers might like to have. I had some old family photos and dad's gold wedding ring, which I thought Ron might want, and I brought them with me.

Forever present on my fingers were my grandmother's silver wedding ring, and my mom's gold wedding band, which were both constant reminders of their love. I thought perhaps Ron might want our dad's ring, so I handed it to him.

As we spoke and shared a meal together, I realized it was a familiar comfort that I had not had in a while. Ron was a philosophy professor, author, and more of a beatnik, and was only a few years apart in age from me. I valued his opinion and listened to his thoughts. And it was on this very day sitting in the restaurant that our conversation turned my life around.

After talking about finances, work, and my divorce and future plans, I took out some writing that I had started years ago while home with a back injury and going through a very difficult time in my marriage. The need to write was my medication to numb and release the hurt, anger, and disappointment in my life, which had then become unmanageable.

My unfinished story lay tucked away in a box, not forgotten, but ignored. After moving from place to place the story got shifted out of the box and onto my desk with the recent move. Like words set to a song that was never sung, my story was not heard, and I knew I needed to write it.

While finishing my meal over cappuccino and espresso ice cream, I asked Ron if he would mind reading a few pages. I wanted him to read it alone without me monitoring his facial expressions while he read, so I excused myself to use the restroom. When I returned, he was smiling and said that he liked my sense of voice, that it was captivating, and that he would love to read more. The response was sincere, and I knew he never held back, always saying exactly what he felt. Although sometimes the truth may hurt, there is always comfort knowing you can trust the words you hear.

Ron paid the bill, and as he walked me to the train station, we made plans to stay in touch. I boarded the train by Union Square and headed home to Queens. Digging deep into my bag I reached for my pen and notepad to write some ideas down that had already started popping into my mind. I needed new ideas on how to start my story instead of using old and familiar thoughts. Finally, I had a beginning. So I begin where my life changed — the day I met Iden.

CHAPTER TWO

THE BEGINNING

'How on earth are you ever going to *explain* in terms of *chemistry and physics so important a biological phenomenon as first love?*'

—ALBERT EINSTEIN

In 1978, I was a freshman at Queens College in Flushing, New York. I was not a purpose driven student, but I wanted an education and knew my academic strengths and weaknesses. Most of my course work involved reading and writing because I was considering a major in English, more specifically in creative writing.

I was 18 and starting college, not knowing much about the world other than Queens and New York City. I hadn't travelled much with my family or on my own. Just a Queens' girl then and now, and perhaps always. So how would I know who Khomeini was, or for that matter the Shah of Iran? And where the hell was Persia?

As I stood outside waiting for my class to begin, I looked up at the beautiful autumn sky and took in a deep breath. Nature always made my anxiety subside, and today I was feeling more nervous than usual with the start of my first college class, Drama 101.

I did some deep breathing and gave myself a pep talk, before I suddenly heard what sounded like gunshots, which startled me from my reverie. I walked around the building and saw several young men with white hoods over their faces chanting, "Death to the Shah." The demonstration frightened me, yet I was unable to move away. As I was staring into the crowd, a young Iranian student handed me a flyer. I grabbed it and shoved it into my backpack, as I ran into the building to find my class as quickly as possible.

After two classes I had a break, so I headed to the Student Union to get a cup of tea and to look over some notes from my prior class. Reaching into my bag to get my wallet to pay for my tea and muffin, I found the flyer that was given to me earlier that day. I read the flyer (which was written mostly in English) and, unbeknown to me at the time, in Farsi as well.

The flyer explained how there was a lack of democracy under the Shah of Iran, and that the citizen's wanted a new democratic system to replace him. I stared at the flyer trying to make sense of it and was also scanning the world map in my mind as to where exactly Iran was located. I took my eyes off the paper and looked up to see the same students handing out more flyers to other students as they walked into the cafeteria. A few of them were headed my way, so I decided to head to my next class to avoid those students and their mysterious dark eyes.

My next class was also in the same building near to the demonstrations, so I quickly ran in. The first-floor classes held mainly foreign students studying English in order to pass an entrance exam into the college. My drama class was in the theatre right next to one of these English classes, and all the students were out in the hall on a break.

As I waited for my class to begin, another student arrived and asked if I could watch his guitar while he used the restroom. I gladly agreed and stood with the guitar leaning on the theatre door. While waiting, I peeked into the windows of my classroom to look around at the stage, and when I turned around a student approached me and asked, "Do you play the guitar?"

I simply said, "No, " before he asked.

"Then why do you have a guitar?"

I told him it wasn't mine and then explained why I was holding it.

The owner of the guitar returned just in time to hear the student say that since he had left his country he had not played, and he missed playing very much. The owner of the guitar happily obliged his wish, opening up his guitar case and handing the guitar to him. A wide smile appeared on the young man's face. Taking the guitar in his hands ever so gently, he knelt down on the floor, balancing the instrument on one knee. His hair was black and shiny, and he had the same dark eyes that I had seen in the students handing out the flyers.

As he started to play, the music filled the halls, and all the students turned to see where the heavenly sound was coming from. Although it was only one guitar being played, it sounded as if there were at least three or four guitars being played all together. It was the most beautiful sound I had ever heard.

After he finished playing, the guitar owner asked the player the name of such a beautiful piece. "Romance d'Amour, " the young man replied. The two guitar players spoke for a bit and made plans to meet again. The guitar player spoke with an accent I had never heard before, so I asked him what country he was from?

"Iran. I am from Iran and my name is Iden."

As he stood up from his kneeling position, he asked me my name. "Patty, " I said, while looking directly into his dark eyes.

That first encounter on a September day in 1978 changed my life and it would never be the same again. The French have an expression for falling in love: "Coup de foudre, " meaning to be struck by thunder. Yes, I was struck by his deep sorrowful eyes, his artistic manner, his mysterious soul, and of course by his handsome face.

After our first meeting, Iden walked through the building halls looking for me; the girl with the guitar. My drama class met two times a week and it only took him a week or so to find me once again, waiting outside the theatre door for my class to begin. I always arrived early and kept myself busy reading a book, but one day as I glanced down the hall something pulled my eyes off the page. It was Iden. I wanted to return to my book but couldn't take my eyes off him. He came right up to me, saying he had been looking for me and was happy to see me again. A little embarrassed and not knowing how to respond, I just said, "Thank you."

After class we made plans to meet for coffee in the cafeteria. Although I enjoyed my class, I found it difficult to concentrate knowing that I was going to meet him. I didn't want to arrive too early at the cafeteria, so I walked slowly, thinking about the things we could talk about. I hoped he wouldn't ask me what I knew about Iran for fear of looking ignorant. Although, after seeing the demonstration, I did some research about the current political situation.

I found an unoccupied table near a window and opened my book, *Beowulf*, and started my assigned reading because I didn't want to look like I was anxiously waiting for him, even though I was. He entered the cafeteria from behind me, placing his hand on my shoulder.

He said, "I recognized you from behind because of your hair."

His touch upon my shoulder was one I will always remember.

Funny how some simple little actions endear our hearts and make us love someone. Iden asked what I'd like, and he soon returned with some tea, sugar, milk, and lemon — because he wasn't sure how I took my tea. He then cut the pound cake he'd ordered to share it evenly.

I thought the conversation would be a little awkward at first, but after the first few introductory questions and answers, the time just flew by. I missed my Spanish class and remarkably did not feel upset. He seemed to have a power over me that made me lose track of time. I felt that I was where I needed to be, and all over a single cup of tea.

From that day on, my life was very different. My relationship with Iden was like riding on a magical carpet. I walked on air and felt the sparks of love for the first time in my life. I no longer felt lonely or not listened to. He soon became my best friend. He was so intelligent, patient, artistic, gentle, and understanding. We did everything together. When we weren't together, we talked for hours on the phone. We took walks in nearby parks and talked, cooked Persian food, studied together, went to foreign movies in the city, and so much more. It was difficult for me to ever imagine a time that I would live my life without him.

As the months passed and I was busy studying, Iden was preparing to take the English exam for foreign students in order to begin his studies at the college. Although he already had a BA in Fine Arts from Tehran University, he was beginning new studies in computer science. He was an accomplished classical guitarist and had been at a musical conservatory with fellow friends and musicians in Iran before leaving it all behind when he relinquished that life to come to America.

The Iranian Revolution happened in December 1978, and Iden's dream of returning to Iran soon diminished. Iden had been raised in a Muslim home, and although he was deeply spiritual, he did not follow any strict Muslim religious rules. The future was uncertain due to the changes in his country. He knew he could not return to the current life in Iran, and the new life he was starting in America held many obstacles.

Queens College became our home. Iden had rented a new apartment close by, so whenever we had breaks between our classes, we were able to go to his place to rest and enjoy being in each other's arms. We were both inexperienced lovers and that was the beauty of our love. It was innocent and held the belief that everything would be just fine because we were young and hopeful. The world seemed balanced, although it was uncertain.

CHAPTER THREE

THE PARTY

'And I like large parties. They're so intimate. At small parties there isn't any privacy.'

—F. SCOTT FITZGERALD

After a few months of dating, Iden asked me to attend a birthday party for a family friend. He explained that Persian parties were a lot of fun, with music, dancing, a tremendous amount of Persian food, and plenty of tea and sweets. I thought it would be a good opportunity to meet some of his friends, learn a little more about the Persian culture, and about Iden as well. I gladly accepted the invitation with excitement.

Iden informed me that Persian women dress up very fancy, but I didn't need to if it was something I did not feel comfortable doing. As a student, I normally just wore jeans. We had never really gone anywhere that I needed to dress up, so he was surprised when I said I would actually love the opportunity to get a bit fancied up. Neither of us owned any party clothes, so we decided we'd buy something new to wear for the occasion.

That weekend I called my good friend Debbie to ask her if she had time to go shopping with me for a party outfit. We decided to meet at Blooming dale's, because she shopped there often and knew where to find everything, especially the sale items.

Debbie was more excited about finding a new outfit for me than I was. We looked at racks of dresses, slacks, skirts, and blouses.

After trying on a dozen or so outfits, a wrap-around skirt and a silky white off the shoulder blouse caught my eye. To make the outfit even better, both pieces were 50 percent off.

After completing our shopping, we had a bite to eat at a little French bistro near where I worked as a waitress. While we talked, Debbie asked many questions about Iden. She still had not met him due to our busy schedules, and by the way I was talking about him, she knew I liked him very much. She was somewhat like a sister to me and knew I had not dated much, so she wanted information about him to ensure I wouldn't get left with a broken heart.

Following lunch, we walked along Lexington Avenue and then rode the train back to Queens. I got off in Jackson Heights and she went on to Forest Hills. Before she exited, I gave Debbie a big hug and she told me to look pretty and have a great time. She also said to take a picture so she could see how I looked, but I think she was more curious to see the man whom I was falling in love with. As the doors closed behind me, I turned around and waved a long goodbye through the windows until the train disappeared into the dark tunnel.

I couldn't wait to get home so I could call Iden and tell him about my shopping day with Debbie. Everything I did and thought about I wanted to share with him first.

* * *

The day of the party arrived. It was the first day of spring, but the air was still cold and windy. I woke up early but decided to stay in bed a little longer. The night before I had worked late after a full day of classes and was feeling tired. Staying up late was always difficult for me, regardless of the event. I preferred to get up with the rising sun and head to bed early. The party started at 7 p.m., and Iden had already informed me that Persians never show up before 8 o'clock. He explained that it was a cultural thing, and instead of showing disrespect it was showing respect to arrive late.

The sun shone brightly into my room, and I enjoyed the warmth on my face as I thought about my new outfit, and how I was going to style my hair.

The smell of the coffee brewing and the hum of the vacuum cleaner were all loving familiarities of a Saturday morning created by my mother. I headed downstairs to the kitchen to have some breakfast and talk to Mom while she did the household chores.

Mom worked in a small boutique in Jackson Heights and put in long hours, cooked, and kept a house in impeccable order. How did she do it all? I admired and loved her so very much. As I came down the steps Mom turned off the vacuum to give me a big smile

"Good morning, beautiful!"

We moved to the kitchen, and I sat down at the counter while she poured us both a cup of coffee.

As Mom began making breakfast, we talked to catch up on things. I watched how she was preparing my favorite breakfast. Toasted Italian bread in a skillet with an egg inside had become my weekend breakfast treat. During the week I usually made do with just toast and coffee. She knew exactly how I loved to eat my eggs. Hard enough not to be running down the plate when you dipped your toast into them, but soft enough to allow the toast to get soft inside the yoke.

While Mom was cooking, I stared at her face, trying to ignore the signs of aging. To me, she was the most beautiful woman I knew. She had amazing style, always smiled, and made everyone in her presence feel important.

As I ate breakfast, I informed Mom about the party, explaining that I would be getting home late and not to worry. We enjoyed our Saturday talks together, especially when we were alone in the house. My oldest brother, Mark, was married and living in the city, and my younger brother, Ron, was attending college in Long Island. On Saturdays, my father always found a place to go to relax from his long week at work. But where did my mother go to relax on Saturdays? She was always the stronger one. She too would have liked to take a much-needed break, to get some relaxation and peace, but she never demanded it, nor resented those who did.

When I had finished breakfast, I told Mom I was ready to help with whatever needed to be done. I was happy to help her, but it also relieved some guilt, since I knew I had not been pulling my weight around the house. I also felt bad about going to the party and having fun while she was at home alone.

It was still chilly, but signs of spring were evident as I looked out the window from my desk, sipping my espresso. Small buds had started to grow on the trees. I smiled knowing the dogwoods and mimosa trees would soon be blooming. With that thought, I couldn't believe my first year of college was coming to an end.

Although it was exciting to know that I would be able to relax a bit, help my mom more, and work more to save for a vacation, I also felt nervous because I had no idea what to major in. I loved acting and reading and writing, but I kept hearing my father's voice inside my head, "And what will you do with that degree to earn a living"?

Mom ducked out to go the grocery store for a few things, so I had time at home alone. Being home alone was a real treat for me, so I decided to indulge myself by taking a long hot bath with lavender bubbles and washing and conditioning my hair.

I lied down for just a moment but was obviously more tired than I knew because the next thing I knew Mom was knocking on my door and saying, "Get up! It is already 4:30." I couldn't believe I had slept for over an hour.

Once dressed and ready, I gave myself a once over. I could hardly believe it when I looked at my reflection in the mirror. Just as I went into my closet to pull out a black jacket, Mom walked in. She looked at me and asked, "Have you seen my daughter?" We both laughed and she gave me a hug, saying I looked just beautiful. Mom put her hand into her apron and pulled out a gold bracelet and put it on my wrist. "I hope Iden appreciates what a beautiful young lady he has."

At 5:30, I still hadn't heard from Iden and was hoping all was okay, but then he called and said that he was running a little late. I told him to take his time and that I would meet him at 6:30. We were both excited to see each other.

Arriving early usually meant waiting, and I hated to wait, but I hated being late even more. My nervousness about being late compelled me therefore to always be early, and so I was destined to wait. In a time before cell phones it was difficult to know exactly when someone you were waiting for would arrive:6:30 meant 6:15 to me.

At 6:45, I saw Iden walking down the station steps and, noticing me, he waved. We embraced and kissed, and as I put my lips on his, I realized that something was different. He had shaved off his moustache, exposing his full upper lip. Kissing him without a moustache was like having a first kiss all over again. His lip was full, and it gave me quite a new sensation. "What made you do it"? I asked

"I needed a new look, " he said.

I told him how handsome he looked in his new black pants and gray madras shirt, and I couldn't help noticing how wonderful he smelled.

Iden told me how beautiful I looked, how proud he was to be able to walk into the party with me on his arm, and that he was looking forward to introducing me to his friends and family. We held hands and waited for the train to arrive.

By 8 o'clock we were in Long Beach, walking down Lincoln Avenue toward his friend's house. On the walk over, Iden explained a little about each of the friends whom I was about to meet. Apparently, some of the people attending the party had worked for the United Nations in New York when Iran had an embassy. The couple hosting the party were friends of Iden's family's, and they had been talking via telephone for a few months.

As we approached his friend's block, I noticed the beautiful Victorian houses with wrap-around porches and lovely gardens out front. I loved porches, and had always imagined having a house where I could sit and sip tea and read a good book.

When we arrived, the aroma of saffron and other Iranian spices came drifting outside. I could almost taste the flavor already. I had eaten Persian food before but had never visited a Persian family to share a home-cooked meal.

Iden rang the doorbell and his friend greeted us with a huge smile saying, "Salam, "and then hugged and kissed us both. As we entered, there was a huge winding staircase with a crystal chandelier hanging over the steps. The house looked like a mini palace. There were Persian carpets on the floors and walls, and furniture that I had never seen the likes of before. In the living room were sofas covered with heavy brocade material, and there were gold vases of flowers everywhere. On the table by the sofa sat a big tea samovar surrounded by platters of fresh fruit, dried fruit, nuts, and candies. I was in awe as I stood looking at the beautifully displayed food and found it difficult not to stare.

Many people sat in another room, eating and talking. Iden brought me a small cup of tea and some sweets. I sipped the tea and noticed he had put a sugar cube on the saucer. He showed me how to put the cube in my mouth and sip the tea, which was wonderful.

As I continued sampling the delicious spread, I took notice of the people, especially the women. The women were beautiful in an exotic way that I had never seen before. Their makeup was perfectly applied to enhance their eyes and full lips. Their clothes hugged their bodies, as if the clothes were designed just for them. Every part of the human body that could wear a piece of jewelry was adorned with an expensive piece. They wore diamond rings on their fingers, rubies in their ears, and gold bangles on their wrists. I thought my outfit looked inferior compared to theirs.

It was interesting to see Iden engage with his friends in a way I hadn't seen with our mutual friends. Feeling a bit out of place, I got up and walked into a smaller room near the living room. It was around 9 o'clock and I was hungry. Iden came in and said, "What happened to you? I was looking for you." He seemed lively and in good spirits. He was usually quiet, but I guess being surrounded by his friends speaking Farsi and listening to Persian music made him feel very comfortable, which was all very understandable.

We sat and talked with some of his friends, and soon I was very happy to now hear that dinner was being served.

I immediately went to the dining room, where large tables literally bulged with Persian food. There were trays of rice with herbs and saffron piled up high in mounds, stews with meat and vegetables, kebabs of chicken and beef, and salads made of tomatoes, cucumbers, and onions. I took a little of everything and grabbed a plate for Iden as well, thinking he was going to join me, but he was busy talking to his friends. Iden soon found me and had his plate filled to the top. I expressed how wonderful all the food was and that one day I would like to learn how to make some of these dishes too.

Around midnight, I was getting tired and felt like Cinderella needing to leave the ball. Iden wanted to stay longer even though most of the guests had already gone home. I understood that he was enjoying himself, but I reminded him that we had a long commute back to Queens and that the trains ran infrequently at this time of night. He informed me that one of his friends had offered to drive us home, which was good news for sure.

An hour later we piled into his friend's car. Iden and his friend sat in the front, and I sat with his friend's wife in the back. She didn't speak much English, so she sat and smiled at me while Iden and his friend spoke Farsi the whole ride home. We pulled up in front of my house and I said my good byes before Iden opened my door and gave me a hug and a kiss goodnight. I did not immediately go into my house, but stood looking up at the full moon, watching the little black car drive down the block.

I entered the house quietly so as not to wake my parents and headed straight into my room to get undressed, not bothering to hang up the outfit previously hung up with so much care. My mom came in and whispered, "Glad you are home safely, " and gave me a kiss goodnight.

As I lay my head on the pillow, I quickly reviewed the night in my mind. I did enjoy experiencing a Persian party but didn't feel that I was there with Iden. I was more of an observer, uncovering a little layer of a person that I was in love with.

* * *

THE DAY AFTER THE PARTY

The day after the party, the phone rang loudly at 7 o'clock in the morning. Our phone was located downstairs near the kitchen, and I was the one who usually answered it if I was at home. Although I was in a deep sleep, I got up and looked at my clock. I immediately thought something had happened to one of my brothers or another family member, since it was too early for a non-emergency call. As I answered the phone I heard, "Salam. How are you?" It was Iden. I thought something had happened to him and asked, "What's happened?" He told me to calm down and that everything was fine. He just couldn't sleep and wanted to know if I could meet him for breakfast at our go-to diner on Northern Boulevard.

"Great! See you in about an hour, " he said and hung up.

As I put down the receiver, I sat on the chair not knowing if I were dreaming or awake. Mom was already up and was in the basement when the phone rang. Even on a Sunday she was up early doing chores. When she came upstairs, she saw me sitting by the phone.

"Good morning. Why are you up so early?" she said.

I greeted her and explained that Iden had called and wanted to meet shortly for coffee. She looked at me and said with a smile, "I guess he missed you already."

I laughed and said that I would tell her all about the party when I returned. I was looking forward to having a leisurely Sunday at home with Mom, but as always, I was also excited to see Iden.

The diner was about eight blocks from my home, and I enjoyed the walk. As I entered, Iden was waving to me, drinking coffee, and talking to the waitress.

"Hey! Good morning! Thanks for coming." he said.

The waitress came to take my order. My stomach was still full from all the food I had eaten at the party, so I just ordered coffee and a piece of toast.

Iden seemed surprisingly energized given our late night and his early start to the day. He had a quiet manner and didn't usually do things so whimsically. He wanted to know if I enjoyed the party. I told him I'd had a lovely time, and that it was nice to meet some of his friends. He mentioned that one of his friends was a classical guitarist and suggested they could play together sometime. He missed playing and wanted to purchase a guitar so he could play again. I agreed, saying that it would be wonderful, since I knew from experience how beautifully he played.

We talked about some other things and spent an hour or so in the diner. I was tired, and although I was enjoying Iden's company, I would have loved to be back in my bed. Iden walked me home and I invited him in, but he said he had a lot of studying to do for finals. I kissed him goodbye and we gave each other a big hug. As he left, I watched him walk down the street. Something about him seemed so unfamiliar, even his walk.

As I entered the house through the side door, I could smell Sunday breakfast being cooked. No sooner had I planted one foot on the kitchen floor, than Mom yelled out, "Pancakes."

Although I wasn't hungry, I gladly accepted a plate because I was hungry to be around Mom's presence more than I was for the pancakes. We talked for a bit, and she asked me about the party, so I gave her all the details. She always listened, which made me feel validated and loved. After our chat, I told her I was going back to sleep and if she needed me to do anything, I would be happy to do it after I got up.

I must have slept way into the early afternoon and when I woke up, I checked my clock to see just how long it had been. It was 2o'clock! I got up and made my way downstairs and I could hear talking and laughing in the living room. I peeked inside and saw Mom, Dad, and Iden all sipping a tiny little cordial glass filled with vermouth. My eyes focused on the drink in Iden's hand because I'd never seen him drink before then.

Mom explained that Iden had called while I was sleeping, so she invited him over for Sunday dinner. I looked at Iden and all I could say was, "Hi!"

Dad went to a cabinet that contained a little bar inside with all kinds of glasses, liquor, and wine, and he poured me some vermouth as well. As a child I remembered how he poured soda into cordial glasses for my brothers and me when we had company to make us feel grown up.

We all chatted for a while before heading into the dining room to eat dinner, which was usually served by 3p.m. and no later. Our Sunday table had grown smaller over the years, with my grandparents passing away, uncles and aunts moving out of the city, and my brothers married and attending college. So it was usually just Mom, Dad, and me and an occasional friend, and now Iden too since we were dating.

My two brothers were not around much, so I think that Iden filled a void for Dad. Iden was also very happy to have this family time together and it made him feel less homesick, which made me happy as well.

When we'd finished dinner, Iden and I went to my room to talk before dessert was served. He said he had a little gift for me and handed me a book of poems by Omar Khayyam. He read some aloud for me and I thought that they were beautiful. Our desire for each other was present, but we just kissed since there was only a door between my parents and us. The kiss helped me feel a connection again to Iden.

Iden stayed a little longer before we said goodbye, for we both had schoolwork to do and we were both feeling tired. The previous late night had caught up to us. Since it was a lovely late afternoon, I walked with Iden to the 74th Street station. As we walked, we talked about the summer and hoped to have a small vacation after a long year of studies and work. He also mentioned he would like to go to Long Beach and walk along the boardwalk with me because he knew I loved the beach. He made me smile with those words.

Patricia and Iden in college days ©

CHAPTER FOUR

THE SUMMER OF 1979

'How sweet I roamed from field to field. And tasted all the summer's pride.'

—WILLIAM BLAKE

The spring semester finished, and like all young college students, plans for the summer were in the making. I wanted to do some traveling, but Iden was on a student visa, and we were limited to staying in the States because there was no Iranian embassy in America after the revolution.

As a young girl my family vacationed in the Catskill Mountains in upstate New York. The mountains were a familiar place for Iden since mountains surrounded his hometown in Iran. We both needed a break after a year of college classes and working. As long as I could be in nature, take some nice long hikes, eat good food, and have quality uninterrupted time with Iden, I would be very happy wherever we vacationed.

After driving a taxi for a year, I knew Iden would enjoy escaping the hectic scene of New York City to find some peace in the countryside. So after deciding to head upstate, I made a reservation at Blackhead Mt. Lodge. I had not been there in many years and returning with Iden made it exciting to share some of my past experiences with him. The owners of the lodge knew me very well since I went there throughout my childhood, and I even worked there as a waitress for a few summers when I was sixteen and seventeen. When I called to make a reservation, they were delighted to hear from me and looked forward to seeing me.

Iden had saved up some money and purchased a used brown Datsun B210. On the day after classes finished, we loaded up the car and made our way to the Catskills. We didn't have a working radio in the car, so we played tape cassettes of all kinds. We listened to classical guitar pieces, the Beatles, French music, and even some Iranian music, all of which Iden had brought with him from Iran. When the music wasn't playing, we talked about many things especially plans for our studies, and what we would like our future together to look like. Hearing us make plans for our future together made me feel hopeful for things to come.

After a three-hour drive, we exited the NYS Thruway on Exit 21 and made our way up the long and winding road to Blackhead Mt. Lodge. Iden automatically took in a deep breath and reached for my hand. "Thank you for bringing me here; it was just what I needed," he said.

The trees were lush and green and made a canopy over the road as we went up the mountain. As we entered the resort, I felt an extreme sense of joy being with him in a place that I loved.

We parked the car and went inside to find the owners, Wally and Eddie. They were both in the lodge's office and greeted me with big hugs as I proudly introduced Iden to them. We exchanged some information about my family and theirs and then we said we would catch up after dinner. They were busy at the moment, and we wanted to get to our rooms and relax.

We unpacked, and even though we wanted to rest, we were both hungry, so we quickly washed up and walked over to the main building, which held the dining hall.

The Catskills were home to many resorts that were owned and operated by families from many different nationalities. Blackhead Mt. Lodge was a German resort and served traditional German food. Memories of some of the food I had eaten there came back to me the minute I stepped into the dining room. I looked forward to having some, since German was not a cuisine that was served in my home.

We sat at a table by a window that looked out onto the mountains. It was a spectacular day, with bright sun and not a cloud in the sky. We read the menu and I was happily surprised to see that the menu had remained almost the same over the years.

Because Iden was unfamiliar with German food, I helped explain some of the dishes on the menu. We could choose from sauerbraten, bratwurst, or wiener schnitzel, all served with potatoes and vegetables. Although he was raised a Muslim and did not eat pork while living in Iran, Iden had developed a taste and liking for sausage. He ordered the bratwurst, and I ordered my favorite, the sauerbraten.

The lodge had a large outdoor wrap-around porch that faced the mountains, and since it was such a beautiful afternoon, we decided to finish drinking our coffee outside.

"Wouldn't it be great to have porch of our own where we could sit, drink our tea and coffee and talk"? Iden asked.

I agreed that it would indeed be lovely. Little did I know that we would have that porch one day, but it would go mostly unused because we never seemed to find the time or quietude to just sit and enjoy it.

After the heavy meal, we took a long walk down the road. We walked in silence, holding hands. It felt so good to be with him and I felt so connected and present. We were in the center of our own universe, living and loving each other.

Upon our return, we simply went back to our room, showered, and got into bed. We wanted to be in each other's arms and to feel each other completely. Our lovemaking was never intense or wild, but always honest and tender.

With a full belly and tired bodies, we slept until the moon shone through our cabin window. We were still full from lunch, so we skipped dinner and just made some tea with an electric kettle provided for us in our room. Iden had brought along his guitar, so he played a few songs while I read, and then we went to sleep, content and peaceful.

After a good night's sleep, we were both up early and took an hour or so walk before heading into breakfast. As we walked, we pointed out everything that caught our eyes. We also took notice of the sounds and smells around us as we walked. There was no need to talk to each other since we both felt we were communicating with life around us.

After an hour of walking we turned back to make it to breakfast before service finished at 9:30. By the time we returned to the resort, we were both hungry. As we entered the dining room we smiled because we could smell the bacon and freshly brewed coffee. Wally greeted us with, "*Guten Morgen*" (good morning in German), and showed us to our table.

While we waited for our breakfast, Wally sat with us and had coffee while we chatted and caught up on in our lives. When the waitress brought us our breakfast, Wally excused herself and said she hoped we'd have a wonderful day.

After breakfast we drove around looking for yard sales while enjoying the scenery. While we drove along in search of tables in front of people's homes displaying their goods, I started to talk about things that were on my mind. I had some concerns about my parents' relationship, my career decision, and our future together. Iden was a good listener, and he acknowledged my thoughts and feelings, although he didn't seem able to express what he was feeling. At times, I felt as if there was much he wanted to say but didn't. He was a bit of an enigma to me, and I was trying to peel away the layers around him in hopes of understanding him better.

After spending a few days roaming about in the Catskills, we headed back to the city. We felt relaxed and ready to get back to work and to attending summer school. Both of my parents did not attend college but were extremely proud that one of their sons earned a business degree and the other one was studying for his PhD in philosophy at Stony Brook University. After spending a year in college I still did not have any idea what I was going to major in, but I knew if I kept taking classes in things I liked and enjoyed, I would somehow find my way into a major. I too wanted to make my parents proud.

Iden was also taking summer classes, driving a taxi, and starting to do some small computer jobs for Persian businessmen he had met through his friends. We spent many summer days after classes picnicking in Kissena Park, going to movies, walking around in Central Park, listening to free concerts, and finding little bistros to have some inexpensive meals.

But of all the things we did during that summer, my favorite time together with Iden was when we went to Long Beach. We would pack a bag with blankets, lunch, and snacks and spend long hours lying in the sun, swimming, and walking along the shore picking up shells and other small treasures. Iden was always careful that I didn't get sunburned, so he would apply sunscreen for me, but never to himself. He thought because his skin was darker than mine, he couldn't get sunburned, but he did.

After a day at the beach, it felt like we were on a mini vacation. He looked so handsome with his dark eyes, dark wavy hair, and tanned, slim, but muscular body. A few times when we were in Long Beach, we went to visit his friends who lived there. We enjoyed our time together with his friends on those summer days much more than the night of the party, and I remember the days with much happiness and calmness. The waves rolled in and out and we were very much following the rhythm of the ocean. It was natural and peaceful.

We spent the entire summer this way and soon the sun began setting earlier and the nights became cooler. Registration for the fall semester came quickly and the carefree summer days were soon to end.

CHAPTER FIVE

GRADUATION

"To accomplish great things, we must not only act, but also dream, not only plan, but also believe."

— ANATOLE FRANCE

With the start of a new semester, I began to find my way in college. Helping Iden with his English led me in the direction of teaching English to non-native speakers of English. I declared my major in applied linguistics and focused on the TESOL (teaching English as a second other language) program. Since I always had a book in my hand and it seemed that writing was the easiest way I expressed myself, I also declared a second major in creative writing.

The years passed quickly because we were both busy with our studies and work as well. Iden was taking his last computer courses and they were very demanding in both class time and in study.

Back in the late 70s, there were no personnel computers, so in order to write a simple program, he had to use antiquated punch card machines that were located in the computer center. Each card represented a single code. To truly understand what that meant, in order to draw a simple Christmas tree, for example, it took over a thousand punch cards.

Iden had to spend hours in the computer center feeding punch cards into a main computer to complete his assignments. His intelligence and hard work were things I found very attractive.

He was able to handle advanced computer classes while working almost full time and keeping straight A's.

Through the help of some friends and family, Iden was given a Green Card, which allowed him to work legally in the United States. He started working for some small businesses doing computer work and only driving a taxi on the weekends. Iden soon moved to a new apartment in a lovely house. The house was so close to Queens College that it allowed us to come home in between classes. I helped decorate his new place with many items from my parent's garage that they no longer wanted. My parents were more than pleased to empty out their garage to help him settle into his new place. They were starting to grow very fond of Iden.

Slowly Iden's apartment started to feel like a home. We added a photo of us here and there and filled vases with fresh flowers weekly. We went to thrift stores and yard sales to find things to help decorate without spending too much money. After his Datsun B210 died, my father found a good used car for sale that Iden bought for a few hundred dollars. It was a 1972 blue Pontiac. It felt more like a boat than a car, but we were thrilled to have some wheels again to takes us away from Queens.

During spring, we were excited to be able to take spontaneous rides to Long Beach. Walking on the boardwalk and sitting on the benches breathing in the ocean air while listening to the waves breaking on the shore took away all our stress. Our relationship was deepening as we spent days studying, working, and enjoying leisure time together. Our conversations were constant and in search of learning more about each other. I especially loved learning about Iran and his family. The few times I spoke to his parents on the phone they sounded so sweet and gentle. His dad spoke French and I was able to have a little conversation with him using what I had learned in my basic French classes.

Over the years at college Iden had made some Iranian friends who had American girlfriends as well. Having an apartment that was nicely decorated gave us the opportunity to entertain friends. Iden constantly surprised me with his ability to cook delicious meals. Standing next to him while he cooked, I would imagine a life with him, and those thoughts made me extremely happy.

During that three-year period we were inseparable. We saw each other at school, and I stayed over many nights. On the weekends I would camp out at his apartment while he worked. Although he kept his place very clean, I would straighten it up a bit and go food shopping to make us dinner when he got home from work. We didn't have cell phones to communicate, but he would find a pay phone and give me a call to let me know when he would be home. Iden never complained about working hard. He drove very long hours and was always pleasant when he got home.

As graduation was quickly approaching, I had to decide my next course of action. Iden applied to a PhD program in computer science at the CUNY Graduate Center in New York City. He thought it was necessary to have an advanced degree and so he also encouraged me to apply for one as well. As I look back to those days, I don't think my present day life would have been as comfortable as it is now without his support and advice.

After graduation, I applied to Queens College's master's program in TESOL. Everything seemed to be going in the right direction. We were both enrolled in a graduate program, working part time in both fields of studies, and saving money. Our relationship was becoming very serious, but there were some concerns I was having.

Although Iden had a Green Card and could study and work in America, I started to wonder if he would want to stay and live here. We talked about it from time to time and he always responded by telling me that the Iran he knew was not the Iran that he would ever want to return to, even though his entire family and friends lived there. I wondered how he could easily say goodbye to his past and begin a new life here in America. I knew he loved America and all it had to offer, but he was an immigrant who had a love for his own country that held his entire life of memories. Would he be willing to give that up for a life with me? I knew Iden struggled with his feelings about making a choice to stay in America or to return to Iran. There were periods of time where he would talk to his family every week, yet at other times, he would not call them for months.

We both graduated in June 1982 and were accepted into our graduate programs for the following fall semester. My parents gave us a small graduation party at my house. Mom and I did most of the cooking and we made a large sheet cake that "Congratulations Patricia and Iden" in big yellow letters, The party consisted of my brothers, uncles and aunts, and a few neighbors and friends. I was happy to have graduated, but even more so to see my parents so proud that all of their children were now college graduates.

Iden and I also wanted to have a small party for our friends at his apartment to help us celebrate. I loved having parties because it brought people together and helped share our happiness. Since most of Iden's friends were Persian and their girlfriends American, we decided to make a combination of Persian and Italian food.

With my list in one hand and Iden's in the other we went shopping for the party on a Friday night. On Saturday morning I rose early, and while Iden was working, I cleaned the apartment and started food preparations. I wanted to enjoy the experience of having my first party, so I planned on having all the food prepared before the guests arrived. Iden had loads of music cassettes, so I popped some in and started to cook.

Iden gave me a call in the late afternoon saying he was still at work and could I start the Persian stew without him. Although I had seen him prepare it many times, I had never made it by myself. I tried my best to make it as equally delicious. While everything was cooking, I decorated the house with colorful balloons and fresh flowers. By the time Iden arrived home from work that night, he immediately said he smelled the stew and begged to have some for dinner that night. "Of course," I said. "You can be my guinea pig!"

I loved watching the expression on his face when he was given a plate of stew with steaming hot rice to eat. He was almost like a child looking into a candy store. He raised a spoonful up to his nose and said that it smelled delightful and looked wonderful. When he finally tasted it, he said it was marvelous. I made sure he was being honest with me, and he assured me he was and that he really thought it was delicious. After a few bites he added that he wished his mother could be here to share a plate with him. I had never heard him talk that way before and it made me want to hug him, so I did.

Iden had a very kind and gentle spirit and was able to show his kindness very easily, but it was hard for him to show his pain. The comment he made about his mother allowed me to witness a vulnerable part of him that I had not seen before that day.

Our party was on a beautiful day in June. It wasn't too hot, and there was a lovely soft breeze coming into the kitchen window that morning as I prepared more food. As I cooked, I watched the curtains swaying back and forth, almost as if they were dancing. Their movement gave me a sense of calmness because I was feeling a little nervous about hosting our first party. While I was cooking, Iden was busy arranging tables and chairs both in the apartment and outside in the backyard. We were blessed to have good weather, which meant we could use the backyard to help accommodate our guests since our apartment was small.

The party began with the opening of the first bottle of champagne to propose a toast to the graduates. I toasted and took a few sips of the champagne before quickly disappearing into the kitchen to bring out the dips, vegetables, and cheese platter. While I was in the kitchen, I could hear bottles of beer opening and laughter. With the food in the oven starting to heat up, I returned to the living room and saw Iden with a beer in his hand. I had never seen that before and he seemed to be a bit uncomfortable holding it. When he saw me looking at him, he asked me if I wanted one as well. I declined, saying I would have a drink of wine later with dinner.

An hour later, the food was ready to serve. Iden and his friends seemed involved in conversation and content to just pick on nuts and cheese and drinking. However, I was hungry and could not drink without putting food in my stomach, so I decided to bring out the food and whoever wanted to eat could take a plate.

When I brought the food out, Iden and a few friends had started tuning up their guitars and it seemed as if I was disturbing their little private party when I called everyone for dinner. I started to serve those who wanted to eat and then I made myself a plate and sat down next to the ladies. Once finished eating, I collected the dirty plates and began to prepare some tea and a pot of coffee to have with our dessert that I would serve after everyone had eaten.

Iden came into the kitchen shortly after saying that he was hungry and ready to eat. He apologized for not eating with me but was enjoying playing guitar with his friends. I told him I was glad he was having a good time and to grab a plate and have something to eat before it got cold. I could tell by the way he was talking that the drinking was starting to hit him. I wasn't annoyed because, after all, it was a party but was just a little confused by his change in behavior. He had never been a joke teller or extremely outgoing, but on that night, he became the life of the party.

With dinner finished, we all headed outside to have dessert. The sun no longer shone in our backyard, which made it cooler and more comfortable to sit than when our company first arrived. The drinking had subsided and we talked about possible vacation ideas as well as plans for the future after graduation. Some of Iden's friends were returning to Iran to visit family and stay for a few months. They asked Iden if he was planning a trip back home. I am sure he wanted to return home to visit his family, but he didn't respond. Perhaps he had plans that he didn't want known.

The day after the party we did not have work or school, so it was a treat to sleep late and linger in bed together until we felt like getting up. By 10 o'clock, I had slept enough but Iden was still sound asleep, so I gently eased my way out of bed in order not to disturb him. He had been putting in long hours at work and studying hard to finish up his degree in computer science, so the few days he was taking off before pounding the pavement for a job were well deserved and necessary.

The first thing I did every morning was make a cup of coffee and sit for a while with my thoughts to plan my day. I sat for a few minutes, reviewing the day before me, knowing our party was a success by how thankful our guests said they were for their lovely time. Yet I had some unsettling thoughts running through my mind.

I shook off whatever was bothering me and finished the after-party clean up. I showered and dressed, ready to start the day, and felt like taking a walk before the sun got too hot, so I grabbed my bag and put on a pair of sunglasses and out I went. I left a note for Iden in case he woke up before I returned.

I remembered I had some library books that needed to be returned, so it felt good knowing I had a direction to walk. It was about 2 o'clock when I arrived home and I could not believe that Iden had just gotten up. He was sitting in his pajamas at the kitchen table drinking tea. I said hi and asked if he'd had a good sleep. I waited for an answer, but none came. He left the kitchen and went into the backyard with his teacup in hand.

Iden was obviously not in the mood to talk, but I did not know why. I thought perhaps the combination of drinking and sleeping too much might have made him feel a little cranky. His mood obviously had shifted from the night before, so I decided to leave him alone. Perhaps the sunlight and fresh air would put him in a better mood.

I got busy unloading the groceries I had bought while out, then went into the backyard and said that I should be getting home. I then asked if he needed me to do anything before I left and he just said, "No, thank you. Let's talk later."

I arrived home around 5 o'clock to find that no one was home. It was odd not having anything to do, so I just sat at the kitchen table waiting for Mom to get home. I was giving myself a few weeks off before I started tutoring again, and then in September I would start teaching for the New York City Board of Education while taking graduate classes.

While I waited for Mom to return, I decided to give Iden a call to see if he was feeling better. I thought it would help me feel better as well. I let the phone ring several times and before I was just about to hang up, he finally answered.

"Hi, Iden." No response came so I said, "It's me, Patty." He didn't seem to recognize my voice.

"Oh! Hi," he said. "Can I call you back? I was sleeping."

I didn't get a chance to respond, as he had already hung up the phone. I felt even more confused by his odd behavior, so decided to get busy doing something to distract my thoughts. I thought I would surprise Mom by starting dinner.

When Mom walked through the door, she was happy to see me and grateful for the meal I was making her after a long day at work. Dad arrived home shortly after her so we all sat down to eat together. Dad opened up a bottle of wine and asked if I wanted a glass. I declined but as I looked at Dad with the glass of wine in his hand, it made me think about Iden. He'd looked so awkward holding his drink, whereas Dad looked comfortable.

It had been a long time since I shared a meal with my parents due to my work and school schedule and spending many days at Iden's apartment. My parents were very accepting of my relationship with Iden, and they never objected to my staying nights at his place. We had been dating for almost four years and they knew we were very serious and loved each other. While we ate, we talked and caught up on what was going on with them and with me.

Mom inquired about the party, and I told her everything had gone well. She then asked if Iden appreciated all my hard work and if he'd had a good time. As I started to answer her, I could already feel the need to lie.

"Yes, Mom."

I also said Iden thought the food was delicious, which he did, and that he was very appreciative of everything I did to make it such a wonderful party, which he was, however, I left out how I had left him today.

I was omitting what I was feeling. I wanted to tell her that I thought he drank too much and slept most of the day, and that he didn't talk to me at all that day. I felt uncomfortable disclosing what I was feeling because I didn't want them to have negative feelings toward him.

After Mom and I finished up in the kitchen, we watched an episode of *The Love Boat*. I sat staring at the TV screen, but instead of watching the show I thought about Iden. He called briefly before

I went to bed and just said that he was really tired and needed the day to stay in bed without any further conversation. In the future, whenever I had problems, I wished that I could still have the comfort my mother always gave me while I sat next to her on her big comfy couch.

CHAPTER SIX

THE DISCOVERY

'In one drop of water are found out the secrets of the ocean.'

—KAHIL GIBRAN

In the fall of 1982, I started my teaching career in Jackson Heights, Queens. I taught days, and two nights a week I spent at Queens College taking graduate courses. It may not have been an exciting life, working, studying, and living my days away in Queens, but it was a routine. I thrived in a daily schedule. Iden on the other hand, was still driving a cab, doing some odd computer jobs, and studying, and his schedule was different every day. He decided to go full time to graduate school in order to finish quickly, so he delayed getting a full-time computer job.

It was difficult to know where and when Iden was going to be somewhere or what he was doing on any given day. Unlike me, he enjoyed the variety of his schedule and struggled to stick to a routine. On occasion after teaching, I'd start walking to the subway to head home and a Yellow Cab would honk and surprise me. I never knew when this would happen, so when I exited school at the end of the day, I would look around for a taxi with Iden behind the wheel. When he picked me up, we would exchange a hug and a kiss and quickly tell each other about our day. If I were hungry, he would whisk me off to grab a pizza or a sandwich. It was always a pleasant, unplanned meeting. His unpredictability was thrilling in a way. Since our schedules were packed with work and study, we weren't able to spend as much time together. Those little cab getaways broke up my daily routine, and it was wonderful to have those few moments together at the end of a long day of teaching.

We spent the next year working and finishing our master's degrees. With some money we had saved, we started to enjoy the benefits of having cash always available. Since I was working and still living at home, I was able to give my parents some money that I knew they could use, although unbeknownst to me, Mom was saving that money for my future; my future with Iden.

I was so busy with work and study that I felt bad about being absent in Mom's life, but I knew she had her work, her home, and her friends to keep her life fully occupied. Dad seemed to enjoy a life outside of home. He had begun traveling by himself and taking weeks off in the winter to escape to Florida. I was amazed how easily Mom accepted all of this without complaint. My house was often quiet, and I felt the absence of my brothers and Dad.

A few months after finishing his master's degree, Iden became quiet and withdrawn. I thought it was to do with the large amount of studying and driving that he was doing, and he was also sleeping very few hours each night. I occasionally mentioned the importance of resting, but he was driven to make money and to finish his degree on time with honors. His work ethic was amazing as well as his acutely sharp learning skills.

One night at his apartment I decided to surprise him by cleaning and cooking a homemade Persian meal that I knew he missed and that he would appreciate after a long day of driving a cab in the hot summer days in New York City. I had finished teaching as well as completing my master's degree in applied linguistics, so I had more free time than I'd had previously.

Iden was usually very neat, but there were dirty clothes accumulating high in a corner and dishes piled up in the sink that needed washing. He had a washing machine in his apartment, so I took a pile of jeans and threw them into the machine, but as I started the wash, I remembered to check his pant pockets for anything he may have forgotten to take out. I put my hand inside and pulled out a prescription bottle with something shaking inside.

For a moment I felt I had trespassed into his life, but I didn't do it on purpose. I wasn't specifically looking for something. Did that make it right? Perhaps the pills were some kind of antibiotic or allergy pill. I pulled the bottle closer and read the label. Zoloft. Take one a day. Dr. Karim. I had never heard of that medicine before, and I completely lost track of what I was doing. My cleaning took second preference to finding out what this medicine was prescribed for. There was no Google, and I didn't have any friends in the medical field. I could simply wait and ask Iden when he got home and tell him truthfully that I had found the bottle while doing his wash. I don't know why I didn't do that, perhaps I was unsure of his reaction even after all these years of dating.

In hindsight, maybe if I had gotten it out in the open then and there, we could have dealt with things earlier on in our relationship. The phone rang and it jolted me away from my dilemma for a moment. It was Iden saying he would be home in an hour.

"Great," I said, "I will make us some Persian omelets."

I immediately took the pants out of the wash, returned the pills to the pocket and tried to pile them up in the corner the way they were before the discovery.

Iden arrived home in good spirits, immediately heading to the bathroom to shower off the day. While he showered, I made a start on the omelets. He came into the kitchen all shaved and smelling wonderful as he gave me a kiss and said, "Something smells great."

Iden's big dark eyes and dark thick wavy hair melted my heart as we stood by the stove in a long embrace. He proudly took the money he made that day out of his pocket and planted it in my hand. He counted $250, which was an amazing haul in one day from a 12-hour shift behind a steering wheel. I told him to sit down and relax and that dinner would be ready soon.

We ate our meal with little conversation, then he asked if he could just go lie down to read the paper without helping to clean up.

"Of course," I said, "Go ahead and lie down. I will clean up and join you later with a pot of tea."

I quickly cleaned up and by the time I went to join Iden in the living room with the tea he was already sound asleep on the couch. I covered him with a blanket, read a little, and fell asleep next to him.

When I awoke, Iden was up making coffee and apologizing for having fallen asleep last night so early. He explained it had been a long, hot day of driving. I told him that there was no need for an explanation but thanked him just the same. Being a Saturday, he was off work, so I suggested we have a quiet day at home and go out for dinner in the city for a well-deserved treat.

After breakfast that Saturday morning, I told him I needed to go to the library to research some teaching methods. When I arrived at the library, I asked for the prescription reference books. The librarian showed me the medical journals and a huge book called *The Pill Book*. I quickly opened it, looking over my shoulder to make sure no one was watching.

I felt like a criminal, lying to Iden as to why I was at the library. I flipped through the pages, finally arriving at the Z section. There it was Zoloft — an antidepressant prescribed by a psychiatrist to treat depression. I had no idea he was feeling that bad. I sat with the book for a while and wondered if I should wait until he was ready to talk about it since, after all, he had kept it a secret from me all this time.

It was the early 80s and mental illness was not talked about as openly as it is today. Should I just tell him about my discovery and accept the consequences, even though my finding the pills was by accident? Either way, I felt confused. If he didn't tell me, I felt I couldn't help him and there would be this thing between us. It didn't feel like he was lying, but I felt hurt because he didn't want to share what he was feeling or his pain with me. Or was *I* his pain?

I was young and in love, and I thought all lovers needed and should share everything with each other, no matter how difficult or painful. I have learned over the years through experience and medical information just how difficult it is to be open about mental illness. Even today, as our knowledge and information about mental illness has become more available to the public, it is still a difficult subject to talk about, even with our loved ones, for fear of judgment.

The librarian asked if I needed help. I was frozen on the last page of the book. "Oh, no thank you," I said, closing the book with a loud thud. I put the book back on the shelf and ran out of the library as fast as I could to catch a breath of fresh air.

I started to walk faster and faster. I just needed to release the anxiety I was feeling. I walked for what must have been over an hour until I started to feel calmer. A lifelong habit I'd developed and has continued throughout my life is exercising to release stress in order to regain my composure.

Before returning home, I tried putting on my happy face because Iden was very perceptive, and he would know if something wasn't quite right with me. As I walked, I decided it would be best for him to approach me about what he was going through. I would be as supportive as I could in the meantime without letting on what I knew.

Arriving back at the apartment, I put on a big smile and said, "Hi, I'm back." I found Iden fast asleep in the living room with a computer textbook on artificial intelligence open on his chest. In my discovery of that small pill bottle, I had also discovered a part of Iden that would eventually open many mysteries hidden within him, mysteries that even he didn't yet know existed.

CHAPTER SEVEN

THE MARRIAGE

'Why love if losing hurts so much? We love to know that we are not alone.'

—C.S LEWIS

After my little discovery, I tried to help my friend and lover, Iden. I tried to make him aware of his strengths, to focus on all his accomplishments and all the possibilities the future held. My career as a pseudo psychiatrist had begun. With his master's degree completed and various job possibilities in his field of computer science, I was waiting eagerly for the day that he could stop driving the taxi.

Iden never really minded driving taxis, and in a way, I think he had mixed emotions about hanging up his driving cap. I suppose it was somewhat comforting to him knowing he had a job that gave him some flexibility. He also enjoyed the free-spiritedness of driving. There wasn't a set schedule, no boss looking over his shoulder, and he went to different places and met different people every day.

The thought of Iden wearing a suit and a tie and having a routine work schedule would be something he would have to get used to, and hopefully soon. He came to America with dreams, of course, but they changed as his needs changed. Thoughts of going back to Iran had changed after the revolution. Although he had my family and me and some good friends here, the security of his old life was no longer present.

I had just started a new teaching position at a new school, and it was initially hard adjusting to the new school. I was teaching much younger children than I was used to at my other school. But I quickly adjusted my teaching skills and adapted to their way of learning.

As the months passed, I eventually found my way and began to feel comfortable and to enjoy my new teaching position. I made some new teacher friends and I looked forward to having lunch with them and talking about things beyond the classroom.

Many of the teachers were young, and we often talked about our boyfriends, finances, and dreams for the future. When I listened to their stories, I sometimes felt displaced. They seemed to have some solid plans in order and had more interesting lives than Iden and I had together. They traveled and went out with other couples on a regular basis. They were always going to parties, weddings, or some other event.

Although it really wasn't in my nature to compare myself to others, it was easy to fall into that trap. Iden and I did do many things with other couples, but we existed more in our own little world.

Teaching children brought me great joy. It was almost impossible to feel sad when you looked into their beautiful faces. Over time, their little faces with big loving eyes carried me through some of the darkest and unhappiest periods in my life. The beauty of children is that they propel you out of your misery because they expect you to be as happy as they are. Their positive energy pulls you out of your sadness. I am very thankful for each and every child that I saw during my career as a teacher.

Iden finally hung up his cabbie hat and was now working for a major hospital as a network manager in New York City. One of his friends knew someone who worked in the hospital and was able to arrange an interview. He was hired on the spot. He had a charisma that was infectious, and he was also very intelligent, so I was not surprised. After the interview he came home feeling excited and hopeful about the future, just as I was too.

We decided to go out and celebrate with some friends to a Persian restaurant. The first person I informed about the good news was Mom. Upon hearing the news, she let out a big scream and said," Hurray"!

Mom was my biggest cheerleader, always urging me on and equally excited as I was about my good fortune.

That night, Iden picked me up in a new but used car. This time it was a Volkswagen Karmann Ghia. It had a stick shift that I didn't know how to use, so I got my first lesson that night. He made me drive all the way to the restaurant. He always encouraged me to try new things and had patience in teaching me along the way.

We arrived at the restaurant a little jolted by my stick-shift driving, but I was proud about my new accomplishment, and he was equally happy about his new job and my new success. As I look back, knowing that someone else truly wants something you want is a wonderful feeling. He always tried to make me happy.

Our friends were already at the restaurant and were happy to see us as we entered. The scent of Persian spices was in the air, and I was looking forward to having a wonderful dinner and a night of celebrating. Iden's face looked light and worry-free. I never approached him about the Zoloft, and he never spoke of it either. It was just left where I found it: in the wash. I didn't even know if he was still taking it or seeing a doctor. Although we didn't talk about it, it was there, present in my mind every time I saw him, judging his mood, his energy, and how much he slept. But that night I didn't worry because he looked and seemed to feel just great and so did I! We had a wonderful time eating kebabs and rice and dancing to Persian music.

Iden had started his job at the hospital and I had my job at school. Everything seemed to be falling into place. On the weekends Iden would talk to his parents to ensure that all was well, and I would have a brief conversation with his dad speaking my limited French, but we were able to connect and relay our sentiment. Over time I was able to learn some Farsi and talk to his family a little more. His parents were very sweet and sounded pleased that Iden and I were together, expressing their desire to meet me one day.

At this point we had been dating for almost five years and we were very much like a married couple, except we didn't live together full time. So the process of going from a couple to being married just sort of happened. There wasn't the "get down on the one knee" thing to profess undying love and popping the question. We just decided to get married. We practically lived together already, we both had a good job with steady incomes, and we loved each other. We decided to get married in March and planned the wedding day for May.

When I told Mom and Dad about our future plans, I could imagine they were thinking about something in my future besides a wedding. I assured my parents that I was not, in fact, pregnant, and that I was ready to get married.

We didn't want a big wedding, nor could we afford one, so we planned a very simple but beautiful wedding ceremony and celebration. Iden was not Catholic and therefore we could not be married in a Catholic church without months of preparations. We therefore decided to get married in the United Nation's Chapel in New York City and hold a small reception at a French restaurant.

Mom and I started the adventure of finding the perfect wedding dress. I had always loved my mother's wedding dress, made with satin and Irish lace and pearls. On my parent's wedding day, they truly looked like movie stars. Wearing that dress, although it fit perfectly, would be a little over the top for the type of ceremony we were planning. Our search took us to all the major department stores, and we finally found a dress we both loved in linen with just the right amount of lace.

After purchasing the dress and shoes, we met my brother Mark's wife, Kathy to order the wedding cake. We went to a bakery on the Upper East Side of New York City and sampled some cakes prepared for weddings.

After ordering the cake, we were all very hungry and headed to a restaurant located on the Upper East Side. It was a long day in the city, and we took the train back to Queens, tired but extremely happy with our accomplishments and our full bellies. The wedding was just a few weeks away and I felt confident that everything was going to work out just fine.

Mark was a Wall Street broker and knew how to dress well. He helped Iden pick out a handsome suit for the wedding. He kindly offered to buy one for him from Barney's. They scheduled a guy's day out to do wedding shopping as I had done a girl's day with Mom and Kathy.

Mark was, and always has been, very loving and generous. His thoughtfulness has been present constantly throughout my life. Iden missed his brothers in Iran and therefore he looked forward to spending the day with Mark. He let Mark do the shopping since Iden had always admired how well- dressed Mark always looked.

With his slim build and dark handsome features, Iden made anything he put on look attractive, especially a very expensive suit. With a joyful heart, Iden treated Mark to lunch to show his appreciation.

With all the arrangements in order, Iden and I got busy writing our vows. We wanted to say a few special things to each other along with the traditional marriage vows.

The month flew by, and our wedding day finally arrived, May 29, 1983. The loud thunder and lightning woke me up very early in the morning. I supposed this would have put a bride-to-be in a bad mood, but I wasn't upset in the least. I was just too happy to let bad weather ruin my day. It was 4 a.m. and since I was already up and too excited to go back to sleep, I decided to enjoy my last day alone in my house.

I made myself a cup of coffee and brought it back to my room. I thought of my parents, especially Mom, and all the things I wanted to tell them. So in order to express my feelings the best way I possibly could, I picked up a pen and started to write each one of them a separate letter expressing how much I loved them and how grateful I was for all they had given me.

I heard a knock on my door.

"Hi, I couldn't sleep any longer."

I happily greeted Mom on this special day. We sat and looked at each other and I saw all the things she wanted to say in her eyes without her saying a word.

"I love you too, Mom."

In the next few hours everyone was up and getting ready for the wedding. I enjoyed a long hot shower and sat in my robe drinking another cup of coffee while putting on my makeup. Once my makeup was done, I went to get dressed.

Dad passed by as I stood up and commented on how beautiful I looked. Mom and I locked eyes and smiled because getting a compliment from him was rare, but when given, it was given sincerely and with love.

Mom went out for a moment and came back into my room carrying a clear box that contained the white orchids I was going to wear in my hair. She put the box down on my bed and then took out a smaller box out from her dress pocket. Handing it over to me she said, "This is something old for you to wear today."

I took the box and thanked her before I even opened it, embracing her and giving her a big kiss on the cheek.

Inside the satin-lined box were two silver hairpins with very tiny diamonds down one side of each pin. Mom told me her mother had worn them, she wore them, and today was my turn to carry on the tradition of wearing the hairpins on my wedding day. As I held the pins in my hands, I could feel the history they contained, and I gladly asked mom to pin them in my hair. I then stepped into my dress and Mom helped me close the many buttons down the back. We looked at my reflection in the mirror and the reality of the day suddenly hit me, I was getting married!

Everyone was suited up and ready to go. I hardly recognized my brother Ron. He was, and still   is, a bit of a beatnik, with long hair, earrings, and tattoos, but on that day his long hair was neatly pulled back, and he looked very handsome. My other brother Mark and Kathy, were meeting us at the chapel.

I stood looking at my family and was so proud to have them with me on this special day. The limousine arrived and we made our way to the city to The United Nation's Chapel. The rain continued as we left the house, and Mom, always trying to be supportive, said, "It is good luck to have rain on your wedding day."

As we headed to the city, we stopped at a red light a few blocks from home. I gazed out the window and saw the 85th Street Park being rained upon; the slides, the swings, the sandbox, and the monkey bars all made me smile. It brought me back to my childhood. And then my eyes caught sight of the seesaw, one end was up in the air and the other was firmly planted on the ground. I remembered the difficult task of my brothers and me trying to balance it. The seesaw cannot be stabilized by two people who are not equally participating in the balance. Life is full of ups and downs, but now I would have someone to help me up when I was down and keep me grounded when I was feeling lost or confused. I wasn't going to live my life alone. In a few hours I would be joined to someone I loved to have as a witness to my life with all its glories and defeats.

A Unitarian minister performed our ceremony to a very intimate group of family and close friends. Iden and I recited our own vows and read some poems written by Kahlil Gibran. Afterward, we headed to a favorite restaurant to celebrate. We started the dinner with a champagne toast where Mark said a few words and my best friend, Debbie, spoke as well.

When dinner was finished the cake was presented. It was absolutely breathtaking, decorated with white marzipan icing with edible silver and pale pink ribbons and pearls and white orchids in the center. The vanilla cake with raspberry filling was divine, and I can still taste it in my mouth to this day. It was a glorious day indeed!

Iden and Patricia on their wedding day 1983 ©

CHAPTER EIGHT

THE APARTMENT

'I loved the house the way you would any new house, because
it is populated by your own future, the family who will fill it
with noise or chaos and satisfying pleasures.'

— JANE SMILEY

Our wedding was a perfect day. Iden and I took a short honeymoon
to Canada. He was not an American citizen and there still was no
Iranian Embassy in America to issue a visa, so we were limited as
to where we could go. We were unfortunately only able to take a
few days off due to our busy work schedules.

We decided to go to Quebec because it was the closest thing to
Paris, which had always been a dream of mine to see. During our
honeymoon we talked about future plans to visit Paris and many
other dreams we had, as most lovers and newlyweds usually do.

We traveled to Quebec by Amtrak. The train ride took about
nine hours, but we passed the time by talking, reading, eating,
and taking short little naps on each other's shoulders. Planning
trips had always been exciting for me. Although I hadn't travelled
much back then, I still enjoyed planning road trips. Before going to
Quebec I borrowed a guidebook on Quebec from the library and
spent time jotting down places to go and things to do. I also took
note of restaurants that offered good food and were affordable.
For the train ride I had brought along some sandwiches, fruit,
cookies, and a few other snacks. When we wanted to have a bite,

we ventured into the dining car to purchase some hot tea. As we sat and ate it was fun to sit and look out the window.

We arrived in Quebec on a beautiful June day. Spring was in full force, and our hotel, Le Manoir d'Auteuil, was directly across from the Parliament Building, and near the St. Lawrence River. The street and the hotel looked as if it belonged in Paris, with fresh lilacs hanging from baskets outside the windows. We were tired from the trip, but excited to take a walk in the city and stretch our legs.

We quickly unpacked and freshened up and I grabbed my little guidebook in case we wanted to do some sightseeing or have a bite to eat. Although I liked having a destination to walk to, I also liked the excitement of getting a little lost and finding my way back. I wasn't a big thrill seeker but having Iden at my side made me feel secure and adventurous.

We found our way back to the hotel after a nice long walk, stopping in a café to have some delicious French onion soup and salad. We were tired, but eager to spend our first honeymoon night together.

When we awoke it was to receive a breakfast of croissants, fruit, yogurt, mini cream pastries, and coffee all delivered to our door as a honeymoon gift. Before we ate, we quickly showered, and I opened all the windows and shutters. The buttery smell of croissants baking filled the room and made me hungry. We had enjoyed our night together, sleeping peacefully in each other's arms after a night of sweet lovemaking.

After a good night's sleep and with our bellies full we wanted to make the most of our four days in Quebec, so we headed down to the river and sat on the benches to watch the international parade of sailboats. We enjoyed the show and the sunshine on our faces and decided to take the funicular at the shore of the St. Lawrence River to the Upper Town. I do not like heights, so taking a chair lift up a mountain about 194 feet above the starting point was indeed scary, but I did it while squeezing Iden's hand and screaming very quietly. It was beautiful, once we got to the top to view the river and its surroundings.

We walked around for hours on Grande Allee, Quebec City's busiest street, observing the beautiful flowers hanging in baskets from every streetlamp, cafes with tables and colorful umbrellas along the sidewalks, artists painting and selling their work, and the myriad of street musicians on almost every corner.

We stopped in some stores along the way because I wanted to bring something back from Quebec for Mom. I did not want to buy a silly souvenir, but rather something she would love. I wanted her to know that I was thinking of her, even on my honeymoon. We passed by a linen store and I suggested to Iden we go in. Everything was made from linen with exquisite hand stitching and embroidery on many items. I saw and bought some hand towels that I knew my mom would love because they had lavender flowers stitched on them, which were her favorite flower and scent.

Iden was always patient while I shopped in stores. He never complained and kept himself busy looking around while I decided what I wanted to buy.

We continued to walk around and enjoy all the sights before we decided to go to Quebec's famous landmark, Fairmont Le Chateau Frontenac, to have a drink. The hotel was extremely fancy, and we felt somewhat out of place, but it made the day feel very special, sipping wine and eating oysters at such a fine place. Iden had never had oysters before, so it was fun watching his face as he sucked his first one down. As a child, my parents took my brothers and I to the Jersey Shore where they rented a summer house with some friends. Dad taught us all at a very tender age how to eat oysters, clams, and lobsters.

We walked around the hotel after finishing our meal, and although it was very elaborate, we were happy to return to our sweet little inn. We planned a sightseeing tour for the next day to see the Montmorency Falls.

Breakfast in the hotel didn't start until 8 o'clock and since we had to be on the bus by 9, we went out to have breakfast. All we had to do was follow the smell of butter to find a place to eat. We spotted an adorable café that served crepes. We ordered one crepe filled with eggs and jambon and another with strawberries, chocolate, and crème.

The bus ride to the falls was only about 20 minutes or so, but it was nice seeing different parts of the city. The Montmorency Falls are at the mouth of the Montmorency River, which is about 7 miles northeast of Quebec City. The waterfall makes a huge plunge into the St. Lawrence River and provides power for the region around Quebec City. We spent some time watching the waterfalls and then took a hike around the falls. Everything was so green and lush since it would soon be summertime. We found a nice place to sit on the grass under a shady tree to enjoy listening to the sound of the river's water splashing down.

One thing Iden and I had in common was our love of spending time in nature; it brought us much peace. We soon went from sitting upright to lying on our backs to relax and experience this beautiful day with all its glorious sights and sounds with each other. As we lay on the dewy grass with the leaves from the trees overhead filtering through the sunlight, Iden reached over to hold my hand and squeezed it tightly, saying he loved me, and I responded that I loved him too. We spent a good part of our time lying there before realizing it was time to head back to the bus to depart.

Upon arrival back at the hotel we were tired   so decided to relax a bit and have a quiet night. We had both bought books with us for the long train ride, so after showering we got into bed and read for a while before we fell into each other's arms and went to sleep.

On our last day in Quebec we did not want to waste a minute, so we rose with the sun and headed out in search of coffee and guafre, which are French waffles. On previous days, we had seen many people walking around eating something wrapped in parchment paper that looked like a pastry. On one of our walks down to the St. Lawrence River I stopped someone who was happily walking by munching away at whatever was inside the parchment paper, so I asked what was she eating. She was a Quebecer, so she answered in French and said, "*Guafre.*"

When she saw that I did not understand she said, "Waffles."

She was also kind enough to tell me where I could buy them.

We found the little shop that was selling the waffles and ordered some. They came wrapped in parchment paper, smothered with butter, drizzled with honey, and dusted with powdered sugar. My eyes devoured it even before I bit into it. It was like no waffle I had ever eaten before. We took our waffles and coffee and sat on a park bench in the early-morning sun.

That night in Quebec we took a horse and buggy ride around the city. We ate grenouille, which are frog's legs. It was the first and last time we would ever eat them, but it was an experience. As we ate dinner, a classical guitarist played French songs and Iden knew them all. I can remember watching his face light up while he listened. We forwent the carriage ride back and chose to walk arm in arm back to the hotel. The memories I have of my days in Quebec with Iden will always be very dear to me; it was an innocent time, a time where our dreams were made, our love was strong, and our future held much promise.

We returned home ready to start a new chapter in our lives. The house that Iden had been living in was being sold and the new owners did not want any tenants. In a few months we needed to move out, so we began looking for a new apartment in Queens.

Our search brought us to my old neighborhood in Jackson Heights. We rented an apartment in a three-family house across from my old grammar school. We slowly decorated our first place together with some of Iden's furniture and possessions as well as my things that I had brought from home. As we saved, we gradually replaced some old furniture with new, and also replaced mismatched cutlery and dishes with brand-new ones to change over from college days to married life.

We both continued to work full days and at night we cooked dinner together and discussed our day. On the weekends we started the day by having breakfast in a diner, doing our laundry, and doing our weekly shopping at the local supermarket. We also made a weekly visit to our neighborhood bank to deposit part of our paycheck into a joint savings account. We were so proud as we watched the amount grow each week.

On Saturday nights we sometimes had our friends over, and we would either have dinner in or go out and grab a bite and see a movie. Mom also spent some Saturday nights with us after her long day working, and Iden enjoyed her company as much I did. We lived in that apartment for almost five years, and it was a happy and peaceful time.

In 1988 we decided we'd had enough of renting and wanted to own something. We wanted to take the next step in our lives. Buying a co-op was the only reasonable choice for us since we did not have a down payment large enough to purchase a house. We had always loved Forest Hills with its beautiful tree-lined streets and cobblestone sidewalks. It had more of a suburban feel to it, and it also had excellent schools, both public and private. Children were part of our conversations as we made plans for our future, but we both knew we needed more financial and job security before starting a family.

Each Sunday, while at my parents' house for dinner, I would scan the real estate section of my father's *Sunday New York Times*, searching for our future home.

There was no rush to buy a new home, so we took our time finding one that was priced right and in good condition. After a few months of searching we fell in love with a two-bedroom apartment in a pre-war building surrounded by lush gardens with benches and water fountains.

We made an appointment to look at the prospective apartment. As I walked through the gardens outside the apartment, I immediately had a feeling of belonging. I tried not to appear too excited when I stepped into the apartment, but it had everything we were looking for. It was a large two- bedroom with many closets and a newly renovated bathroom and kitchen. It also had many windows offering good natural light.

After viewing the apartment, Iden and I told the agent we would get back to her with our answer and found an empty bench nearby to sit and talk it over. The price was high, but we did not have to fix anything, and it was in a perfect location and setting. We crunched some numbers, figuring out our mortgage and maintenance payments. As Iden was doing the math I was focused on the fountain spraying water. My mind leaped ahead to a future day when I would sit here with Iden and with a baby in a carriage.

We made an offer to the agent the following day and it was accepted. I immediately called my parents. They were extremely happy and couldn't wait to see the apartment. Over the next few months we were kept busy packing up our belongings in our Jackson Heights apartment, and on the weekends, moving some things to our new place in Forest Hills.

Although Iden was excited, he seemed a bit nervous, and it appeared as if he were having second thoughts about the purchase. When I asked him if he was okay, he just replied, "Sometimes I worry that something bad will happen because we are so happy."

I tried to reassure him that being happy doesn't have to lead to misfortune. He just smiled and said, "I hope so!"

By June 1988, we were fully moved into our new apartment and slowly got acquainted with our new neighbors There were six apartments on our floor, and we were blessed to have very caring and thoughtful neighbors living alongside of us.

Some of them were elderly and loved to talk and would often invite us in for tea and cookies, and some were young couples like ourselves who had recently moved in as well. Sometimes we would have drinks together on a Saturday night or go out for dinner. We also traded in our old Jackson Heights Saturday routine for a new one since moving to Forest Hills. Instead of eggs in a Jackson Heights diner, we now had lox and cream cheese on a bagel sitting in our dining room.

Our neighborhood was lively and filled with parks, supermarkets, restaurants, a movie theater as well as many mom-and-pop stores that sold everything from designer clothes to gourmet foods. After purchasing just a few items, the owners knew you by name and it made the neighborhood not just a place to live, but also a home.

Four months quickly rolled by, and September ushered in another school year. We had made some new purchases replacing the old with the new and it was a place that I was happy to wake up to and return to at the end of a long workday. I loved having some of our favorite things around the apartment, such as plants, books, paintings, candles, and photos of people we loved. We also had a lovely handmade Persian carpet that Iden's family had sent us as a wedding present. Gradually decorating our apartment brought me much pleasure.

Iden's job as a network manager was becoming increasingly more demanding. He had now been given a pager, which would invariably go off at all hours of the night, and most of the time it required his immediate attention.

I always needed a good eight hours of sleep, and Iden did as well, but due to his work he was sleeping less, and when he was sleeping it was interrupted. During the week he would sometimes only get five to six hours sleep some nights, but on the weekends, he would make up for those lost hours by sleeping into the afternoon. Whether it was a lack of sleep, or too much sleep in a given day, it sometimes put Iden in different moods than I was used to. Oddly, with very little sleep, he would appear to have more energy and when he slept a lot, he would appear lethargic.

Our Saturday routine of grabbing a bagel and doing weekend chores together was slowly changing because of Iden's changing sleep patterns. Things still needed to get done, so while he slept on the weekends, I did the errands and chores and waited till the evening to enjoy time with him. I wasn't feeling sorry for myself because I didn't mind doing things alone, however, I was starting to feel distant from Iden and the strong connection we previously had was slowly unravelling.

By late September I was pregnant with our first child and was due to deliver in early May. My periods had always been irregular, so when I was a few days late I waited with anticipated hope.

Becoming a mother was something I had always wanted, and Iden too looked forward to becoming a father. Whenever we saw couples with babies in a carriage, we would always make a comment about how beautiful the baby was and how lovely it would be to have a child in our lives.

After the second week of my missed period I bought a home pregnancy test on the way home from work. I rushed passed the doorman without my usual greeting and ran up to my apartment. Once inside I read the directions, and without even taking off my coat I headed into the bathroom. One minute seemed like an hour and as I kept my eyes glued to the little stick. Slowly, I saw a small blue plus sign emerge. I was pregnant. In that very second, I felt my world had changed. It had changed just by witnessing that little blue plus sign.

Bubbling with enthusiasm I couldn't wait to phone Iden and tell him the news. I called his office, but he was not in, so I left a message with his secretary to ask him to please call me back as soon as possible, assuring her that all was fine.

I was so excited I couldn't help but pace my living room floor. My standard routine when I got home was to change into sweats and a tee shirt, call my mother to catch up on the day, and ask what she was making for dinner to give me inspiration. It was soon approaching 4 o'clock and I held off calling Mom because I knew I wouldn't be able to hold back the good news and I wanted Iden to be the first person I told. I turned on the Oprah show for a distraction, and after watching half of the show I still hadn't heard from Iden. I called Mom because otherwise, she would worry that something had happened to me. I apologized for calling late and blamed it on staying at school to finish some necessary paperwork. Every part of me wanted to tell her the news, but I didn't, and I rushed off the phone.

Finally, around 6:30 Iden walked through the door. His faced showed a day that must have been rough because he looked beat. He changed out of his work clothes, and I made him a cup of tea before telling him the news. Iden always liked having a cup of tea when he arrived home after work and before dinner.

He came and sat next to me, and I asked him how his day went. He said it had been very busy and he'd had to deal with a lot of problems at work. When he asked me how my day had been I said, "Great. Do you know why?"

He asked why and I looked directly into his eyes and grabbing hold of his hands I said, "Because we are going to have a baby!"

Iden looked at me and didn't say anything for a moment. He then embraced me and gave me a sweet long kiss. After the embrace he asked me a bunch of questions:

"How are you feeling? When is the baby due? When do we go to the first doctor's appointment? Can you still work?"

And he asked many more questions late into the night. I assured him that I was feeling just fine, and that I would arrange a doctor's appointment as soon as possible.

We spent the evening talking about the things we would need to do to make the apartment ready for the arrival of our baby. We also talked about our finances and if we could afford for me to stay home to take care of our baby. From that day on, every time I walked into my apartment I imagined coming home to a baby, already feeling all the love it would bring to us as well all the love we would give to him or her.

CHAPTER NINE

ELIZABETH

'The child must know that he is a miracle, that since the beginning of the world there hasn't been, and until the end of the world there will not be, another child like him.'

—PABLO CASALS

Having a nervous disposition always kept my stomach in mild upset. So now being pregnant, the bathroom and I quickly became good friends. For the first three months the nausea was always present, morning, noon, and night. I was permanently out to sea. I no longer took the train to work because that was an accident waiting to happen, and no one needed to witness that scene so early in the morning.

Iden happily gave me a ride to work, and it was a pleasant way to start our day. Words of encouragement and reassurance just before we said goodbye made me feel that all was good and safe in my world. Teaching was becoming a challenge because I couldn't leave the classroom every time I felt sick. It was difficult to predict when the waves of nausea would hit, and I desperately tried to fight it off by munching on Saltines and sipping ginger ale.

At the end of the day I was exhausted, and I had the good fortune to catch a ride home from other teachers who lived in my neighborhood.

A week before Christmas, I came home from work and felt an overwhelming need to take a nap. I lay down on the couch and didn't wake up until Iden came home from work. He was very concerned since he had never seen me sleep during the afternoon. I explained that I was just very tired and needed to rest for a few hours and reassured him that I was fine. I headed to the bathroom to wash up before starting dinner.

In a matter of minutes, the world seemed to stop suddenly when I saw blood on the toilet tissue. I screamed for Iden, and he came running into the bathroom.

"Blood," was all I could manage to say.

He immediately picked up the phone to call my doctor for an appointment as soon as possible. I tried to hold back from crying, but just couldn't control the tears. I was frightened. Iden remained calm and reassured me that everything would be okay.

We arrived at the doctor's office and waited for what seemed like hours. As I waited, I was looking at all the pregnant women sitting with me.

Will I ever look like that? I thought.

The nurse called us into an examination room, and I changed into a gown and started to shiver. The room was cold, and I was nervous. The doctor came in and asked me a series of questions. He then examined me and gave me a sonogram. All the while I kept looking at his face to detect any sign of what might be going on. Suddenly we heard the baby's heartbeat and we both cried with joy.

"Everything is going to be just fine," the doctor said reassuringly.

The two of us cried as we hugged each other. After I got dressed again, Iden and I sat in the doctor's office. He advised us that I needed to stay home and stay off my feet. He also told me to make another appointment in two weeks for another sonogram. The doctor answered our many questions with much patience and understanding.

Driving home, I told Iden that although I was relieved about hearing such good news about the baby, I was nervous about not working. Growing up middle class and hearing my parents talking about finances gave me constant concerns about our financial security. Although Iden was earning a good, steady income, I wanted to continue working until I was at least into my eighth month. The baby was due in June, so I had the whole summer to be at home before we had to make a decision about child care. Iden reassured me that I had to follow the doctor's orders and that our finances would be just fine with me not working.

The following day, I called the school and explained my situation to the principal, who was very understanding, although somewhat disappointed. He said, "The faculty, and especially the students will miss you!"

Hanging up the phone I had mixed feelings. I was sad to leave my teaching position because I enjoyed my job and seeing my coworkers. Our daily chats always started my day with some good laughs, and I would also miss seeing my students, whose beautiful faces always gave me much happiness. However, I was also happy to feel safe at home, waiting and preparing for our baby.

I spent my pregnancy lying on the couch, on the sofa, on the love seat, or wherever else I could lie down to pass the time. I also went out and took small walks around the beautiful gardens surrounding our building every day. Iden bought me loads of books and magazines to read to keep me occupied. I quickly became glued to *What to Expect When Expecting*. Every day I would read over the sections that pertained to the weeks of my pregnancy. I asked Iden to borrow some cookbooks from the library too. Since I had so much time on my hands, I wanted to experiment with new and different cuisines that I had not previously tried.

I was settling into a new way of living and liked it. Mom helped me pass the days with frequent phone calls and visits on her days off from work. She would always bring something delicious for lunch, and while we ate, she would tell me stories of her own pregnancies with my two brothers and myself. It was always a good time, and those afternoons were golden for me.

The months seemed to pass quickly, I was feeling stronger and less nauseous and was now clearly showing signs of being pregnant. At my sixth month checkup we were asked if we wanted to sign up for Lamaze classes. Iden was very excited to do so. He loved watching medical shows, had a very strong stomach, and he wanted to be with me during the time of labor and delivery for support. He actually enjoyed going to my two-week checkups to hear how the pregnancy was progressing.

After each doctor's appointment we would stop off at a Bagel Nosh to have dinner. We routinely ordered an everything bagel with tuna salad and a brownie to share for dessert. For some reason, this is what both Iden and I craved while I was pregnant. Even to this day whenever I eat a bagel with tuna I can't but help recall those days of being pregnant.

We started our Lamaze class as I approached my eighth month. We arrived with a pillow in hand and watched a movie about childbirth for our first class. At least two husbands almost fainted and one got sick. Iden couldn't take his eyes off the movie and watched with periods of holding his hands over my eyes. We had some good laughs on our way home after each class, talking about the couples in our class. Iden liked to imitate the way people acted and he always depicted them correctly.

Spring was now in full bloom, and I was just a few weeks away from my due date. I had not gained much weight in the first two trimesters, but I was making up for it in my third. Iden was trying to get home earlier so we could take a walk before dinner and sit on the garden benches to admire the daffodils and crocuses covering the grounds. Large baskets filled with flowers hung from the old-fashioned lamp posts, which reminded us of the streets of Quebec.

Some days, new mothers with their infants would sit by me and impart their knowledge of labor and child-rearing with me. It seemed that in just a few months after giving birth, a woman was transformed into being an expert mother of her child. No other job teaches so quickly.

Other days, I would sit next to the older residents of my apartment complex and listen to their stories of child-rearing. Everyone has a story, and it was a pleasant time hearing each one and realizing that in a couple of weeks my own new chapter was about to begin.

May 28th was my expected date of delivery, but it was now June 1st, and I was scheduled to have a stress test performed in a few days. It was almost impossible to do anything except wait. Iden called several times a day to check in with me. He bought me a beeper just in case he wasn't at his desk, which being a network manager, he very often was not. Iden also did most of the household chores, which I could no longer do. I was still able to rattle around a few pots and pans to make something delicious to eat. He was increasingly being given more responsibilities at work as well. During my pregnancy he was generally in good spirits and he eagerly awaited the birth of our first child.

On one warm and stormy night, I woke up to announce the time had come. My water broke and I was feeling contractions. We called the doctor and quickly left for the hospital. My labor was long and hard and Iden was at my side coaching me along throughout the entire labor to welcome Elizabeth Pari (Farsi for little angel) into our lives.

Iden cut the umbilical cord, and the doctor handed her to me and lay her on my chest. After giving us a few moments, nurses washed her and swaddled her in a blanket and a hat.

The nurse handed Elizabeth to Iden as he sat in a chair and the doctor took care of my post-delivery necessities. I turned my head to look at her and at him. She had huge cornflower-blue eyes, and as we locked eyes at that moment, I fell in love in a whole new way. She seemed to have an old soul behind her newborn eyes. She was alert and moved her eyes taking in everything and everyone in the operating room. Iden held her like a dad who had held many babies before. Happiness and love were written all over his face. We looked at each other and knew that our lives had changed from that moment to something even more beautiful than before.

Elizabeth's birth was a blessing along with her pleasant disposition. Although I was nervous about breastfeeding, she immediately latched onto my breast and nursed gently, which gave me a beautiful sense of comfort and belonging. From the time she was about three months old she started sleeping through the night. When she woke in the early morning, she would cry softly to let me know she was up and ready to nurse. Because I was breastfeeding, Iden didn't have many opportunities to feed her, but I was pumping breastmilk and filled bottles to give him the experience of feeding her as well.

We slowly shifted from a married couple into a family. After Iden left for work I sometimes felt nervous being left alone, but as I started to feel better physically, I was able to start a new routine for myself. At first it was difficult to leave the apartment because of timing. By the time I fed her, changed her, and then got myself showered and dressed it was time to start the process all over again. But little by little I found my way and got a good schedule going.

Some days I would sit in the park and talk to other mothers, exchanging stories, and now I felt so proud to have my own story to tell. I also loved watching the children play on the playground. My eyes always went to the little ones playing on the seesaw. Who liked going up high and who liked coming down fast? And of course I always watched to see who liked to try and balance the seesaw the way I did with my brothers years ago when I was a young girl.

Other days I would take walks to Austin Street to look in the store windows at all the pretty clothing for women and children, designer furniture, and gourmet delicacies. For a minute or so, I wished I could buy it all. Not so much for me, but I would love to buy some of those pretty lace dresses for Elizabeth and a desk big enough to hold all of Iden's computers and his assortment of hardware and software.

Sometimes I would go into the gourmet chocolatier and purchase one piece of dark chocolate with almonds. Even though it was just one piece, the storeowner valued each piece and each customer and he would wrap it in beautiful tissue with a matching bag. I would open the bag carefully because I didn't want to tear it. The smell of the chocolate was a treat in itself, and I would savor each bite. Iden wasn't much of a candy eater, but he did like dates and nuts so I would occasionally buy some at an organic market to surprise him.

Although we were managing fine, we had to stay on a strict budget to make ends meet. Most of the mothers whom I had met since Elizabeth was born seemed to be in a better financial situation than Iden and me. They talked about babysitters, dining out, and taking cabanas on the shore for the summer. Although I was very content with my new little world, it did make me think of having some luxuries one day.

Elizabeth was a very easy newborn, allowing us to do our chores together on the weekends. In the afternoons after our chores and errands were complete, we sometimes went for a walk and sat and talked under the shade of a tree in Forest Park, and many times we took her to our old stomping ground, Kissena Park.

We would also forgo doing errands on beautiful summer days and head out to Long Beach. We bought a big beach umbrella to protect Elizabeth from the sun and took turns bathing. The ocean was a place for us to let go and to feel refreshed and relaxed. After a day at the beach we would return home and shower before heading out to a casual restaurant for dinner. After putting Elizabeth to sleep we would watch a movie or just enjoy time in each other's arms.

We spent Sundays at my parents' home to keep up the traditional afternoon meal together with family. Since Iden and I started dating we always had Sunday dinner with my parents, and now with Elizabeth, they were even more excited for our weekly visit. Seeing my parents' loving care with Elizabeth was a very endearing sight. It was surprising to see my dad acting in a way that I never remember him doing with my brothers or me.

Both of my brothers were now married and each busy with their own families, but they would still join us for dinner every now and then. Dad's brother, Uncle Dominic, would always be at the Sunday dinner table as well as a cousin or two and some family friends. My parents loved to have company, and I guess I inherited that as well. It always made me happy to have family and friends over for dinner.

The family dinner table was a time for catching up on the week's events: jobs, family, plans, finances, and world news.

My parents' Sunday table was filled with delicious food, wine, conversation and love, all of which refueled me and prepared me for another week. Iden always loved these days too, especially because he did not have his immediate family near him. My family became his family. My parents loved him like a son, and he loved them as his parents.

Fall soon turned into winter along with the cold and gray days. Going for walks was still part of my daily routine, but of course the time sitting outside on benches and talking to neighbors and friends was over. So I started inviting mothers and babies over to socialize. Before the mothers would arrive, I would put down a soft comforter on the living room floor so the babies could play while we talked. I'd invariably host the get-together, making sure there was plenty of coffee and goodies to eat.

Most of the moms had enrolled themselves and their babies in classes at our local community center or at the YMCA. Since we were living on a budget and trying to save as well, I didn't sign up for these classes and thought these home social gatherings were enough for both Elizabeth and me for the time being.

Elizabeth spent most of her waking time with me, but when her daddy came home from work, she would turn and look at him and start to giggle, putting her arms up for him to hold her. Her first word was 'dada,' and we were so happy when she started to utter it at six months old. More words came as the months passed quickly by. As Elizabeth neared her first birthday, she was walking and talking more every day and big plans were underway for her first birthday party.

Although we didn't have a large apartment, we invited family and good friends who we wanted to help us celebrate our daughter's first birthday. The night before the party, Iden and I rearranged the furniture to accommodate a buffet-style luncheon. We hung balloons and streamers and set up a bar area with soda and wine. We set up little folding tables with nuts and chips and placed candy dishes filled with chocolates on them. Iden designed a play list of songs and tuned up his guitar in order to sing "Happy Birthday" to Elizabeth at cake time. Although we had a stand for his guitar in the living room, he'd rarely picked it up since his work had become so demanding.

Usually when Iden came home from work he ate dinner and then played with Elizabeth until we put her to bed. After doing some work on the computer he would fall asleep watching TV. He did enjoy playing his guitar on the weekends after breakfast, when he could sit around in his pajamas and have Elizabeth and me as his audience. When he played, Elizabeth watched him intensely and would sing along with whatever words she knew. It was a very happy sight to observe, and I could feel my heart grow a little whenever he shared this uninterrupted time with her. It was a priceless time in our lives.

After setting up for the party and getting Elizabeth bathed, fed, and dressed I went to get myself ready while Iden played with her. As I was showering, I felt a little dizzy and nauseous, and I thought perhaps it was because I was anxious about the party and wanting to have everything turn out well. After getting dressed I made some toast and tea and Iden and I decided to take a little stroll with Elizabeth since it was such a beautiful day. I thought some fresh air might also help me feel better.

My parents were the first to arrive with handfuls of things for the party. Dad, being artistic, always made decorations for us for our birthdays, and so he started the tradition for his first grandchild by making a beautiful watercolor door decoration of Elizabeth's favorite stuffed animal. Her favorite stuffed animal was a very large rabbit that she slept with every night given to her by my dad. She was very excited to see it, and we immediately hung it outside on our apartment door, with pink and white balloons surrounding it. The rabbit was holding a cake with one candle on it, and written on it were the words, "Happy 1st Birthday, Elizabeth!" The number one was not painted on, but rather was a number cut out and taped on so the decoration could be used for consecutive birthdays to come. It is still in my daughter's possession many decades later.

The other guests soon arrived, and the party got underway. It was great to have Mom arrive a little bit earlier than the other guests just to make sure everything was in order. Soon the apartment was filled with music, talking, and laughter. I was busy with my mother being hostess, so Iden, Dad, and my brothers took turns watching

Elizabeth. She was such a sweet and easy baby that it was really not a problem. She was very social and enjoyed eating, talking, and dancing. A real party girl indeed!

By the time the birthday cake came out and we sang "Happy Birthday," I started to feel a bit nauseous again. Although I was having a good time and no longer felt nervous or anxious, I couldn't get rid of the feeling. I began to think perhaps I might be getting a virus and was looking forward to the end of the day.

Iden played the traditional American birthday song on his guitar, and then he played one in Persian. Elizabeth sat on a little chair in front of him with a birthday crown on her head and clapped her hands throughout both songs while I videotaped them. After the cake was sliced and served, Elizabeth opened her gifts and was so excited with her presents. She received books, toys, clothes, art supplies, and my parents bought her a little kitchen play center. That play kitchen became her focal playing center from that day on and for many years thereafter.

My parents stayed after everyone left to help me clean up, and Mom was pleased with the day and all the gifts Elizabeth had received. I was pleased how everything had turned out, but I was also glad when everyone was gone because I felt I had to lie down. I told Iden that I wasn't feeling well and he said that he would finish cleaning up and take care of Elizabeth by giving her a bath and putting her to sleep. I went to sleep around 7 o'clock and didn't wake up until the following morning.

Upon waking I had the same feeling as I did the day before, and soon realized that it was the same feeling I'd had almost two years ago. It was a Sunday morning and Iden was up with Elizabeth making breakfast. He knew I wasn't feeling well so they had closed the bedroom door so as not to wake me. I went to the kitchen and Iden asked how I was feeling. I didn't want to say anything until I knew for sure, so I just said a little better. He made me a cup of tea and some toast, although I didn't feel like eating anything. I told him that I would like to take a walk to get a few things that I needed at the store. I walked to our nearest pharmacy and bought a home pregnancy test. When I came back, I immediately went into the bathroom, tore open the package, and took the test. I needed a few minutes to wait for the test to know if I was pregnant or had a horrible virus. The little blue sign soon appeared, and I was very excited.

Although we had not planned this pregnancy it was a blessing.

"How are you feeling?" he asked when I came out of the bathroom. "You really don't look well."

I didn't know any other way to say it. "I am pregnant."

He was holding Elizabeth and put her down to give me a kiss and a hug, saying that next year we would be having two birthday celebrations. We spent the day discussing many things and what the future might look like for our growing family.

That night I got up to use the bathroom and saw that Iden was not lying next to me. I found him in the living room watching TV. He said he was having trouble falling asleep and wanted to watch some TV for a while. I asked him if he was worried about anything and he said, "No, but I might take on some consulting work on the weekends."

The plan of my returning back to work after Elizabeth's first birthday did not seem to be in our future. We were very good about managing our money, but children brought extra expenses, and I had not worked in over a year. We wanted to bring this second new life into the world with as much joy and love as we did with Elizabeth, but I felt there was a little sadness that had come over Iden the very moment I told him we were having another baby.

CHAPTER TEN

CLAUDIA

"Anxiety in children is originally other than an expression of the fact that they are feeling the loss of the person they love."

— SIGMUND FREUD

Living without fear allows us to experience a big life along with making many mistakes as well. With making mistakes comes deeper understanding of who we are and what we need and want in life. With my second pregnancy I knew what to expect and was not consulting *What to Expect When You Are Expecting* every day. Elizabeth was almost two, and was walking and running, and she easily kept me in shape chasing after her at the playground, and on our daily walks.

Most of the mothers I knew were also pregnant with their second child, and therefore our conversations focused mainly on what life would be like with a second child. Some of the mothers were planning to return to work after the birth of their second child for financial reasons, while others clearly just wanted to get back to life beyond child care.

Although I was perfectly content being a stay- at-home mom, it was time to get back to work for financial reasons. With a second baby on the way and with our hopes of buying a house in the near future, Iden and I discussed my going back to work. We were not comfortable leaving Elizabeth or our newborn in day care, so Mom, who was working part time these days, offered her babysitting services three days a week. The other two days I was scouting around for a possible neighbor who might be interested in a part-time babysitting job. Our second baby was also due in early spring, which would allow me time at home with my newborn before returning to work in September.

Many of my friends had hopes of buying homes in Westchester or Long Island before their children started school, so they wanted to get back to work as soon as possible to start saving. Iden and I were perfectly content living in Forest Hills and had hopes of buying a house on one of the beautiful tree-lined streets of Forest Hills Gardens. We both wanted to be near to my parents for obvious reasons but living in Forest Hills offered many other benefits. It was an easy commute to work, it was safe, it had playgrounds and parks, and had great private and public schools. We also had developed relationships with other couples with children.

My second pregnancy was very different than my first. I did not experience months of nausea and I did not have any bleeding that kept me on bed rest. I was healthy and I had a big appetite from the moment I conceived. During my pregnancy with Elizabeth I had only gained about 20 pounds, but with my second pregnancy I had already gained 20 pounds by the time I was in my fifth month. The doctors reassured me that the weight gain was fine, and after having a routine sonogram Iden was relieved to know I wasn't carrying twins.

Our days waiting for the birth of our second child were very busy. Iden's work schedule at the hospital and his consulting work for some small companies made for a late-night return home a few nights a week. On the weekends we had our usual chores and errands, along with Iden working from home as well. Elizabeth would often go a day or two without seeing him.

As we ate breakfast she would ask, "Where is Daddy?"

I would always say that he was working and that he would be home soon, reassuring her that he loved her very much. I could tell she missed him. I too missed sharing the things and what new words our daughter was saying, what she learned to do, and what she laughed at during the day. When he returned home on those late nights, he would greet me with our usual hug and kiss, but he was tired and just wanted to eat and sometimes even ate at the computer finishing up urgent work for a client.

In the middle of April, we were all sleeping late on a Saturday morning when the phone rang. I picked it up and heard the word, "Salam." I immediately handed the phone to Iden, telling him it was a call from Iran. He said, "Salam," and I could tell by the look on his face that he was hearing some bad news. He took the phone into the living room and continued to talk. I heard his voice change as if he were holding back tears. I went to check on Elizabeth and then went to sit on the couch next to Iden, trying to figure out what had happened using my limited knowledge of Farsi.

The conversation ended abruptly and Iden started to cry. He sat down on the carpet and said his brother Rahman had died in his sleep. He was only 38 years old and had suffered a massive heart attack. He grabbed and hugged me and cried a very painful cry. Although I had only met Rahman once before, I thought he was a very sweet and extremely educated man and Iden loved him very much. Rahman had developed a drinking problem and had recently separated from his wife and child. Therefore, he was not in the best physical and mental condition for a man of his age.

After the news of his brother's death there was an obvious change in Iden. Of course after a sibling dies it is expected there would be a period of grieving, especially because Iden was so far away from his family. But Iden's sadness was darker; it removed him from his life and his family's life.

Iden became frozen in his grief. He got up every morning and went to work and when he returned home, he pretty much just ate and went to sleep. There was no music, no conversation, no laughter or making future plans. I knew he needed time to heal, and the best thing I could do was to let him know that I loved him.

Elizabeth and I became a duo, doing mostly everything together, while leaving Iden alone on the weekends to deal with his loss. At times I desperately tried to bring him out of this dark period by asking him to take walks with us, making foods he loved, visiting my parents, and having his friends over, but nothing seemed to work.

Looking back, I realize how little I knew about depression. You don't just snap out of depression or will yourself out of one. It was painful to see Iden suffering, and I thought it would all be okay after he had mourned the death of his brother. Or can you ever stop mourning the loss of a loved one? I didn't know how to console him, and I was at a loss as to how to help him. There were times when I started to feel sorry for myself because I was feeling as if someone had died in my life as well. Where did Iden go? I didn't know if he was still taking Zoloft or seeing the psychiatrist anymore. Although we had been married for over six years, I still felt uncomfortable asking him.

One warm Saturday in April, Iden woke up and seemed to be feeling better. It was apparently so because he was up before me. He was smiling and suggested that we should go to Central Park since it was a beautiful day and that we had not taken Elizabeth there recently. I immediately agreed, even though I didn't feel I could walk too much because I was in my ninth month and was quite large.

I was so happy to see him in a better mood that I agreed to do anything to celebrate the change and to give Elizabeth a nice family outing. We packed lunch, loaded up the car, and headed to Manhattan.

Central Park was a place that held many memories from my own family. Dad loved New York City and he often took me to explore Manhattan with him. The park was our favorite place to go. It had so many things to do, especially in the warmer days of spring and summer.

We were lucky to find a spot not far from 5th Avenue and 60th Street. We unloaded the car, and with the stroller holding all our bags, we made our way toward the park. Elizabeth now loved to walk and run everywhere. The park was bursting with spring flowers and trees with greens leaves and budding blossoms, lovers and friends sitting on benches, music playing, and families like us strolling along with their children.

We headed first to the zoo and then arrived just in time at the sea lion habitat to catch them being fed. Elizabeth enjoyed this show so much and Iden and I enjoyed observing her happiness.

We then found a bench to sit and have a snack before heading to the carousel. Iden had to do the ride with Elizabeth because I have motion sickness even when not pregnant. Every time they came to where I was standing Elizabeth called out, "Mommy, look at me!"

We made our way toward the boathouse to see the sailboats and find a place to have a picnic lunch. As we sat watching the children sail their boats, I noticed the expression on Elizabeth's face. She was excited about seeing the children sailing their boats, but not as much as seeing how happy her father was on that day. She constantly placed her hand into his hand and held it ever so tightly the whole day.

We ate our picnic lunch and sat for a while enjoying the warmth of the spring sun on our faces and the harmony among us. We packed up our belongings, almost skipping back through the park to our car.

As we walked back to the car, I was feeling a little uncomfortable and suggested we stop in a restroom for both Elizabeth and me before the car ride home. Just as we exited the restrooms, I felt water trickle down my leg. I told Iden that my water had broken, and he was very excited but remained calm. Elizabeth felt a sense of urgency and started walking and talking fast. While in the car, we made plans to stop home first to grab the bags I had prepared in advance for myself as well as for Elizabeth. Elizabeth would stay at my parents' home while I was at the hospital.

I wasn't feeling strong contractions, so I knew we had some time. I would rather arrive later than sooner in order to avoid waiting in a labor room for hours. On the ride home we explained to Elizabeth that we were taking her to Nanny and Poppy's home so Mommy and Daddy can have her baby sister or brother, assuring her that we would soon be back together. Elizabeth loved my parents and felt very comfortable in their care. I called my doctor when I got home and he said to arrive in a few hours, no later because after your water breaks it is necessary to give birth to avoid complications. I called my parents as well and told them our plans. They too were excited to have a new grandchild arriving and to have Elizabeth stay with them.

Claudia Shireen (Farsi for sweet one) came into the world kicking and screaming as all babies do, but her scream as the nurses later told me was one not to be forgotten. When they handed her to me it was difficult to look into her eyes because she was crying so hard. My two girls from the minute they arrived were very different in their appearance and demeanor.

Claudia was very colicky, and it took supreme effort to get her to nurse calmly. She would nurse so strongly that I developed mastitis in a few weeks and needed to be hospitalized to receive intravenous medication. When I took her to the pediatrician, he explained that she wasn't gaining enough weight and perhaps I should consider bottle-feeding her. Since I had nursed Elizabeth, I wanted to do the same for Claudia, but it was not working well for either of us, so I supplemented it with formula. Finding a formula that she was able to tolerate became a difficult task. Before Claudia was born, I thought I was a woman of patience, but when she entered my world, it taught me that I had very little.

Over the years, Claudia would always be the child who needed a little extra care. She walked and talked later than Elizabeth, but still in the normal range mode. Many loud noises, strangers, and new places seemed to upset her, and she needed someone to hold her to be quieted down. Elizabeth was very proud to be an older sister, and she immediately took on the role as helper and protector. Although she was not yet two when her sister was born, she wanted to help feed her, wash her, and to play with her.

As I watched the girls play together, I was amazed at Elizabeth's maturity. Elizabeth could make Claudia stop crying and start smiling in minutes by making silly faces or just by holding her. Elizabeth would often say, "Look Mommy, she is happy now!"

Elizabeth was born with dark brown hair, but it was now almost platinum blonde, and her beautiful blue eyes still remained. Claudia was born with dark hair as well, but had her dad's dark, big, cherry- colored eyes. If you looked at both girls quickly you would never think they were related, but if you watched them for a while, you could feel their sisterly bond and notice that they smiled the same way.

Although I did not have to work after many sleepless nights of dealing with a colicky baby, I still ran after a toddler who was up and ready to go the minute she opened her eyes. My morning routine was to feed Elizabeth first and give her some love and attention, while I walked around with Claudia in a snuggly wrapped around my chest, trying to get her back to sleep. In order for me to shower, I would have to put Claudia in the crib. Even though she cried, I knew she was safe.

While I was in the shower Elizabeth would play by the bathroom with the door open and inform me on the state of her sister. Early on Elizabeth learned how to take care of her family members and I learned to shower and dress in under five minutes. I got really good at having the double stroller all packed up with the diaper bag and all the necessities the night before. Thank goodness Claudia loved being in the carriage, and as soon as we went outside the crying would stop. She became quiet and would fall asleep, allowing time for Elizabeth and me to talk and play at the playground.

Pushing the stroller around with two children quickly got me back into my skinny jeans. My friends and I would take turns sitting on the benches watching the infants and putting our toddlers on the swings and seesaws. We no longer went to coffee shops because we took up too much space, so we would bring Thermoses of coffee and bags of cookies and snacks to munch on while we talked and played with our children. Since I was always the more anxious mother, I was the one who went with the older children and pushed them on the swings and ran around playing tag, while my other friends watched the sleeping newborns.

The months passed by quickly, and we were used to surviving with little sleep and having raccoon eyes. When Iden got home from work he relieved me and helped me with Claudia even though he had put in a full day at work. Iden and Claudia had a unique bond that started very early and was always present throughout her teenage years and into adulthood. His love for Elizabeth was evident as well, but she was easier to be around without the demand for excessive patience. Iden had more patience for Claudia, and she responded to him and was more content in his arms. He would often get her to fall asleep in his arms while we ate dinner and shared a few quiet moments together.

Mom always told me never to compare my children because no two children are exactly alike. Elizabeth and Claudia, although sisters, were as different as different can be. When Claudia was old enough to sit in the swing at the park, she didn't like to go too high, whereas Elizabeth wanted to touch the sky and she would say, "Higher, higher, Mommy!"

Both Claudia and I had the same dislike of the seesaw. She did not like going up or down and would like to sit and be balanced while sitting on Iden's lap while Elizabeth and I sat on the other side.

Claudia was almost one, so we set to planning her birthday party. Iden reminded me that last year he said we would be having two parties around this time of year. I couldn't believe how quickly the time had passed, although I remembered Mom telling me that when you raise children, the days are long, but the years fly by quickly.

We had a lovely party for Claudia, and she behaved well that day with very little episodes of crying. It was beginning to feel like the colicky period would soon be over. Iden played "Happy Birthday" on his guitar with Elizabeth strumming along on her toy guitar as well. Seeing Iden surrounded by his girls and his music made it a very happy day for me and for all of us.

Although Iden and I had made plans for me to return to work after Claudia was born, we both thought it would be in our best interest to wait until the girls were enrolled full time in school. Right before I was scheduled to return to work, I broke down and told Iden I didn't have it in me to leave the girls and do the running around that was necessary for me to go back to work. Even though Mom had planned to watch them a few days a week I was struggling to be confident that I could do it all. I wanted to be there for them, especially in these early years.

Iden was making good money between his job at the hospital and inside jobs doing consulting. Although he worked long hours during the week and even on the weekends, he never complained.

He was equally happy having me remain at home with the girls as I was.

Elizabeth soon turned four and was ready to start prekindergarten. Claudia was turning two and attending Mommy and Me classes at a local community house. Most of my friends had returned to work, and we no longer had those impromptu gatherings in our apartment. I wanted to give Claudia the full benefit of my alone time with her because most of my time was spent with both her and her sister.

I knew the days of my staying at home would come to an end because Iden seriously wanted to start looking for a house. Since the girls were born, we had filled our apartment, and our two-bedroom apartment was no longer big enough. Every room was taken up — carriage, toys, playpen, crib, etc. —and the closets were filled with diapers. We dreamed of having more space and a yard for the girls to play in and perhaps even a porch. I wasn't sure when I would be returning to work, but I knew it needed to be soon.

I wasn't sure if it was due to working so many hours or the demands of family life, but Iden's moods seemed to change. He went from being involved and talkative with the girls and me, to being distant and aloof and needing time to be alone. The girls clearly felt the lack of his presence.

It wasn't as if Iden didn't want to spend time with us, he just didn't seem capable of it and didn't seem aware of what his behavior was doing to his family. When he was feeling down, I became more anxious because I felt alone, and I had to pretend to my girls that their dad was fine so they wouldn't feel anything was wrong. But children are very perceptive, and they were able to understand that Daddy wasn't always happy. They needed me to help them feel stable.

Elizabeth, being older and a little stronger in spirit, could sail through each little storm, a little weathered, but not discouraged. Claudia, on the other hand, started to feel the uneasiness and it settled inside her, perhaps not noticeably at that time, but years later the evidence of our struggle would surface.

Patricia with Claudia and Lizzy 1993 ©

CHAPTER ELEVEN

CHILDHOOD

*"The most effective kind of education is that a child should
play amongst lovely things."*

— PLATO

In 1994, Elizabeth was enrolled in prekindergarten in a local
Catholic school. We weren't sure where we were going to start
her education from kindergarten onward, but for now we decided
this school would be perfect because it was close to our home and
many neighborhood friends' children were in the same class. The
public schools in our neighborhood were the best, and although
we were concerned about her receiving an excellent education, we
also wanted a school that provided a sense of community.

Elizabeth was a very bright, social, and happy child, and she adapted
easily to new situations, so we knew she would do fine wherever
she went. She attended the morning session of prekindergarten that
went from 8:30 to 11 o'clock, Monday through Friday. Since we
only had one car, I made the eight-block walk to school and back
twice a day with Claudia. Iden normally took the train to work, but
now he was seeing clients after work at least three times a week so
it was necessary for him to use the car on a daily basis.

I tried to arrange classes for Claudia in the nearby community
house during the time Elizabeth was at school to make fewer trips
back and forth, especially in the winter. In inclement weather Iden
would leave for work a little later and drop Elizabeth off at school.

Elizabeth loved school and quickly made new friends. We received golden reports about how well behaved and bright she was. She was already reading and writing, but more importantly, her teacher always commented on how kind and helpful she was to her classmates. With her new love of reading, we went to the library every Thursday after school and took out the limit of books that we were allowed to borrow. We easily went through them all in a week.

After dinner we had a nightly routine of bathing and reading before bedtime. Claudia would sit on my lap with Elizabeth in front on her little chair pretending to be the teacher and read a story. Many of the books were too difficult for her to read, so she either made up the words, or I would read it for her. Although Claudia enjoyed listening to the stories, I think she enjoyed looking at Elizabeth's face while she read, especially if she made funny faces to make Claudia laugh.

The first year of school went by quickly and summer soon arrived. We decided to take our first vacation in upstate New York. Iden and I had always loved the mountains and nature, so we decided to rent a small cabin in Bolton Landing in Lake George with some friends for the first two weeks in July.

The two-bedroom cabin was situated right near the lake with a wraparound deck. The cabin grounds had a playground, a pool both for adults and children, and lots of green grass to play and run around on. Each cabin had an outdoor barbeque pit where we made many dinners and roasted marshmallows at night while telling stories and listening to Iden play his guitar under a sky of a thousand stars.

One of our friends knew how to operate a boat, so we rented one and rode around the lake finding places to dock and swim and even to do some fishing. The days on the lake made us bronzy, and Iden started to improve and began to smile every day. Since he was born in the mountainous city of Tabriz, the mountains were in him, and he seemed to feel at peace surrounded by the Adirondacks.

The children loved being outdoors and sharing our meals on the deck with our friends and the view of the beautiful lake. Some nights we went into the city of Lake George to do some of the touristy things. We played arcade games, went on horse and buggy rides around the town, and sat in the town park to listen to outdoor concerts while eating large waffle cones filled to the top with our favorite ice cream.

On July 4th we all went into town to sit in the park and listen to a concert while watching the fireworks. We took a large blanket to sit on to enjoy the festivities. The girls had fun playing, but as soon as the first bang of the fireworks exploded, Claudia started hysterically screaming, while covering her ears and trying to run away from where we were all sitting. We tried to soothe her by picking her up and talking to her, but nothing seemed to work.

Elizabeth was enjoying herself along with the other children. Iden decided to take Claudia back to the car to soothe her and to allow the rest of us to enjoy the show. I suggested he wait a little to give her time to adjust to the noise to see if she would eventually calm down, but he couldn't deal with her being so upset, so he whisked her away. I know he loved Claudia very much and wanted to make things better for her always, but in the future, we would continue to disagree about how to handle Claudia's phobias.

We spent many wonderful vacations in Lake George and continued to spend at least one week a year up there until the girls were teenagers. Many times Mom came along with us. Having her

Lizzy, Iden, Patricia, and Claudia at Lake George in 2000 ©

with us was a real treat for my girls, for Iden, and especially for me. She encouraged Iden and me to take a walk together, sit by the lake, and even go out for dinner, just the two of us, something we rarely did.

Another school year began, and Elizabeth started kindergarten. We decided to keep her enrolled at the same school because we had all become fond of the teachers and the nurturing and safe environment of the school. We had discussed my returning to work but thought it best to hold out for one more year until Claudia started school. We both knew that Claudia was a little delicate and needed some extra support dealing with her phobias, which increased as the years went on. She was afraid of clowns, life-size characters at parties, and anyone wearing a mask. Halloween was especially difficult. But Claudia was an extremely loveable child and always had a smile on her face.

The few times we went to Disney World were very difficult with all the Disney characters around and with the fireworks at night. But Iden and I got through each crying event the best way we could. We felt bad at times for Elizabeth because we couldn't participate in all the things she wanted to do. But Elizabeth was mature and understanding and was always accepting. She didn't like to see her sister upset and she rarely complained about any change of plans.

In order to make some extra money, I was able to do some babysitting of siblings of students in Elizabeth's class who were Claudia's age. It was a good opportunity for Claudia to play with someone her own age without her sister around, and it gave me some extra money to buy little extras for the girls, and Iden.

Since I was a teacher, some of the parents had also asked me to tutor their child in reading and math. I made a schedule for after school to do homework with the student while Elizabeth did her homework and Claudia played or, on occasion, over the weekends at the student's home. With this extra money, I was even able to save a little.

Elizabeth sailed through kindergarten doing well and showing early on that she was going to become not just a student, but also someone who would pursue an education with determination to become a lifelong learner.

As summertime once again rolled around, we looked forward to our family vacation upstate. One night in June, Iden came home from work and said he wanted to discuss something with me after the girls had gone to bed. Although I could sense it wasn't bad news, I was anxious to find out what he wanted to discuss.

After the girls were asleep, Iden made two cups of tea and we sat at the table ready to talk. He started by saying how much he missed his family and that he wanted to take a trip to Iran to visit them this summer. It had been four years since his brother died, and he needed to go home. He thought it would be great for us to finally meet his family.

The political situation in Iran was no better, but it wasn't any worse. Iden had now become an American citizen, but we could only travel to Iran on his Iranian passport, since the United States at that time did not issue visas to Iran. The whole time he was talking, a hundred thoughts and questions ran through my head. I waited until he was finished speaking before asking any questions because he was talking excitedly, and I didn't want to interrupt him. He explained that we needed to fly to France with our American passports and to stay a few days with his brother, Ahmad, who lived in Paris with his wife. After leaving Paris we would fly to Iran on his Iranian passport. "Wow!" Was all I could say. I couldn't help but have visions of the movie *Not Without My Daughter*.

I asked Iden questions, and he gave me the answers, perhaps the answers he knew I wanted to hear, but not necessarily the correct ones. He said he had been saving money from his work as a computer consultant and we just had to purchase the airline tickets. We would not need to stay in any hotels since we would be staying in Paris with his brother, and then once in Iran we would be staying with family. Many of his Iranian friends had already taken the trip with their American families, and they said it was safe and that they'd had a very good time.

The only thing I needed to adhere to while in Iran was to cover my hair, therefore I was required to wear a headscarf. Since our daughters were young, they could forgo the covering. Deep down I was frightened, but also very excited because I had always dreamed of going to Paris and meeting Iden's family. I hoped this trip would allow me to touch a part of Iden that had seemed unreachable.

Everything seemed to happen quickly. To leave by mid-July, we needed to start making the arrangements as soon as possible. Iden needed to go to Washington, DC, to visit the embassy in order for us to be placed on his Iranian passport. Even though the girls didn't really understand where we were going, they knew there was a new excitement in our home. They understood that they were going to be meeting a new set of grandparents and many new aunts, uncles, cousins, and friends of their father. They were also excited about taking a very long plane ride across a very large ocean.

Packing was hard because I wasn't sure what sort of clothes I should take. Iden encouraged me to take my regular clothes along with some dresses, because Iranians loved to have parties. I also needed to buy a shirt with long sleeves to cover my arms while walking in the streets. Tehran in the summer has temperatures in the hundreds, so the material had to be lightweight, like linen. I also purchased some pretty scarves as well.

I made sure to pack necessary medicines for the girls in case they became sick, even though Iden reiterated the fact that his whole family were doctors, so if any of us got ill we would be in good hands.

I was concerned how I was going to break this news to my family. On a Sunday afternoon after our meal as we were having dessert, I broke the news to them. My parents thought it was a very unsafe trip to take, and they were especially concerned for the well-being of my children. The Iranian hostage situation was long over, and things were safe for tourists, especially for Americans, to travel to Iran.

My parents asked Iden many questions about Iran, more than they had ever asked in our total 10 years of marriage. Their concern haunted me the entire trip, and I prayed their ominous look was nothing more than parental love.

With our suitcases packed, passports, tickets, and all the other necessities organized, we were ready to leave on our adventure. I had also bought some small gifts to take for his sisters and brothers that I thought they might not be able to purchase in Iran. Little did I know that once I arrived in Iran and visited the bazaars, that there really wasn't anything they could not purchase in Iran. The bazaars were filled with many goods from herbs, jewelry, carpets, and everything under the sun. My gifts suddenly did not seem at all impressive, although they were very much appreciated.

We left New York in mid-July on a Saturday flight to Paris, and to this day I have never had such an amazing feeling as we descended into Paris. Iden's brother and his wife and a few nieces and nephews were waiting for us at Charles De Gaulle Airport. When we greeted his family, it was such a new experience to meet people with the same facial features as Iden and my daughters. Iden greeted his family with big hugs and kisses and then he introduced us to his family. We were all tired after a long flight, so we went back to Ahmed's home located near Saint Germaine.

The girls were amazing travelers, and my first priority was to get them a good meal and some much-needed sleep. Iden's brother had cheese and bread and a Persian stew with rice waiting for us when we arrived at their apartment. The two-bedroom apartment was redesigned for us so we could all be in one room, while Ahmed, his wife, and 10-year old son shared their bedroom. We washed up and enjoyed the meal together, combining French and Persian cuisines. We drank some tea before the girls, and I said good night and went to sleep while Iden stayed up a bit longer chatting with his brother.

Ahmed had many similar features to Iden. Since Ahmed had studied and lived in Paris for many years, his accent was much different than Iden's. His English was also very good as well as his wife's, so we were able to hold good conversations. When Iden and Ahmed were talking among themselves they spoke Farsi, every now and then switching to English.

It was wonderful watching Iden looking so full of life and happy. Since we were in Paris for just a few days we did not do all the touristy things since we had the benefit of having someone who knew the city well to show us around. We walked down the Champs-Elysees, saw the famous monument Arc de Triomphe, sat in the Luxembourg and Tuileries Gardens, and ate delicious waffles.

One day we were able to leave the girls with Ahmed's wife, Rana, and have an afternoon visiting the Musee d'Orsay.

We mostly ate meals at home prepared by Rana, but we also sat in sidewalk cafes drinking coffee and eating delicious pastries while people-watching. The girls were well-behaved and enjoyed all the attention given to them by their older cousin. It was nice having an older child who could keep them occupied while we strolled the streets of Paris.

The time flew by, and we were soon ready for the second part of our journey. Ahmed took us to the airport, and we said our goodbyes. We had such a great time in Paris and saying goodbye to Iden's family and to Paris was difficult for all of us. Three days in Paris for a girl from Queens was just a tease. I knew I would have to return to this beautiful city again.

Iden and his brother hugged and shed many tears of happiness. Ahmed hugged our girls and I noticed that both he and Iden possessed a gentleness that was very sincere and sweet. As I said goodbye to Ahmed I felt as if I were saying goodbye to an old friend. He looked at my face and noticed I was a little nervous.

"Don't worry! Everything will be just fine, and you will enjoy your time in Iran," he said, as we ended our embrace and went through security.

We boarded Air France to Tehran. Air France was one of the few airlines that flew to Iran after the Revolution. We did not show our American passports, but Iden showed his Iranian passport with my picture and pictures of our two daughters. On the plane were Iranians as well as many non-Iranians and I heard them speaking many different languages. It was comforting to know that my daughters and I were not the only non-Iranians on our way to Iran.

The flight to Iran would be almost six hours long and we were very fortunate to have seats together with some empty ones between us. I settled the girls in and gave them some crayons and coloring books that we had bought in Paris.

I stayed awake and watched Elizabeth and Claudia sleep a most peaceful sleep. Iden looked at me and tried to convey with his eyes that we would be fine and to try to relax. Whether it was his soothing look or a deep feeling of trust, I soon fell asleep and was woken by the flight attendant informing us that we were soon landing in Tehran and to please sit upright.

The girls were still sleeping, but I slowly woke them up and tried to inform them in the best way they could understand that we were in another country meeting more of Daddy's relatives. Before the plane landed, the women began adorning themselves with headscarves. Elizabeth asked why I was putting a scarf on my head. I explained that it was something all the women in Iran did, even though it wasn't something we did where we lived. She just looked at me and said, "That's nice."

When we landed in Tehran and stepped into the airport it was clearly evident that my daughters and I had entered a whole new reality than we had ever previously experienced. Women wore burkas, and some had scarves covering their hair. Many men wore long black shirts and most of them sported moustaches.

After claiming our luggage, we were soon greeted by almost 20 people. It seems to be a custom in Iran that when a relative comes to visit, you bring as many people as possible to greet your guests. After a very long trip it was overwhelming to meet so many strangers. It took an hour or so to meet and double cheek kiss every person while listening to Farsi and hearing Iden's name being called out a hundred times. The girls were very good about receiving all the attention. I was very surprised at Claudia's ability to meet so many strangers without issue. We finally made our way to the hotel. Iden's family is from the north of Iran, and since that required another eight-hour car ride, we planned to stay in Tehran awhile to relax and meet some relatives that lived there.

We stayed at what was once a Sheraton Hotel but was later renamed Hotel Homma after the revolution. It was a spectacular hotel with a mix of Western and Eastern décor. A very large painting of Ayatollah Khomeini hung prominently behind the reception desk. Iden's sister, Pari, and her husband Youness, had reserved a suite for us and it was absolutely beautiful. We had two full bedrooms and two bathrooms with Western toilets, a kitchen area, and a beautiful balcony. His whole family was staying on the fourth floor with us, and we practically took over the entire floor.

We planned to stay in Tehran for almost a week to meet his cousins and to do some sightseeing, but for now all we could think about was eating a meal, taking a shower, and getting some rest, even though we had slept on the plane. The whole experience from the time we left NY until now had left us exhausted.

I unpacked, gave the girls a shower, and ordered room service. I was surprised at the delightful meal that appeared at our door with a beautiful white tablecloth. We had chicken kebabs with rice and freshly baked pita and yogurt sauce, followed by a big pot of tea. Our girls were good eaters and quickly ate up the tender meal and almost fell asleep with their last bite. We closed the blinds from the hot afternoon sun and put the girls to bed.

Iden and I went out on the balcony and smoked a cigarette. As I inhaled the cigarette I also took in the sights, sounds, and smells of Tehran. The palm trees, the smell of pita being baked in the streets, a cloudless blue sky with a fiercely bright sun, and the Alborz Mountains were all new and beautiful sights.

The next morning, the girls were still sleeping, but I did not see Iden. I walked around the suite but did not find him anywhere. I washed and dressed and got the girls up. They were in good spirits and wanted to know where Daddy was. I said we would go and look for him and reassured them that he was probably visiting with one of his family members.

As we walked down the hall, a door stood open, and I could hear talking and quickly recognized Iden's voice. He and his parents were sitting on the floor sharing breakfast together. When his parents saw us, they immediately told us to come in and join them. The girls were happy to see their dad and get hugs from their newly met grandparents. We enjoyed the hearty breakfast together, and although our communication was limited, we could still feel their love.

We spent a glorious week in Tehran visiting relatives and enjoying the parks and the sights of the city. His family made me feel much loved and welcome and it was lovely seeing Iden so content. We went shopping at the bazaars and were overcome by all the goods for sale. Everything was beautifully displayed in the shops, including jewelry, clothing, electronic devices, kitchenware, spices, perfumes, leather goods, and, of course, carpets. Carpets in the bazaars are piled one on top of the other in huge piles over 10 feet high. A seller uses a ladder to turn over carpets for you to look at if you are interested in buying one.

On one outing to the market with Iden's sister and her husband, they asked us to pick out a carpet that we liked as a belated wedding present. I looked at over a hundred hand-woven carpets, one more beautiful than the other, until finally settling on one that I fell in love with.

Walking in the streets of Tehran under the shade of big palm trees and a brilliant sun with gutters of running water along the side of the streets, smelling the roasting ears of corn on open fires, and listening to afternoon prayers are images that will always be etched in my memories of Iran.

One day while still in Tehran, Iden and his family went to visit the grave of his brother Rahman, and Iden thought it best that I stay behind at the hotel because it was undoubtedly a sad occasion and not necessary or suitable for our girls to attend. He arranged for us to spend the day with his cousin and we went to visit Niavaran Palace, once the home of the Shah and his family. His cousin and his wife picked us up at the hotel after breakfast and we drove to the palace, which was about a 45-minute ride.

The palace was very impressive, even though it had not been looked after and had been stripped of many of its royal possessions after the revolution. We took a walk around and found a park for the girls to play in, later returning to the hotel where the girls and I fell asleep in one bed and awoke when Iden returned from his day out to say good night.

Our time in Tehran quickly came to an end and we headed up north to Iden's hometown of Ardebil. Our last day in Tehran we spent lounging in the hotel lobby drinking a la crème glacee, ice cream sodas made with coffee, which were so delightful. There was Persian music playing and my girls were very happy learning Persian dance moves from their cousins. Iden and I sat with his family, and they asked many questions about life in America.

A few hours later we retired to our rooms to pack and get ready for our trip up north near the Caspian Sea. I was looking forward to being near the sea and having an opportunity to go swimming and to see Iden's hometown.

After a short nap we all showered and got dressed for dinner in another hotel nearby. Before leaving for dinner Iden and I went out on the balcony while the girls where happily entertained by Iranian cartoons. We shared a cigarette together and he expressed how happy and appreciative he was of me taking this trip with him. Although he spoke with happiness, he seemed sad, and I asked him what was on his mind. He said it was a shame that his family was so far away and that he had really loved all of us being together. I responded by saying it had been an amazing and loving experience and that hopefully we could see everyone again either here or in New York. We gave each other a strong hug and a kiss, and we went back into the room where our two girls were singing a Persian children's song.

We met Iden's family in the lobby to share our last dinner in Tehran. During dinner I looked at my daughters' faces sitting on their aunt's and uncle's laps, and I too wished that we had Iden's family in New York.

We walked the few blocks back to our hotel and said our goodbyes to family members who were not heading up north with us. Iden put the girls to bed and lay down with them and I could hear them as they talked and laughed together. I went outside and lit a cigarette, looking out over the city and up to the sky with its crescent moon. One moon for the entire world to share, but how unfortunate we were not able to share peace and understanding to have families stay connected. I puffed my smoke up into the sky and felt ready for part three of our journey.

Early the following morning we packed the car with our luggage for the trip up north to the Caspian Sea and to Iden's hometown. His parents and his sister, Pari, and her husband, Youness, were taking the trip with us. Iden, his sister, the girls, and I packed ourselves into a very small Peykan for the trip. His parents and Youness went in another.

We headed through the Alborz Mountains, leaving the city of Tehran behind. The mountains were unlike any other mountains I had seen in upstate New York. The mountains are large, brown, barren slopes void of any trees and vegetation. As we drove through the mountain roads the girls were excited to see goats roaming about. We made a few stops to use a restroom and buy drinks in a small mountainside shop along the road. Iden's family warned us not to buy any food from these shops because they were afraid that we might get sick.

As we were driving, we listened to a cassette of Abba songs, which Iden played over and over because there was no radio reception in the mountains and that was the only English-speaking cassette his brother-in-law owned. If I ever hear an Abba song it immediately takes me back to that car ride up north to the Caspian Sea. "Oh, Fernando" and "Dancing Queen!"

We arrived in a city near the Caspian Sea called Rasht in mid-afternoon. His family had rented a lovely villa on the lakeshore. The villa had a huge wraparound porch and the air smelled salty and fresh. The inside decoration was more casual than that of the hotel in Tehran. We settled into our rooms and the girls, although tired, were very excited to go walk on the sandy beach and play on the playground on the villa grounds. Iden was very tired due to emotional fatigue rather than physical, so he took a nap while the girls and I walked on the beach and had fun exploring. It was so relaxed up north. Many women weren't wearing any headscarves and were walking in the water with their bare legs exposed.

Since it was so warm, the girls wanted to change into their bathing suits and put their feet in the water. We went back to the hotel to find that Iden was fast asleep, so I quickly changed the girls into their swimsuits and left quietly, leaving Iden to rest.

The girls took a few dips in the water, splashing and screaming with joy. I didn't know if it was appropriate for me to put on my swimsuit, so I just rolled up my pants to my knees and went in with the girls.

We dried off and headed to the playground. They had a circular ride that you pushed with your hands and ran around as fast as your feet could go before quickly jumping on and sitting down until it stopped. We played on that for a while, then the girls found a seesaw. Elizabeth enjoyed the seesaw while Claudia held on to me for dear life, although she tolerated it to make her sister happy.

After expending all our energy, we returned to our room to rest a bit before dinner. Iden was still sleeping, and the girls were very good about remaining quiet. The girls and I showered and laid down for about an hour before we were awakened by a knock on the door to let us know that it was soon dinnertime. Iden was up, showered, and dressed, and he looked very handsome. He had some good color after walking about in the Tehran sun and he looked rested and happy. He wore a black linen shirt with grey linen pants and sandals and his black hair was a bit wavier due to the seaside air. We looked at each other and smiled. I knew that he knew I loved him very much.

Hungry and excited to be eating in a new place, we all walked downstairs to meet his brother and his wife in the lobby before entering the restaurant. The restaurant was simply decorated with windows looking out to sea. As soon as you entered you could smell the delicious spices and fish being grilled on open fires. The room was a little dark and candles adorned every table to give the room an elegant and cozy glow. As soon as we sat down, we were brought freshly baked pita bread and butter with various types of herbs such as radishes, mint, and scallions. There was also a plate of feta cheese, yogurt, and eggplant dip.

Although my girls were young, they had developed very sophisticated palates and enjoyed feasting on these appetizers. Iden ordered for us, and I knew he would order well. While we waited for our food, we watched the sun set on the sea and Iden's parents held our girls lovingly while singing a child's song to them in French. The food, when it arrived, was an amazing sight. There were grilled sturgeon kebabs on top of white rice with fresh vegetables and grilled tomatoes.

Little did I know that sturgeon is prized for its caviar, and the Caspian Sea was known for the bulk of the world's catch. Even the girls ate the flaky, soft, and deliciously marinated fish with much enjoyment. After we finished our meal, we left the restaurant and took our tea and honey cookies on the porch to take in the last moments of the night sky.

We drank our tea and sat looking at the sea and each other. No words were needed to understand the love we all felt. Many years have passed since that trip to the Caspian Sea, and the girls still remember those loving summer days with their Iranian grandparents by the sea.

After a few peaceful and delightful days at the sea we departed to Ardebil, Iden's place of birth. Ardebil was a four-hour trip from where we were, so we enjoyed a leisurely and satisfying breakfast before embarking on another trip. We left the oceanside and headed to a mountainous city and another exciting opportunity to discover more about Iden's past. The trip was somewhat like putting pieces of a puzzle together, only the pieces were scattered all over and not directly laid out in front of me.

The smell of the sea was soon long gone as we drove through the Alborz Mountains again. Unlike the mountains in Tehran, the mountains up north were greener with many types of trees. Many olive trees and special palm trees with large dates grew along the sides of the road. The girls and I marveled at the palms. Iden was driving and he suddenly pulled the car over to a roadside shop and said, "Let's walk around and see if they have some dates for sale."

We all stepped out of the car for a much-needed stretch, and Iden took the girls into the store. Iden's family pulled over as well and took a walk with us. The store was like a farm stand, only it was selling products only made from olives, figs, and dates. There were baskets full of freshly harvested dates, figs, and olives and the owners gladly offered us samples of all of their goods. The figs and dates were nothing like I had ever seen or tasted in America. The girls tasted them and thought they were eating candy because of the intense sweetness of the fruit.

The olives were also very large and had many different colors, textures and tastes. Even the store had a sweet smell like a candy store. Some of the dates and figs were stuffed with walnuts and pistachios and were simply delicious. Iden purchased some of the products and I also bought some fig jam and a fig hand cream. We were given hot tea in small glass cups and no sugar cubes were necessary because of the sweetness of the fruit that lingered in our mouths. We all said, "*Khoda hafez*," goodbye, but literally meaning "God take care," and as we left the store, we received hugs from the grateful owners.

With our legs stretched and with our little snack we were ready to continue our trip up north. The girls and I took a nap. A little before we arrived at Iden's sister's house, I opened my eyes and saw the green mountains hugging the winding roads and beautiful flowers of all colors growing wild along the roadside. The air was cooler and the wind on my face felt delightful.

Iden's sister had arranged for us to stay at her home since it was larger and had American toilets as opposed to the more traditional ones found in Iran, which are more like American outhouses. A gate surrounded Pari's large home of many floors. Persian rugs were scattered throughout on the shiny marble floors.

Both Pari and Youness were doctors and they had recently built this new house. Everything smelled new and looked hardly lived in, but it was tastefully decorated with Persian décor. The backyard was also lovely, with a swimming pool, gardens, and swinging chairs that the girls immediately jumped on.

After taking a brief tour, we went up to the second floor where Iden and I were staying with the girls. We were given two rooms with an adjoining bathroom. We weren't sure if the girls would sleep without us since it was a new place, but we thought we would give it a try and leave the doors between the rooms open. We washed up and were invited to sit in the backyard for tea while Pari and Iden's mom got busy in the kitchen preparing lunch.

Pari had a housemaid, so she was keeping the children occupied and helping in the kitchen. We were shortly served a tasty lunch of cutlets and salad with pita. It amazed me how quickly such a meal was put together.

With the mountains surrounding us we sat eating our meal with our children and Iden's family. I felt connected to each and every one in a very special way. We spent the rest of the afternoon walking in the neighborhood admiring the abundance of nature growing everywhere. We had had a long day and planned on visiting Iden's home the following day with his parents.

Iden's home was a 20-minute drive from Pari's home. Their home was drastically different, although charming. It did not have any gates or walls surrounding it, but it was a modest three-bedroom house with many trees and flowers. His parents were proud to show me Iden's room that he had shared with his brother Rahmen. It had been left untouched since Iden had left for the States almost 17 years ago. As I stepped into his room, I was overcome and discovered new information about the man I loved.

Paintings that Iden himself had painted adorned the walls, yet I never knew he was an artist. Bookshelves filled with books in English and in Farsi stood along the walls along with pictures of old girlfriends and friends, and his guitar and music stand with sheet music were still displayed. I could almost hear the music being played. I sat on his bed, which was covered in a lovely Persian blanket. I lay down on it for a moment and tried to imagine Iden as a young man in this room. I wondered what Iden's dreams were as a young man and if our family and life together were a part of it. As I lay there in my reverie, the girls and Iden walked in startling me back to reality. I immediately got up, hugged him, and told him I loved him. The girls asked their father many questions and we all sat on his bed for a while.

Iden's mother prepared a traditional meal of koufteh, which is a meatball stuffed with rice and herbs in a tomato sauce served with yogurt and vegetables. His mother watched me as I ate, and it was easy to see that she was pleased being in her own home and cooking again for Iden and his family.

His parents were the sweetest people, and I felt sad that my daughters did not have the luxury of growing up with them. Iden asked if we could spend the night at his parent's house. He said his parents had asked him to ask me because they wanted to spend some special time with all of us. I was happy to do so, and when I told the girls they were excited as well.

We stayed the night and extended our stay two more nights. His mother laid out blankets and pillows and some extra carpets for makeshift beds in the living room, so Iden and I and the girls could all sleep together. The girls spent days with us walking through Iden's hometown, visiting neighbors, schools, and other places that were all part of his childhood.

On our last night in Iden's childhood home, I offered to cook a traditional Italian meal for Iden's parents to show my gratitude for their genuine, loving hospitality. His parents watched the girls as Iden, and I took a walk to a local market to purchase the necessary ingredients to make spaghetti and meatballs. The stores are not like those in America. There isn't one big supermarket where you are able to buy everything you need. We went to a butcher, a produce market, a cheese store, and a bakery. Persian food uses many similar ingredients such as tomatoes, pasta, meat, and fresh herbs, so finding what I needed to prepare the meal wasn't as difficult as I had thought. It was also nice taking a walk with my husband through his hometown, listening to the stories that evoked memories from his childhood.

When we arrived back at Iden's home, the girls were writing their names in Farsi and eating some fruit in the backyard. The weather in Ardebil was much cooler than Tehran, making it more tolerable to be outside during the summer months. I unpacked the groceries and began cooking. Iden's mom sat next to me speaking Farsi and helping me chop onions, garlic, and herbs and mix the meat into meatballs and make a salad.

While the food was cooking, she took me into her bedroom and opened a jeweled wooden box, taking out a little red velvet bag and handing it to me. She said, "For you."

Inside the bag, were four 18-karat gold bangles. I immediately put them on and gave her a big hug, saying, "Merci." She also handed me another two pouches, one for each of the girls, which contained two smaller bangles. Again I gave her a hug and a kiss and used my limited Farsi to thank her and to let her know I loved her.

I showed the girls their bangles and they put them straight on. We all showed up at the dinner table wearing our bangles and smiles. Iden was sitting out back talking to his father and playing his guitar. Everyone seemed to enjoy the meal very much. Iden and I cleaned up the dishes while his parents sat in the living room and put on some Persian cartoons for the children.

We returned to his sister's house and spent the next few days together taking walks and visiting more family members and friends. Our time in Ardebil was coming to an end and instead of taking the long ride back to Tehran, Iden's sister had arranged for us to fly back with them. I knew saying goodbye to his parents would be hard, so the children and I said goodbye with a hundred hugs and kisses, and we gave Iden some private time to say his goodbyes. His sister had a friend pick us up at the house and we drove to the airport with tearful eyes. We all were uncertain if there would ever be another time like this when we could all be together.

We arrived in Tehran in about an hour and half, and although I had enjoyed the trip there by car, I was happy to be back sooner because it allowed Iden to have some time after an emotional goodbye with his parents.

On our last day in Tehran we took a walk to Park Said, stopping along the way to buy some little souvenirs from stands in the street. We wanted to have an early night because we had to arrive at the airport by 4 in the morning. I was a little apprehensive about our departure and I had visions of us being pulled over to the side and not being allowed to leave.

It was already crowded at the airport, even at this early hour, and soldiers of Iran's Revolutionary Army were standing guard, which was somewhat intimidating. We said our goodbyes to his sister and her husband and to the many cousins who came to say their farewells. The goodbyes were long and tearful, but I could see Iden was ready to head through security and settle himself down before our trip back to Paris. We passed through security without any problems, and I was relieved to be on the other side of the feeling of danger.

We didn't have long to wait before boarding the plane, and just before takeoff Iden held my hand and, looking into my eyes, said, "I do not know when we will ever come back."

Trying to sound confident, I said, "Don't worry. We will, I promise." With that we all closed our eyes and took a much-needed nap.

We landed in Paris in the late afternoon and once again Ahmed was there to pick us up at the airport. It was great to see a familiar face and not have to meet someone new again. Even though I had only spent a few days with Ahmed and his family before leaving for Iran, I felt very comfortable around them and so did our children. We stayed in Paris for a few days before we had to return to the States. It was mid-August, and the streets were filled with tourists, but Ahmed knew where to take us to have some quiet walks and talks and good places to eat.

Ahmed was very curious to hear my thoughts about my experience in Iran, and I was very happy to inform him that I'd had a wonderful time and would remember this trip with deep fondness. On our last day in Paris we did look at some tourist attractions and we did some more shopping for souvenirs for my parents and a few friends.

We left Paris on August 20th, making the time away almost a month. Elizabeth and Claudia were superb travelers, and from then on, any trip we took was considerably easier. Everyone was quiet on the flight home to New York. Iden was not engaging in conversation, so I left him to his own thoughts, and I occupied the girls with some toys. We arrived at Kennedy Airport with more luggage than we had left with because we had received so many gifts from his family, including the Persian carpet. We had to wait a long time for our bags to be inspected and to go through customs. We finally arrived home at 2:30 in the morning, exhausted, but overjoyed to be home.

It was a remarkable trip, but it was time to get back to reality. The girls would be starting school in a few weeks, and I was preparing to return to work. Elizabeth was a first grader and Claudia was starting prekindergarten in the same school. To help make the transition back to work, my mother offered to watch Claudia three days a week, and my good friend Debbie would take care of her on the other two days.

I had grown accustomed to my life as it was, so I had some hesitation and anxiety about starting a new routine. I hoped the girls would adjust easily to the new routine as well, especially Claudia. We had about two weeks to settle back in after being away for so long. I did some school shopping, and I spent the next two weeks at school setting up my classroom and getting reacquainted with the old staff as well as meeting new teachers.

On the Saturday before school started, I took the girls shoe shopping. Iden stayed home because although he still had some time off, he was working remotely from home. I could see he needed time alone, and I was more than happy to take the girls out on a beautiful September day. After shopping and playing in the park we had lunch and made a stop at church to pray for a good beginning to the school year. The church was empty, and I liked it this way, to be able to sit and be still and to have a moment of silent meditation.

When we arrived home Iden was sleeping on the couch, still in his pajamas. We made a lot of noise, but he was in a deep sleep. He said he was feeling very tired and he moved to our bedroom. I told the girls that Daddy was working late and needed to rest. He lay in bed for most of the day, only getting up to have some dinner.

Iden sat at the table but didn't really eat anything; he just played with his food and went back to bed. I saw the pain on his face and began feeling that tightening in my stomach. I knew that he would experience extreme letdown after leaving Iran and being with his family for almost a month, but it came crashing down much quicker than I thought and there was nothing that I or anyone else could do to bring him back up.

After returning to New York, Iden suffered his first major bout of depression in September 1995. It was difficult for us and especially for him. He went about his daily routine of going to work, coming home and having dinner, and then going to sleep. He was functioning, but not living. I too was going through a tough time managing the girls, their homework, working, and doing all the household chores alone. I missed him both physically and emotionally. I felt more afraid than angry and was embarrassed to share this information with anyone.

For some reason I felt people would judge Iden and me for not being strong enough and perhaps even thinking something was wrong with our marriage. It was the mid-90s and mental awareness was not openly discussed and the information available was limited. I was not properly informed, so I went to my neighborhood library and borrowed books on depression.

I finally decided to speak to Iden about his depression and asked if we could talk after dinner one night. When the girls went to sleep, I asked him what his doctor thought about the way he was feeling?

"What doctor?" he asked.

"Your psychiatrist!" I said.

He didn't deny it: He just wanted to know how I knew that he was seeing a psychiatrist. I told him about my little discovery many years ago and that I wanted to respect his privacy, but I needed to intervene and that if I didn't know what was going on I couldn't help. He told me that I was helping and thanked me for taking on all the responsibilities with the girls, our home, and my work. He further told me that he was suffering from major depression and that he was taking antidepressants to help him. He then went on to explain that he'd suffered from depression in the past, but not as severe as what he was experiencing now. His psychiatrist told him that the trip was very emotional, and it was to be expected for him to be feeling this way. I asked how I could help.

"You do enough," he said.

He stood up and I could tell that this was the end of the conversation. I went over to give him a hug, but it was not returned. He just said, "It will take some time."

After Iden left, I sat looking out our dining room window and opened it to let the cool autumn air in. I lit a cigarette and tried to convince myself that this too shall pass and that everything would get back to normal again. It took quite some time to pass, almost one long, painful year.

During that year, the girls and I became a trio, doing everything together. Our weekly schedule was always the same: school, homework, dinner, watch some TV, and read before bedtime. They eventually got use to Iden being there but not present. Claudia was adjusting to prekindergarten very nicely and Elizabeth was pretty much on her own every night finishing her homework with diligence and confidence.

On the weekends I took the girls to visit my parents in Jackson Heights to allow Iden some time alone. I always encouraged him to come along because I thought going out would do him good. But he declined, saying he would rather be at home and wasn't capable of socializing. My parents had growing concerns about Iden's absence on our weekly visits, but I reassured them that he was just working harder and needed to rest. I hated to lie to them, but I did not want to violate Iden's privacy, even though I needed to share with someone what was going on.

There were also many events, like birthday parties, weddings and dinners, that we were invited to and did not attend. I made up excuses why we weren't attending. I missed Iden's company and I missed the company of others. When necessary, I left the girls with Iden, but I usually found the girls sitting in front of the TV with Iden sleeping on the couch, so I rarely left the girls with him because he simply could not take care of them. We were all struggling and I just didn't know how to help.

Unfortunately, remaining silent made matters worse, but I didn't know any better back then. The girls were growing fast, and their childhood would never come again. We had worked so hard to give them a good foundation in order for them to grow into loving, respectful, and confident individuals and I didn't want them to start feeling anxious because their father was slowly becoming disconnected from us.

Our family life was just no longer the same. I knew Iden loved us all very much. I have never doubted his love, even for a minute. His love was pure and honest. He just wasn't able to give all of us his attention during this time of his life. When I would walk around the neighborhood with the girls, I would see children walking with both their dad and mom and I longed for Iden to be at my side holding my hand and the hands of my girls. He was not only my husband, but also my best friend and I was experiencing a deep sense of loss.

Feeling sorry for myself, I would sometimes say things that I should not have said, but the pain of loneliness can create anger.

"Just get up and move a little, maybe you will feel a little better!" I would say to him after returning from a full day out with the girls. "Taking medicine to help your depression is one thing, but you need to do something to feel better." He would just ignore me and not respond.

The girls continued to do well despite Iden's lack of participation in their lives. Mom was a great help to me during this difficult time. She not only took care of Claudia three days a week, but she also started to prepare meals and do some odd jobs around my apartment to relieve the stress she saw on my face.

Iden drove Mom home each evening after babysitting, and because there was no conversation, she would often ask me what was going on with him. She said he'd always loved to talk about the girls and me or about work, although lately all he would say is hello and goodbye. Once again, I had to lie. I just said that he had been working hard and had been very tired. It pained me to lie to her.

Mom was a very strong woman and telling her the truth would have been such a relief for me, plus I know she would have been very understanding while offering sound advice, but the words could not flow out of my mouth.

Throughout the year I filled the girls lives with as much joy as I could. I went to their friends' parties, to kiddie movies, to the library, to parks, I taught them to ride their bikes and went to visit friends and family alone. Every day that passed I prayed and waited for Iden to feel better and to return to his girls and me and to the living. I missed being a family.

Patricia and Iden ©

CHAPTER TWELVE

OUR HOUSE

"I long, as does every human being to be at home wherever I find myself!"

—MAYA ANGELOU

Just as night turns into morning, Iden's depression lifted, and he was feeling better. The music was playing again. It was playing in the car and in our house throughout the day. He even started playing old familiar songs on his guitar as well as learning new ones. It had been a very long quiet year, and it was good to have the house vibrating in better spirits. We started to resume our social life again by having friends over for dinner and attending events. It was no longer just a trio with the girls and me, but rather a family.

Now that Iden was feeling better, he was always planning to do things and to visit some friends. I was happy to be back in the social scene, although it was a bit hectic running around every weekend. When I wasn't up for going out and preferred to have a quiet night with just our own family I would ask Iden if it was okay to stay home. If I had insisted, I am sure Iden would have stayed home too, but he would often ask if he could go visit a friend by himself. Of course I wanted him to see his friends and have much-needed time out, but he would often return home very late and smelling of alcohol.

Elizabeth was now in second grade and Claudia was in kindergarten full time. The babysitting schedule became easier because my friend Debbie picked both of my girls up after school at the same time and watched them until I came home from work. Sometimes I wasn't in the best of moods when I arrived home, but my daughters' sweet smiles quickly put me in a better mood. Their kisses and hugs obliterated my weariness. Although I enjoyed teaching, it was a very emotional and physical job, and some days were very long and difficult. Iden was still working at the hospital as a network manager and still ran a second job as a computer consultant, and he now had many clients.

Our main goal was to save enough money to put a substantial down payment on a house in Forest Hills, as our family had become very fond of living there.

We approached looking for a house in the same way we did when we were looking for our apartment. After church and before heading to my parents' for Sunday dinner, we searched *The New York Times* for open houses and circled the ones we could afford and the ones we wanted to see just for curiosity's sake. One of my favorite things to do, even today, is go to open houses. The girls enjoyed looking at each prospective house and choosing which rooms would be theirs and I would walk around each room trying to see myself living in each home we visited. We really enjoyed those Sunday outings together.

After almost a full year of looking at houses, after church one Sunday as we were walking home, we saw a sign for an open house. I didn't think we should look at it because it was on a block with many expensive homes, but Iden insisted. I didn't want to be disappointed, but Iden said, "Let's just go look," so I agreed.

The real estate agents gave us information about the house, and when I noticed the price, I felt hopeful. Although the house needed a lot of updating, it had good bones, and the price wasn't far off what we wanted to spend. I listened to the real estate agents talk and I could tell that they had the same accent as Iden, so I asked them if they were Persian. The agent said he was and then started to speak to me in Farsi. I quickly informed him that I didn't speak Farsi, but my husband was from Iran. The agent approached Iden and introduced himself and started talking Farsi. The girls and I left them to talk and went to look around the house.

The house was a brick Tudor with four bedrooms, two bathrooms, an enclosed porch, and a basement with a kitchen, bathroom, two bedrooms, and many closets. There was also a large attic that had been converted into another bedroom, but it was now used primarily for storage. The backyard had a two-car garage, a full deck, and a beautiful garden with many trees and a Japanese garden. I immediately envisioned myself sitting out on the deck drinking tea in the early summer mornings with Iden.

The kitchen was a good size and held potential but needed renovation. It was the most important place for me to feel comfortable. The girls were very happy running up and down the stairs and in and out of the house. By the time we finished touring the house, Iden was just starting because he had been talking to the agent for so long.

The girls and I waited outside on the steps, and I took in all the sights and vibes of the neighborhood. I looked to see if there were children playing or riding their bikes up and down the block. As a child, my fondest memories were the days I spent playing with my friends and brothers on my block. I tried to imagine if this was a place that Elizabeth and Claudia could also spend many days that could be stored in their minds as happy childhood memories.

A new chapter began in our lives as we became homeowners along with many new hopes and dreams. Our hearts were full of happiness and our minds were busy with all the ideas we envisioned for our new home. Home Depot became our new hangout. We hired a contractor that was recommended by our agent, who eventually became a good friend of our family.

Our house was located on a beautiful tree-lined street with gardens out front already decorated for the fall holidays with pumpkins and chrysanthemums. During the week Iden would stop by the house checking in on the construction progress, and on the weekend we would all go together. On one of our weekend visits, Iden was busy talking inside the house with Marcos, the contractor, while the girls and I were outside busily raking leaves and tending to the garden. The girls enjoyed using the garden tools and getting their hands dirty too, especially Claudia. Their joy gave me so much happiness.

The chilly fall air made our cheeks rosy and gave us all huge appetites. After we cleaned up inside the house, I asked Iden if he wanted to grab a bite at the diner on Metropolitan Avenue, which was just a few blocks from our new home. Iden wanted to stay with Marcos, and I could see they were well into a six-pack while they were working and talking, so the girls and I had lunch alone.

As the cold weather settled in, the girls and I no longer went to the house, only Iden went to check on the progress of the renovations. Saturdays were our family time, but since we bought the house, we didn't get much time together. Saturdays were becoming more about Iden having some downtime with a friend and some beers, arriving home in the late afternoon.

Although I liked the idea of Iden having some guy time, I felt it was an unusual amount of time spent away from us. When I mentioned this to him, he became very defensive and said that I was trying to control him. I tried to explain that the girls and I liked having time together on the weekends since all week we really didn't see much of him. I also noticed he had developed a habit of buying beer and putting it in the refrigerator.

The autumn days were gone, and winter was soon upon us as well as the holiday season. We were hoping to be in our new home before Christmas in order to have all of our family and friends celebrate with us in our newly renovated home, fireplace and all. We were set to move in on December 10th. I was over the moon on the day Iden came home and said that although there was more work that needed to be done, we were all set to move in a week ahead of schedule.

We had already sold our apartment but we were paying rent since the new owners were not yet ready to move in. As happy as I was to hear the news, I felt a sudden sense of panic. I had to work, take care of our girls, and pack all our possessions on my own because Iden worked late during the week, and on the weekends, he spent all his free time at the house and at Home Depot. I knew he was working just as hard, but I needed him to be with me a bit more during this moving period. I was quite capable of packing on my own, but it would have been nice to have some help. I realized he needed to ensure the work was being done properly and in a timely manner, but it made me feel I was on my own without a partner to share the important family moments.

With the purchase of our home this became a reoccurring feeling throughout our marriage, causing me to feel disconnected from Iden. More anxiety was added to an already anxious time in our lives. So I put myself to work and started making a to-do list. I was a list maker and a planner, but I wished I had someone to make a list with and to go over it with, but Iden wasn't available because lately he never seemed to be around.

On a snowy, freezing December Saturday morning we moved into our new home. When we stepped inside, the smell of paint and lacquer on the wooden floors came to greet us like a new neighbor. Everything was new. Thanks to my organized packing with notations on every box, the movers were able to place the boxes in the proper rooms and I was able to unpack everything easily. We had over a hundred boxes and yet our possessions hardly filled the rooms.

My parents were there on the day of our move to help take care of the girls while we unpacked. I unpacked the kitchen and then set up the bedrooms and bathrooms, leaving boxes filled with decorative items aside for another day. I wanted to make sure we had our essential needs sorted.

As I was setting up the girls' room with Mom, I went to look for Iden. We only had two days to get things in order before work on Monday. I found him in the basement talking to the workers. When I asked if he could come upstairs to help, he made some comment under his breath and the workers laughed. I told him how tired I was because I had unpacked almost half of the boxes by myself, and I didn't think it was the appropriate time to be talking to the workers.

My parents were getting tired trying to occupy the girls with no TV and few toys. It was too cold for any outdoor activities, and everyone was getting hungry and needed to eat soon. It should have been a joyful day, yet I was tired and thinking perhaps it was a mistake to buy a house and I started to miss my apartment.

Patricia and her mom, Gloria ©

CHAPTER THIRTEEN

CHRISTMAS EVE

*;There is no Ideal Christmas; only the one Christmas
you decide to make as a reflection of your values, desires,
affections, traditions."*

—BILL MCKIBBEN

As the months turned into years, so the newness of our home
turned into familiarity. The smell of freshly painted walls had now
faded, the shiny lacquered floors had dulled a bit, and we had
managed to fill every empty space. Although the girls had their
own bedrooms and we had a full basement and a family room,
they always sat on the dining room table looking into the kitchen.
Even my Mimi sat by the table with them while I prepared our
evening meal.

Every day after work I would pick the girls up from school
and as soon as we entered the house another job began. The girls
immediately changed out of their school uniforms, grabbed a snack,
and started their homework. My first task was to take Mimi out
for a much-needed walk, which allowed me to relax a bit and clear
my head before helping with homework and starting dinner. As I
cooked, the girls and I would talk about their day. Elizabeth always
finished her work quickly and was always willing to help Claudia
with her homework and studying. Claudia was having problems
completing her homework independently and needed support to
finish her assignments. I had mentioned this to Iden, and he said I

was comparing her to Elizabeth, and I shouldn't think too much of it. Elizabeth was bright, but also loved learning, whereas Claudia was as he said, average, and that she was doing just fine. He wasn't at home while we struggled through every homework assignment, although he did hear me arguing with her on the weekends while we studied for a test because she was unwilling to focus and put effort into her studies.

After dinner, the girls watched TV while I cleaned up and made lunches for the next day. We often took our nightly walk with Mimi together, especially in nicer weather. I enjoyed these walks after the daily chores were finished so we could talk without worrying about having to be somewhere or do something. I had just gotten my first cell phone and on these walks, I would reach out to Iden to see when he might be home.

Since our schedules were so different, we rarely had family dinners during the week. Sometimes if he had a big project going on he would not even be home to see the girls before they went to bed. On our walks I would look into the windows to see families sitting down to dinner and I felt a little sad for the girls because they missed that important family time with their dad. I missed that time with Iden as well. When Iden returned home after a long day, he was tired, but always smiled and was happy to see me. If the girls were still up, they would come running down the stairs to see him and give him kisses and hugs. Even though their time together may have been short, it was enough to feel his love.

When the girls went to sleep, Iden and I found some time to catch up on the day while we sat in the kitchen as he ate his dinner. Most nights, even after putting in a full day at work, he would receive calls from work, needing his assistance to fix a computer problem. He would take the call downstairs in the basement where we had made an office with all his computer equipment. Many nights I would head up to bed while he still worked, and he would fall asleep on the sofa without coming upstairs. I would awake during the night not feeling his presence, so I would go downstairs to wake him to come to upstairs to bed.

Before we knew it, Iden's routine of arriving home late and then retiring into the basement to work and sleep became our new normal. Our weekends were somewhat the same, even though Iden was home. The girls and I would rise early and start our day with a special breakfast that I had no time to make during our hectic weekday schedule.

The girls loved chocolate-chip pancakes and Iden and I usually had omelets. The girls tried to wake Iden to share breakfast with them, but I would tell them he was tired, and he needed to catch up on some rest. I was making more and more excuses for his absence. So the girls and I would eat together, and I would leave his breakfast to be eaten later.

The girls were old enough to be left home alone for short periods of time, with Elizabeth now 12 and Claudia 10, but they still needed supervision while I was doing errands on the weekend. Many times I left the house with Iden asleep, only to return home to find he was around the block at our neighbor's house sitting and talking to our friend Marcos and having a few beers.

I didn't mind Iden having a friend that he felt comfortable talking to. I also knew he needed some downtime away from work, but the girls and I also needed him and would have liked to know when he was going to visit his friends. The drinking was becoming another new routine, something he never did in our house or with me.

Sometimes I would call Iden and ask him to come home because I needed some help with chores or because the girls wanted to see him, and he would say he would be home soon. He often came home a bit drunk and would then go downstairs and make some phone calls to Iran while I spent the day doing the chores, schoolwork with both the girls, and my own preparation for work. On days like this, I hoped that the evening would be filled with some family time.

When dinnertime rolled around, Iden found his way upstairs. Sometimes he would play his guitar or watch TV with the girls. Just before I served dinner, I would peek into the living room and see the girls sitting on either side of him each one holding one of his hands. It gave me that sense of togetherness as a family that had been missing over the past few years.

The dining room table brought my family together and it was a place that brought me comfort and love. When we all sat together to share a Saturday meal, I felt happy. It brought me joy to see my girls talking and laughing with Iden. Their faces were lit up because they, like me, missed him and relished the time with him. I wasn't sure why I felt our family was coming undone. I didn't want to feel that way, but I did, and it scared me.

I did not mind having problems as long as we were able to communicate and work together as a family to solve them. We used to share everything together and I could feel him holding back and I felt us drifting apart. I began to feel like a single mom, but my biggest concern was about Iden's ability to take care of himself.

After a long week of work and taking care of the girls, Mom offered to come and stay on the weekends at my house. She noticed my stress and the absence of Iden on the weekends and wanted to help. Her visits helped to take away some of my loneliness and they also allowed me some time alone to take a walk or a run, or to meet a friend for coffee without the girls. The girls loved having their Nanny around too because she gave them her undivided attention and she allowed them to be as silly as they wanted.

Mom and Iden had a very good relationship and whenever they were home together, I often find them sitting out on the porch in the warmer months or sitting by the fire during the cold winter months talking. More recently, though, the conversations had grown shorter and sometimes they would argue, mainly when discussing our girls, his work, or other family matters.

One weekend, when Mom and I were sitting having our afternoon cup of tea, she asked me what was going on with Iden. I explained that he had been working very hard because he wanted to provide for us. When he was home, he was very distant and often stayed in the basement, not wanting to join us upstairs, even for meals.

Mom offered some suggestions and basically said that I should allow him to have his alone time, but she also encouraged me to talk to him. She suggested I ask him what was going on and to let him know how I felt about his change in behavior. I let her know I had brought it up on several occasions with Iden and he usually responded by saying he was tired and needed to rest. I did not mention to her my concerns about his drinking and, looking back now, I wish I had because perhaps it would have brought the issue up with my dad too, so he might have talked with Iden about it.

Dad had a strong personality and could be intimidating, in a good way. When I brought up my concern with Iden about his drinking, he would always reply that there was nothing wrong with having a few drinks with his friends. Having an occasional drink with a friend wasn't the problem; it was that he was now drinking after work and I was finding empty vodka bottles in his bag and in the car.

As the months passed, Christmas was approaching and I was hoping that the holiday season would bring more family time together. Elizabeth and Claudia were now in a preteen phase of development and were going through many changes, both physically and emotionally. Elizabeth started her period and Claudia was having more difficulty with schoolwork, which was causing me great concern.

A month or so before Christmas I started to make my holiday to-do list. Iden had become more withdrawn and quieter and probably heading into depression. When I asked about his mental state and if he were keeping his doctor's appointments, he'd say he was taking care of things and I shouldn't worry. But I did.

Being a perpetual planner, I needed to get things done for the holidays by myself since Iden was clearly not in the holiday mood. I was getting used to doing it all and started to accept that this was my life for now, never sure if and when it would ever change. Christmas time should be a joyous time and I wasn't going to allow Iden's mood to take away my joy.

With a bit of prodding, Iden put the outside lights up and we all went together to pick out our tree. The girls insisted that he help decorate and he did, but I could tell he was just going through the motions. I remember when we first bought our house, we bought two trees. We were so excited to put our tree up that we bought it too early and it started to dry up. So the night before Christmas Eve we had to get another tree and redecorate it before our company arrived.

There was a big change going on within Iden, and I didn't know what it was, but we seemed to be entering a whole different life with him compared to the one we used to share. He rarely made it home for dinner and when he arrived home from work, I could tell he had been drinking.

Iden also began to have irregular sleeping patterns. After work he would remain in the basement watching TV until late and he was also going into work later and later. I tried many times to talk to him about my concerns, but he always said he was okay and that I was making too much of things. I only wish I knew then what I now know about alcoholism, so I could have gotten the help he needed sooner.

The Iden I had grown to love, my best friend and who I believed would be my life partner, was no longer present. Yes, he was physically present and went through our daily routines, but he was absent emotionally for me and for our family.

Christmas Eve that year was on a Sunday, so I had the weekend to prepare. I was fortunate to have some extra time to clean, cook, and do further wrapping without rushing. The past few years I had been hosting the holiday at my house since I had a larger space than my brothers and parents, and I really enjoyed having our traditional family celebration.

Our girls still enjoyed the excitement of decorating the tree and guessing what present was inside each box. They also enjoyed looking at the decorations on the tree from my childhood that my parents had given to me. My parents no longer put up a tree, so most of their decorations went to Mark and me since Ron did not put up a tree. Every ornament had a story and as I hung them up, I would tell them to my girls.

All the houses in the neighborhood were ablaze with holiday lights, and the girls and I enjoyed looking at them at night while we took our nightly walks with Mimi. On the rare nights that Iden walked with us, it was very special indeed and it almost felt like a

Christmas gift to us. This particular year the houses looked even more beautiful because of the recent snowfall. This all made it impossible not to be in the Christmas spirit, but Iden was far from feeling joyful.

After all dinner preparations were finished, the girls showered and dressed in their new black velvet dresses. The designs of the dresses were different, and they wore different color bows in their hair. They also put on whatever jewelry they wanted to accessorize their outfit and even a little makeup. When they were ready, they went and joined their dad while I got ready.

I took a long hot shower and let myself stand under the water for some time. I then put on my holiday outfit of black velour pants with a red sweater. As I was getting dressed, I could hear them singing Christmas songs. I came downstairs to find Iden lying on the couch watching TV. The girls were happily sitting on either side of him. Claudia was combing his hair and Elizabeth was tickling his feet, but it seemed as if no one was touching him. I reminded him that our guests would be arriving soon so he would need to get ready. He went downstairs and I could see that he was dreading the whole night ahead.

About 20 minutes later I called down to Iden to see if he was ready. Over the years we had renovated the downstairs bathroom and Iden used that one and the girls and I used the one upstairs. He didn't respond, so I went downstairs to check on him. He was still not showered or dressed and was just watching TV. When I asked him what was going on he said he was feeling a little down and needed some time and that he would be upstairs later.

The girls and I greeted my family and my friend Annie. I made excuses for Iden, saying he would be joining us later. We had a drink and talked before I brought out the appetizers and made the pasta. I sent Elizabeth down to the basement to check on Iden and she returned to say he was in the shower. My family kept asking when Iden would be joining us, but it wasn't until we had worked our way through the pasta and almost finished the main dishes before Iden came upstairs. He was showered and dressed and looked handsome as always, but he was clearly not showing any holiday cheer. My parents loved him, and they were happy to see him, but he did not reciprocate the greetings.

Iden didn't want any appetizers or pasta, saying that he wasn't hungry and that he would have what was now being served. As he sat down, he poured himself some wine and started eating and drinking but was very quiet

After dinner, the girls helped me clear up then we moved into the living room to talk and to open our gifts. We opened all our gifts to and from family on Christmas Eve, but the girls' presents from us were opened on Christmas Day. It was truly a blessing to see the gifts my daughters received and to watch their excited faces as they tore open each beautifully wrapped package. Iden seemed distant, as if he couldn't wait for the whole night to be over.

We finished the night off with dessert and the girls played with their new toys and looked at all their gifts. The table looked beautifully set with a three- tiered cookie tray of homemade Christmas cookies, Italian fig cookies, pastries, and cheesecake. Iden did not partake in any of the desserts but chose to drink his tea in the living room and put on the TV.

My parents made several comments about his behavior and I just blamed it on his being tired due to working long hours. My parents missed his company and they also missed his guitar playing of holiday songs and our family sing-along. We sat and talked more before Mark and his wife left to attend midnight Mass, and then Ron and his wife and Annie soon left as well. My parents stayed behind for a little bit longer.

My parents, the girls, and Iden and I sat in the living room and continued to talk. Mom commented on how delicious the food was and what a wonderful night it was to be here with our family. Dad was having a conversation with Iden, and I heard Dad ask him, "What's going on with you?"

Iden answered by saying he was feeling a little down, but he would be okay soon and that this feeling would pass. Dad asked if he was taking any medicine or seeing a doctor and Iden answered yes to both questions.

Dad continued to ask Iden a bunch of other questions, trying to probe him as to why he was feeling this way but wasn't able to get any answers. Mom and I cleaned up while they talked in the living room and the girls went upstairs to put on their new pajamas and get ready for Christmas morning.

After my parents left, I went upstairs to talk to the girls and to read them the traditional Christmas Eve story *'Twas the Night Before Christmas*. Every year I bought them a different version of the story, which I still continue to do. They were too excited to sleep so they stayed together chatting while I finished cleaning up downstairs. Iden had already headed to the basement and when I went down to see him, he was lying on the couch. I sat next to him and asked if there was anything I could do to help him. He said he was going through another major depression and was feeling horrible and that he was sorry. I also asked him about his medicine and if he was in contact with his doctor and he said he was taking care of it and not to worry. But I was worried because he was not well, and I felt totally helpless.

Iden's sadness affected us all and it was frustrating not being able to help him in any way. I left him downstairs and went to finish cleaning up. Before starting I sat at the kitchen table and poured myself a glass of wine before I saw Elizabeth holding Claudia's hand. They asked if Daddy was okay. I looked at their concerned faces and could only imagine how they must feel. I hugged them and assured them he would be just fine, saying he just needed some rest time, and he would be just fine real soon. "Now go upstairs and get some sleep and get ready for more gifts from Santa tomorrow," I said, trying to sound happy for them.

I got out our Santa dish and told them we had almost forgotten to leave cookies for him. The girls put some cookies on the dish and Elizabeth looked at me, knowing I knew that she longer believed in Santa, although she still continued the belief in front of her sister. I sat and cried on a night that should have held happiness and magic, yet all I felt was despair.

After finishing up in the kitchen and putting the dining and living room back in order, I sat by the fireplace to look at the

Christmas tree. It held memories of past Christmases, with my many childhood ornaments hanging on the branches. Next to the old ones hung new ones creating memories for my daughters that I hoped they would carry into the future to share when they put up a Christmas tree with their own families. My sadness lifted when I remembered the love I felt at Christmas as a young girl with my family and the past ones I had shared with Iden and my girls. So once again I allowed the joy of this holiday to work its magic and make me feel hopeful.

CHAPTER FOURTEEN

SEASONS

'When we are no longer able to change a situation, we are challenged to change ourselves.'

—VIKTOR FRANKL

Winter slowly gives way to spring without us seeming to witness all the small changes happening around us. And then one day we wake up and see all the beautiful flowers in full bloom and our world is colorful once again.

The winter was a difficult time for Iden and consequently for the girls and me as well. Iden's depression started in December and lasted until the middle of April. He described his depression as lacking color just like winter, where everything was gray. During those months, Iden arrived home earlier than usual from work, greeting us without affection or words. He entered our home to descend into his own world downstairs, only coming up when dinner was served.

The girls were very happy to have him in any capacity sitting at the dinner table, but they noticed his quietness and his lack of attention. The girls still offered kisses and hugs that he gladly accepted but was not able to respond back in his usual loving way. All I could do was feel his pain and be supportive in the best way possible.

I tried to involve him in conversation, to take walks with Mimi, to watch a movie, or do anything that might help change his mood.

All of my suggestions fell flat, and I started to realize that there was little I could do to help his depression lift except to let him know that I loved him. During this time, he preferred to sleep in the basement because his sleeping patterns were different from mine. He fell asleep after dinner and then awoke during the night and would stay up for a few hours watching TV until he went back to sleep.

Without any physical connection, the distance between us grew even further. I missed lying next to him in bed because we would always sleep with some part of our body touching to let us both fall asleep feeling that special bond between a husband and wife.

With the coming of April came spring break from school and work for the girls and me. I looked forward to these breaks so I could spend quality time with both the girls and with my parents. We celebrated Easter with just my parents, as my brothers usually visited their in-laws or took a vacation. I bought egg-dying kits along with other art supplies to make decorations for the front door.

Spring break also gave me time to do some much-needed gardening. The girls and I bought some impatiens to plant in the front garden to make our house look pretty and spring-like for the holiday. Claudia always loved getting her hands dirty and enjoyed nature, while Elizabeth just liked to sit and read a book while watching us work and enjoy being together.

The girls needed a break from schoolwork and activities, so they really enjoyed lounging around in their pajamas and watching TV, something they didn't get to do too often. While they kept busy, I was able to catch up on spring cleaning. I enjoyed cleaning because it gave me a sense of calmness. I guess since I felt things in my life were a bit out of order, having everything clean and in place gave me some sense of security and helped ease my anxiety.

One day after I finished my chores, I got the girls to come outside to help me in the garden. It was such a beautiful day outside and they had been inside most of the day. They got changed and we grabbed our garden tools, heading to the front yard, taking Mimi with us. Other neighbors were out gardening as well, and we spent some time chatting with them before getting busy. The sun felt good on my face as I sat on the front steps soaking in the warmth after the long winter.

Although Iden's depression was causing me to feel lonely and sad, I wouldn't allow it to take away the happiness I was feeling with some of life's simple pleasures, like gardening with my daughters. As we emptied the flowers from the trays and started to turn the soil, I heard a car horn and I looked up to see Iden pulling into our driveway. His face seemed different. He was actually smiling and seemed to be in a better mood. The girls were excited to see their dad home early and in good spirits.

Iden explained that it was a holiday weekend, so all the employees had gone home early. He said he was hungry and went in to fix himself a sandwich, saying he would be out soon since it was such a beautiful day. As he left, I stood there for a while a bit confused as to what was going on. How could his mood change overnight? Iden soon returned after a change of clothes with a sandwich in one hand and a soda in the other to sit on the steps talking to us as we all worked.

As we were planting, Iden said that his Persian friend John had invited us to his house in Hunter, NY, for a few days and that he would like to go. I had known John for several years, but I never really liked him. There was something about him that just never sat right with me. I knew his girlfriend and a few other family members would be there and I liked them very much, so I agreed. They were always very kind to the girls. It would be nice to be out of the city and in the country for a few days. The girls got excited knowing that we were going on a mini vacation, but I think they were more excited knowing that we would all be together for a few days.

Easter Sunday we all got dressed up and attended Mass and then bought some pastries at our Italian bakery before heading home to finish preparing Easter dinner. I had made some vegetables and salads the night before and was now making a rack of lamb and potatoes. Iden was sitting with the girls playing his guitar. While I was cooking, I heard the music stop and saw him walk out onto the deck in the backyard. Through my kitchen window I heard him speaking Farsi, so I was sure he was talking to someone in Iran. He was on the phone for almost an hour before he came back inside, and I asked him if everything was good.

"Yes," was all he said.

Iden hadn't spoken to his family in a long time. During his months of depression, the calls to friends and family overseas virtually stopped unless they called him to say hello, but even then, the conversations were very short. I was happy to see his good spirits and was wondering if he was taking a new medication. I didn't understand how his mood could change so much overnight.

My parents were arriving soon, so I finished preparing dinner in order to enjoy our time together instead of being stuck in the kitchen. It was a warm day, so I sat on the deck with Iden and the girls. When my parents arrived, they joined us outside to talk, have a drink, and to snack on a few appetizers before dinner. After sitting for a while we all came in and Mom and I went in to serve dinner. Iden, the girls, and Dad went to sit in the living room.

As Mom and I were preparing the food she said how nice it was to see that Iden was feeling better. Dad soon joined us to ask for another Manhattan, his cocktail of choice, and also made a comment about Iden's behavior, saying he never heard Iden talk as much as he was talking that day. Dinner was delicious and it was the first meal that I'd seen Iden eat with an appetite in a long time.

We sat and talked after dinner over some fruit and nuts before going out for a walk and returning home to finish our night with pastries and espresso. Iden told my parents about our little getaway, and they were happy to hear that we would have a few vacation days in the mountains. Dad always worried about the weather and said to make sure to take along some warm clothes because it was still cold upstate this time of year.

After my parents left, the girls and Iden sat out on the porch playing with Mimi. I cleaned up the kitchen. I could hear Iden on the phone with Iran again and I could hear him laughing. I soon joined them in the backyard and Iden was still on the phone. I took Mimi for her last walk for the night with the girls and gestured to

Iden to see if he wanted to join us. He covered the phone and said he would see us later. He was talking to a friend that he had lost contact with over the years and who was now living in Canada.

When we returned home, Iden was back inside the house playing his guitar in the living room. The girls went up to their rooms and I asked Iden if we could talk about plans for the next few days for the trip upstate. We spoke for a while, and I asked if he wanted to watch TV with me. I went upstairs to change into my pajamas and got ready to relax after a busy day of cooking. Elizabeth was in her room reading and Claudia was at her desk drawing. When I returned downstairs Iden had put some pillows on our big L-shaped couch and I could smell popcorn popping. He had also changed into comfortable clothes.

These small actions lifted my heart and made me feel that my friend had returned to me. Although Iden didn't usually care to watch romantic movies, we did that night. We watched *Serendipity* while munching on popcorn and talking. The girls came down to grab some popcorn and sat and cuddled with us before heading back upstairs to bed. After the movie we went upstairs to bed. It had been a long time since I remembered going to sleep at the same time as Iden. The girls were already in bed and my home felt peaceful and safe.

Iden and I had not been physical with each other in a long time, so we were both eager to be in each other's arms. We made love with a rare passion, almost as if it were happening for the first time. I had missed him, and it felt that everything was taking a turn for the better.

We left for our mini vacation very early on Tuesday morning, planning to return home on Friday. The weather continued to stay dry and mild, so I was hopeful to get in some nice walks in the country. We loaded up our minivan with our bags, some extra blankets and pillows, and some books and games for the girls. I also picked up wine and some Italian and Persian sweets as a house gift. Hunter is a three-hour drive from Queens, so we were planning to reach John's house by around 1 o'clock in the afternoon.

As soon as we left, Iden popped in some CDs and Claudia immediately started complaining about the Persian music and wanted to hear her CDs. I told her we could listen to Daddy's music for a little bit, and then switch to her music soon. She was becoming more difficult when not able to get what she wanted, and I tried hard to use compromise as a way for her to understand the concept of sharing. However, Iden did not like to hear her whining and would often get angry with me over my method of parenting, so he would give in to her bad behavior.

I didn't want the day to start out with an argument, so I just let him do what he wanted to keep the peace. Elizabeth would also tell Claudia to stop acting like a baby and then they would start fighting. So for the sake of having a good start to our much- needed family time together, I remained quiet. The music played, Elizabeth read and fell asleep, and Claudia kept asking for either something to eat or asking to stop to use the restroom. Iden was very patient and did all she asked, but Claudia's behavior was bothering me as well as Iden's response to all her demands.

We arrived at John's house a little after 1 to find his parents, girlfriend, and his nephew and wife at the house as well for the week. His house was large and situated by Colgate Lake. The house was situated high on large timber beams, allowing for a spectacular view of the mountains. It had a large wraparound porch with many lounging chairs to catch some sun almost all day long.

We took a tour of the house and then we were shown to our rooms. The house had five bedrooms and four bathrooms. A bathroom connected our room and the girls' room. I was delighted to have a view of the mountains from our room. The girls were very excited as well as Mimi to have so much space to run and play in. I had a 50-foot leash for Mimi so she could run and play and not get lost. We all went out onto the deck and were served some snacks of cheese and nuts and fruit with some cold drinks. John offered me some wine or beer, but I was happy with some tea, although Iden happily took the offer of a beer.

It was a vacation, and I was glad to see him relaxing with friends. It was also nice to be in a beautiful place enjoying our time together. That's what I loved the most. It never had to be anyplace special or fancy, it just needed to be all of us together.

After a light lunch deliciously made by John's mother, we all planned to take a walk to the lake. I helped John's mother clean up the kitchen and tried to express how lovely the food was, but her English was limited, although I think she knew what I was saying. It was wonderful to have a meal served to me and I was hoping I could get an opportunity to watch her and help her cook so I could learn more Persian dishes.

We took a long walk around the lake and saw many pretty houses. Iden and I held hands while we walked, and he said, "This place makes me happy because it reminds me of my hometown with all the mountains, trees, and flowers."

The girls and I picked wildflowers, while Mimi chased all the chipmunks and insects as they walked and flew by. We walked over a footbridge and threw stones into the water to see who could throw them the farthest.

Later, we sat in the living room, which opened to the kitchen. John's mom served us hot tea and homemade honey cookies and the guys started to play their guitars. I sat and listened as I talked to John's girlfriend Nina. She asked if I would like to help make dinner after I had told her about my desire to learn how to prepare more Persian meals. I happily agreed.

That evening they were making a dish called koresh-e bademjoon, which is lamb stew with eggplant, a dish that Iden loved to eat, and I was equally excited about learning how to make. The girls followed Nina and me into the kitchen while Iden, John, and his dad stayed in the living room playing their guitars. Elizabeth and Claudia enjoyed staying in the kitchen while I cooked because they wanted to help as well. We all got busy washing vegetables and cutting and slicing. We gave the girls some ingredients to mix into the yogurt to eat along with the stew. We were so busy cooking and talking that I didn't realize that the music had stopped and when I looked up the guys had disappeared.

I wasn't worried, but I did wonder where they had all gone and why Iden didn't say he was leaving. I felt comforted knowing he was with his friend and that he just didn't just leave to go off by himself.

We finished the meal preparations and about an hour or so had passed before the guys returned, talking and laughing. I asked them where they had gone and Iden said just for a walk. We sat and talked for a bit and watched TV and then Iden took the girls to a game room on the lower floor to play Ping-Pong, foosball, and air hockey. It was nice to have some quiet time without the girls and to chat with Nina.

Nina started the fire even though the day was somewhat warm, but the night temperatures drop quickly in the mountains, and it was pleasant to feel the warmth and comfort of the fire. The stew and rice cooking slowing filled the house with delicious aromas and soon everyone was upstairs asking when dinner would be served.

The darkness in the mountains is so different than that of the city. Just before dinner we went out onto the deck and looked into nothing but darkness until we looked up and saw a night sky illuminated with millions of stars, which was unknown to us in the city. I stared at the sky thinking about the brightness above and the darkness below, thinking that at least night and day were predictable.

Dinner was delicious. I thanked Nina and John's mother in a few Farsi words that I knew to let them know how much I appreciated them helping me learn a new Persian dish. We sat and talked some more while drinking hot tea and eating the sweets that I had brought up from Queens when Iden told us he had some news.

He started by giving thanks to John for having us to his home and treating us so kindly. He went on to talk about how much he loved being in the mountains because, as he told me earlier, it reminded him of home. He then said that that afternoon John had taken him for a walk and showed him a house that was for sale next door. The owner was a friend of John's and asked if he knew anyone who might be interested in buying a home in Hunter. After Iden told John how much he loved being here, he'd taken Iden to see the home. Iden immediately fell in love with the home and made an offer to buy it. The owner was in a hurry to sell it and had said the price was below market value.

As I sat there listening to Iden speak, I couldn't believe, first, that he'd considered buying a home without consulting me, and second, where we would find the extra money to purchase a second home. Elizabeth would be starting private high school and Claudia would soon follow shortly thereafter. We would have a big tuition payment due each month, plus we spoke of doing some renovations in the kitchen that we couldn't afford when we first moved into the house.

I was very upset and asked Iden if I could talk to him privately. He said something in Farsi that made everyone who understood Farsi laugh, which made me angrier since I was sure it was something about me. We went into our bedroom, and I asked him how he could think about buying a house without talking to me, and where was all this extra money coming from? He said he had been working very hard and had managed to save some money.

After a lovely day, I felt all the happiness drain out of me. Of course the girls were happy and Iden told them that tomorrow we could all go look at the house to see if we liked it and what we thought, but I already felt that what I thought didn't seem to matter. He had made up his mind that he was going to purchase the house.

The following day we all got up early and went to meet the owner and look at the house. The house was a very sweet home with a beautiful view of the mountains and a lovely landscape. It was very pretty, and I could see myself spending summer days there, going to the lake with the girls and taking walks as we did today.

Although Iden said he had saved money, I never knew about it, and I really wanted to talk about our finances before he went ahead and made the purchase. The owners wanted to sell it quickly without waiting for mortgage approvals and other details that took time since they were moving shortly to Florida. Iden explained that he had saved money from all the consulting work he was doing, plus he was planning to take a small home equity loan to pay for the house.

We had become comfortable financially and I liked that feeling. We had to ensure education payments for our girls, so extra debt always scared me, and I didn't like the idea of taking a loan. Iden assured me it was a good investment and said not to worry. But I did worry. I always worried, especially about our financial security and his well- being.

We returned to John's home and Iden told the news to everyone about the purchase of the home. They could all tell that I wasn't happy with that idea, and then Nina pulled me to the side, saying that sometimes it is difficult being married to a Middle Eastern man. He feels he can make all the decisions, and that when they go right, he is the one to thank, and if they go wrong, the woman is to blame. I told her I didn't think we had that kind of marriage and that I wasn't sure why he was acting like this.

The next few days we spent at John's consisted of Iden on the phone talking to our accountant and banks and talking to the owners of the house. This decision took away the joy of our little getaway, but I tried to look happy for the girls, and didn't want to make a scene in front of strangers. At night in our bedroom I told him that I was not comfortable with his decision, and he said he was, and that everything would be just fine. He had a way of making me believe what I didn't think was possible, was possible.

We left early on Friday morning, and I was happy to leave to get back home and talk in private with Iden, and to look at numbers to see how much we would owe and learn about our new monthly payments.

On our drive home I was very quiet, and the girls kept asking their dad questions about the house. Elizabeth, being so wise, asked if I were happy with the buying of the house. Not wanting to take away the girls' joy I said, "Yes!" I also said I was just a bit tired and had a headache, so I closed my eyes.

After arriving home and unpacking the car, Iden and I waited till the girls were asleep before we talked, which led to a big argument because I didn't feel like it was the right decision to make. I suggested that we rent a place for a month to see if we enjoyed vacationing there. He disagreed and there was nothing I could do or say to change his mind. So that night we went to bed not speaking. A family getaway that started out so well, ended with that not-so- pleasant feeling again.

By the beginning of May, we were now the owners of two houses. Iden was very excited, and we made plans to start some work on the new house and to do some landscaping. The girls and I were also anticipating going to many yard sales and antique shops nearby to decorate our new place in the country. I also had a lot of land to cultivate a small garden with herbs and vegetables. What seemed like a wrong idea was slowly fading and making plans together for the house was enjoyable. I allowed myself to feel the joy, although I still worried about our finances.

CHAPTER FIFTEEN

THE DIAGNOSIS

'Life on Earth is at the ever-increasing risk of being wiped out by a disaster, such as sudden nuclear war, a genetically engineered virus or other dangers we have not yet thought of.'

— STEPHEN HAWKING

Spring slowly changed into summer, bringing many changes outside in the world as well as in my home. Iden was no longer depressed. His mood definitely shifted upward, which was evidenced by his increased energy and lack of sleep and his desire to talk to everyone. He was not outgoing by nature, and it was surprising to see him engaging in conversations with people at stores and in the neighborhood whom he would never normally speak to. With the elevation of his mood, he also seemed to be getting slightly agitated by things that had never bothered him before.

School was now finished, so the girls and I were at home and looked forward to enjoying the easy and peaceful feeling that summer brings. The girls and I loved to go to the beach a few days a week, head into the city to visit museums and parks, spend time with my parents, and on the weekends, we eagerly anticipated our time together in our upstate house. The renovations were complete as well as some clearing of land to make a driveway. We had bought new beds and inexpensive living room furniture and decorated with many items we had lying around in our house and from things we found in yard sales in Hunter.

Mom joined us on many weekends, and it was always a pleasure to have her near me providing extra help and company. I was happy that I could give her some much needed time away from the city to enjoy a swim in the lake, a daily country walk, and stargazing at night on our front porch. Iden would often take Fridays off work, and we would leave very early in the morning, and arrive back home on Sunday afternoon. He often suggested that I stay for a week by myself with the girls. We had purchased a Jeep for the house, but I didn't feel comfortable being alone.

On Saturday mornings, Iden liked to do things around the cabin. The girls were happy staying in, but most of the time being as young as they were, they wanted to go out and have some fun. So I would take them to the lake, on walks, and into town for some shopping. When I returned home, Iden was usually at our friend John's house. When he got back after a long visit, I could tell he had been drinking, and often he would need to take a nap.

I had become concerned about Iden's drinking so asked him what was going on. He told me I was making too much of it and that he enjoyed spending time with John. I understood that a drink with friends was a nice way to enjoy your time, but he was having more than just a drink or two.

When John's girlfriend Nina was visiting, we would go to their house for dinner. The girls and I both enjoyed her company and playing in the game room. John had recently bought some horses and Nina would let the girls feed them carrots and apples and brush their hair. I usually left around 10 o'clock, but Iden preferred to stay longer.

One particular night, after the girls and I had returned home from a visit, and we were all asleep, we were woken by a loud crash as Iden had come home so drunk from John's that he fell as he came in. I managed to get him undressed and into bed. He started talking nonsense about his deceased brother Rahman and about political issues in Iran. I stayed with him until he fell asleep.

I could not get back to sleep because I was extremely upset by his behavior, and I was seriously concerned about his mental well-being. The next morning when he awoke, he said that John gave him too much to drink and that he would never let that happen again. From that day on I despised John even more.

While our weekends upstate were not always unpleasant, it was always good to return home and be away from John's harmful influence. Although the girls and I liked being in the country surrounded by nature, we also enjoyed our summer routine in the city. The girls would relax in the morning, and I did some gardening and other chores. We would then either head to the beach or find some other activity of their choice. Since it was the summer, and we were on a different schedule, we ate dinner at a later hour, as many times we waited for Iden to come home so we could eat together.

We all had cell phones and I asked Iden to call me when he was leaving work so I could plan our meal so we could eat together. Most of the time he was very good about answering my calls, but in the passing weeks he was answering my calls much less. Even the girls tried to call him, thinking he might answer. Our summertime meals became just the three of us more often than not.

If Iden was still not home after we had finished dinner and had not answered his phone, the girls would go sit out on the front steps to wait for him. Soon it became a guessing game as to when he would be home, and if he had been drinking or not. His drinking caused me a lot of anxiety. I was concerned about him driving and getting into an accident. We were arguing a lot about his lack of responsibility, and not answering his phone to let me know when he would be home. When he did not answer, all I could do was wait until he got home safely.

Once again, I tried to talk to Iden about his drinking, but he said I was trying to control him and that he did not have a drinking problem. I began to feel I did not know this man that I was married to. He said that his boss and coworkers often invited him out after work for a bite, and he felt obliged to go. His dinners out were more than they were at home, and our arguments over this matter left me feeling very upset and confused as to why he didn't want to be with his family.

One particular weekend during that summer, he got up very early on a Saturday morning and said he wanted to go upstate by himself, and that he would be back on Sunday afternoon. He already had a bag packed, and his guitar in his hand, I asked what it was all about and why hadn't he talked to me the night before because the girls and I thought we were all going to our house together that weekend. He said he needed some time alone and told me to stop being so controlling as to what he could and couldn't do.

Hearing those words made me stand still for a minute. I couldn't think of what to say. He grabbed a cup of coffee and left. As soon as he'd left, I tried to call him on his phone, but he didn't answer. I wanted him to come back and talk to me to figure out what the urgency was for his needing to leave. I tried many times throughout the day, but he never answered his phone.

When the girls got up, they asked where their father was. I made an excuse that the house had needed something repaired, so he went alone. They were disappointed, but I pretended all was well so they would not be concerned. During the day, Claudia wanted to reach out to her dad, and she tried calling him, but he didn't answer, and Elizabeth started to ask why he wasn't answering his phone. We tried to figure out where he was and what he was doing. Later on I had learned that he would escape to our upstate house to binge-drink with John and would sometimes take a friend from Queens.

Iden drank most nights after work, and I started to think even during work hours. He'd arrive home late most nights smelling of alcohol, and sometimes the girls wouldn't see their dad for days at a time. The girls and I started calling him at around 5 o'clock after work during the week to see if he would answer. He would usually be home at a reasonable hour if we were able to contact him. If he did not answer his phone after 6 o'clock, the girls knew their dad would not be home until late and only I knew why.

The girls were beginning to sense the rifts and Elizabeth knew something was wrong. After a few months of this behavior I suggested we should see someone because he was no longer acting responsible as a husband, father, or to himself. Some nights he arrived home well after midnight and we struggled to sleep, not knowing where he was or what may have happened to him. I tried hard not to involve the girls, but they were old enough to know better and would wait up until he came home. There were only so many lies I could tell them until they figured out what was really going on.

As the summer days of 2001 were almost over, the girls and I started to do back-to-school shopping. They also took trips with me into my school to help me set up my classroom for the new school year. I was sad to see the summer over because it allowed me to be with my daughters, and I was able to do more of all that I loved doing without the hectic routine of work.

I was desperately trying to keep myself grounded, and not to allow the anxiety I was feeling about Iden's behavior to affect the girls and myself, although it was a daily struggle. I experienced a sense of loss because Iden was no longer the friend and the person who I knew and loved, and he was creating an unstable family life. I started to create a life of my own and he was on the outside.

September 11th was a beautiful crisp, sunny day with a cloudless blue sky. I walked Mimi early that morning and as I walked, I looked up at the sky and thought how wonderful a day it would be if I could stay positive and hopeful. The new school year had just begun. The girls were adjusting to their new grade, and I was adjusting to the new students in my classroom.

I arrived at work a bit later than usual because I had overslept, which had never happened before. I enjoyed getting to work at least an hour before my students arrived so I could enjoy a quiet cup of coffee and review my day's lessons and prepare any materials I may have needed. So feeling a bit harried I met my class and started my day feeling a bit more anxious than usual.

I had made a few phone calls to Iden, and he hadn't answered, but I tried to not allow that to upset my day, but it did. When I met my class, the faces on the students always put me in the present moment helping me to let go of all my worries and fears. The morning routine consisted of unpacking, checking homework, saying the pledge of allegiance, and getting reading for our morning meeting time. I was teaching a kindergarten class at that time, and we had just gathered on our carpet when we heard the announcement that there was an attack on the World Trade Towers.

Iden was working downtown, and I tried to call him, but got no answer. My next call was to my neighbor who immediately picked up and said she was on her way to my daughters' school to pick up my girls and stay with them until I reached home.

After dismissing our students safely, school staff were sent home. Since I had a car, I was able to drive home, but all train and bus services had stopped, and the roads were slow moving. As I was driving, I kept trying to reach Iden to no avail. I arrived home by 1 o'clock and picked up my girls from the neighbor's. My girls were very concerned and upset, and rightly so. I tried to keep myself together for them.

I was still not sure what had happened, and I had no idea where Iden was and if he were in any danger. The girls and I hugged and kissed each other and went home and waited and waited for Iden. I kept trying to reach him on his phone, but he didn't answer. I thought for sure something had happened to him otherwise why wouldn't he answer his phone. I watched the news and they reported that cell phone service might not be working so I thought perhaps that was the reason.

Afternoon led into early evening that led into late evening, and still there was no word from Iden. It was getting very late, and the girls were nervous about their dad's well-being. I tried my best to make excuses, but my fears were getting the best of me. We were very tired and kept the television on showing all the news since we had arrived home. We didn't go upstairs to sleep, but rather decided to sleep on the living room floor to wait for Iden to come home. We took all our blankets and pillows and arranged them one next to the other with Mimi lying next to us.

Although the girls were young, they understood the gravity of what had happened, and were especially anxious about their dad. We were in and out of sleep that night and at around 5 o'clock in the morning we heard the front door unlock. Iden came in with a brown paper bag containing bagels and said that they kept all the IT people at the hospital in case the computers were needed in the operating room or for monitoring computer systems during a disaster.

I was relieved to see Iden alive and well and we all got up to give him big hugs and kisses. I asked why he didn't try and get in touch somehow. I knew cell phones were not operating, but the hospital had landlines as well as us. He said he couldn't get through. We spoke briefly, and then we all laid on the floor and slept. When I awoke Iden was already up and watching the news, and I could see that he was crying. He was very upset as we all were, but he seemed inconsolable.

The world and New York City especially slowly tried to get back to life. Everyone seemed to know someone who was killed in the 9/11 tragedy and every story brought more sadness. It was indeed a very stressful time, and many people were suffering from post-traumatic stress disorder following the event. Iden became very depressed and needed to take some time off work. I would leave in the morning and come home, and he would still be in his pajamas and had not eaten all day, nor walked our dog. It was difficult seeing him in this condition, but at least I knew where he was, and I did not need to worry about his drinking. When he was depressed, he did not drink. During these dark periods he just slept and tuned out the world, including his family.

Iden was making visits to his doctor and said that he was taking new medicine so he should be feeling better soon. A new normal took hold of our family life. Elizabeth and Claudia knew better than to bother their dad, but they would try and cheer him up in the best way they could, but nothing seemed to help. I tried to make dishes that he enjoyed eating because he had no appetite, and his weight loss was becoming very noticeable.

Claudia was displaying more and more anxiety and I was becoming very concerned. She needed constant affirmation that I would be picking her up after school at 3:30 in the afternoon, even though I was never late. She was also becoming fearful of things she never was previously, and she had started to feel like she was sick every day. She was also not doing well in school, and she was somewhat socially immature compared to her peers. I tried to talk to Iden about her, but he could not offer any advice or help given his present condition.

Sometimes after I dropped the girls off at school I would drive to work and have a cry in the car. Before I entered the school I would sit in the car and smoke a cigarette to try to put all my worries out of my mind. I would also give Mom a call and she would always say something that allowed me to start my day over in a better way. How I miss those early morning phone calls listening to my lifeline on the other end. My job as a teacher did not allow me to wallow in my thoughts. I had to remain focused and in the present, which helped me forget my worries until three o'clock in the afternoon at least.

Iden returned to work after the winter holidays in January, still depressed, but he decided it was time. And so over the next few years, there were episodes of major depression and episodes where his mood was elevated, during which he did some serious binge drinking

Elizabeth started high school and Claudia was now in seventh grade. Claudia was struggling academically so we decided to have her tested to see if she had learning disabilities. After a few months and many tests, it was revealed that she had some focusing issues due perhaps to anxiety. With that result came more anxiety for myself because I blamed our family situation as the cause for her anxiety.

Every day after work I had to help Claudia with her studies and pray that Iden would be home safe. It is hard to believe that we all spent years living in this vicious cycle. I wanted to get help so I asked Iden if we could go to therapy. Our marriage was falling apart, which was the glue that gave me strength to hold my life together. Our family was also falling to pieces. Elizabeth, although an excellent student, was showing signs of anxiety in a different way. She became a perfectionist in her schoolwork, needing to get a 100 percent on every test.

I found a therapist in Forest Hills who participated in my health insurance. Iden and I talked about it, and we decided that it would be a good idea to go and see a professional to get some help. The first visit was a bit awkward because we had never been in therapy together before, although Iden had been seeing a psychologist alone for years.

After a few visits, the therapist starting probing and asking questions. Trying to be honest, I answered exactly how I felt. Iden thought I was attacking him when I mentioned his drinking and his irresponsibility of coming home late and not answering his phone causing the girls and me to worry. On a few occasions he started yelling, and the therapist had a difficult time calming him down. I knew after those sessions that the disagreement would continue after we left the therapist's office. We tried not to carry it into the home, but it was inevitable. And so ended our therapy sessions.

One night after everyone had gone to sleep, I couldn't sleep so I turned on the television and started changing channels when I saw something about depression. It was the first time I heard the terms bipolar and manic depressive. I listened as the interviewer asked questions to the interviewees. They described themselves as having periods of depression that changed suddenly into a more elevated state that sometimes caused some serious addictive and aggressive behaviors. As they were speaking, I was doing a mental check off comparing their behavior to Iden's during the low and high episodes. I immediately Googled bipolar disorder and started reading the information I found and although it was frightening, at least I felt that I had found some answers for his behavior.

After my late-night discovery, I held onto the information because I wasn't sure what to do with what all that I had learned. Claudia started experiencing some severe anxiety problems that stopped her eating properly. I thought she should see a psychiatrist and Iden agreed. There must have been a time when Claudia was eating at school, and she felt like she was choking. It scared her, and from that time on she started to avoid all foods that were hard and required chewing. She only ate things like soup, mash potatoes, applesauce, and a few other soft foods. She was losing weight and becoming even more anxious because, although she wanted to eat, her fear of choking prevented her from doing so.

It was difficult to find a child psychiatrist that we all liked. After talking to a few doctors, Iden got a recommendation for a doctor in Brooklyn Heights who was said to be excellent. I looked him up to see if he participated in my health plan, and, unfortunately, he didn't. Iden and I decided to go ahead and make an appointment anyway because we were both concerned about her physical and mental well-being.

We met the doctor during Iden's lunch hour because his office was only a few blocks from Iden's work. I took the train with Claudia to his office and waited for Iden there. The doctor met with us first, asking us questions and although I waited for Iden to respond, he was very quiet, so I did most of the talking. He then had us wait outside and asked for Claudia to come in. As we waited, we talked, and we both agreed that he seemed very nice, and we thought Claudia would also like him. After her session we all went in to talk and he told us he would see us next week. He had given Claudia a book to read and a journal to write down her thoughts and feelings to share with no one but herself.

We left the doctor's office and walked Iden back to work. He kissed us goodbye, and we watched him walk away. He was such a handsome man, but his face could not hide the struggle that he apparently was feeling. He just seemed so far away and removed from life and from us.

A year or so passed by and Iden had a very long depression with some periods of elevated moods. He was drinking more and more, even now in depression. Claudia continued to see the psychiatrist and her eating was improving, although her anxiety seemed to increase. She became anxious about so many things, which became unpredictable to know when she was going to have an anxiety attack. Sometimes it was about taking a test, a friend not answering a call, taking a train, going to a party, and just about anything. During one session with the doctor, Iden could not get away from work, so I went alone with her.

After Claudia's session, the doctor asked to talk to me alone, and asked me a few questions about what was going on at home, because Claudia had shared her concerns about her dad and about the disagreements that I had with him. We spoke some more, and I told him about Iden's depression and episodes of mania. He asked me if he was seeing a psychiatrist and I said that he was. I felt awful talking about him, but it was essential information that he needed to know in order to help Claudia. He said the next time Iden was present we would talk some more. Before leaving I asked if he thought Iden might be bipolar. He just looked at me and said that he would see us all next week and we'd talk some more.

At the beginning of summer, Iden was experiencing mood swings quicker than before. Previously, he would have months of depression followed by a few months where he was his old self again, neither up nor down, before heading into an episode of mania. But over the course of the past year, he seemed to go through each cycle much quicker.

We had an appointment with Claudia's doctor one day when Iden showed up somewhat agitated over some things that were going on at work. After Claudia finished her visit, she went into the waiting room so the doctor could speak to Iden and me alone. The doctor asked me a question and I mentioned something about Iden's behavior over the past week. Iden got very angry and started yelling at me. The doctor told him to calm down and asked if he was taking his medicine properly. Iden stormed out of the office, and I stood to go after him. The doctor looked at me and said that Claudia was being affected greatly by Iden's unstable moods, and also by our arguing. In not so many words he told me that my priority should be to take care of my children and myself. Before I left, he also said Iden needed to get himself some help as soon as possible.

We left the office in a hurry so I could catch up with Iden. I called out to him as he walked down the block. It didn't look as if he was going to stop, but he finally did, and turned to look at us. I grabbed Claudia's hand and we ran to catch up with him. We stood there staring at each other and then he said that he didn't appreciate the way I attacked him in the office. I apologized. I'd only answered the doctor because he'd asked me how things were at home. Iden didn't want to talk further, saying he had to get back to work because there was a huge problem. He'd had a huge disagreement with his boss over some work-related issue. We said goodbye and I reached out for a hug and a kiss, but he walked away before I could touch him. As always, I watched him walk away, but it felt as if he were leaving us for good.

On our way home I tried to make light of the situation and said to Claudia that Daddy was under a lot of stress at work and not to mind his behavior. I told her that he loved us both very much and that all would be okay. She tried to believe, but I could see her fear as well as she could see mine.

Knowing how much Claudia liked doing projects I told her that when we get home, we would have lunch in the backyard and that we could paint some wicker furniture I had bought at a garage sale to put on our deck upstate. Elizabeth was working at the Forest Hills Stadium in the restaurant. She wasn't old enough to be a server, but helped with serving water, bread, and clearing off tables. She enjoyed making some money, plus being around some friends. She took her job seriously and was very proud when she got her tips and a paycheck.

It was nice having the time with Claudia alone just to be with her and to do something special together. We made lunch and took Mimi out back with us to eat it. Claudia always loved music and dancing so after lunch we brought out the boom box and cranked up the tunes and did some dancing. It was good to see her laughing. We then took out the wicker chair and table and set them on an old plastic tablecloth and started to paint. It was a beautiful summer day and the honeysuckle fragranced the whole backyard.

I thought of Iden and how nice it would be for him to see Claudia enjoying herself. He loved her very much and they had a very special connection, and I knew this would make him happy knowing she was having a good afternoon after the rough start in the morning at her doctor. I decided to give him a call to check in to see how things were going at work. I called his work phone, but it immediately went to voicemail, so I then tried his cell phone, and it also went straight to voicemail. This wasn't the first time this had happened, but of course it got me a little worried because he left agitated after the doctor's visit and also from issues at work.

I tried not to let my apprehension get in the way of having a nice day with Claudia. We took a little break from painting to take Mimi for a walk, and as we walked, she asked if we could call Daddy. She said she felt like talking to him. She had her cell phone with her so I thought perhaps he would answer her call since he still might have been angry with me from this morning. She dialed his cell phone, and it too went to voicemail. She left a sweet message saying that she was having a good day and wishing that he were here with us. She asked him to please call her as soon as he heard the message. We finished our walk and had some ice tea and some oatmeal cookies before finishing the painting of the chairs.

By 4 o'clock there was still no word from Iden. Claudia had asked him to call. Trying to reassure her that all was okay I said he must be very busy with work today and as soon as he gets a free minute, he would call us. Elizabeth arrived home from work and came into the kitchen to chat for a bit and I filled her in on the day's activities at home, leaving out the drama of the morning. Claudia was upstairs watching TV and talking on her phone with a friend.

Elizabeth went to change and shower before dinner, but no sooner had she gone upstairs than she came down again and asked, "What's going on with Daddy, and why isn't he answering his phone?"

I turned around and immediately said, "What are you talking about?"

She said that Claudia told her about us trying to get in touch with him and that we hadn't spoken to him since after the doctor's appointment. Her fears and mine were the same. Always worried that perhaps he might be drinking, because whenever he didn't answer his phone and it goes straight to voicemail something seemed wrong. She asked what happened in the doctor's office because Claudia had also mentioned our disagreement. Elizabeth told me I shouldn't have said anything to upset him. She always thought that what we might say and might not say could make her father drink or not drink. Her comment upset me, and I explained that I was just giving information to the doctor to help Claudia. Elizabeth said she was calling her father and that he might pick up his phone for her. She dialed his number and I foolishly hoped he would answer, but it also went to voicemail.

By 6 o'clock we had tried several more times to get in touch with Iden and we were all upset at him not answering our calls. In our minds, this meant one thing and that was that he was out drinking. He had never left work to drink before, or so I thought. He would usually drink with some coworkers after finishing work. It was dinnertime and I tried very hard to carry on with our life while waiting to hear from him. The girls brought their phones to the table even though that was not usually permitted, but I understood the need to keep vigilance in case there was a text or a call from their dad. I also had mine in my pocket. Although I had made their favorite for dinner, pasta with meatballs, the girls hardly took a bite.

Elizabeth was asking what if this happened or that happened, and I tried to reassure her that we would hear from him soon. I cleared the table of the uneaten food, and we went and sat in the living room. Claudia sat in our bay window looking out to the street for Iden's car. I put on the TV and tried to find something to watch while we waited, when suddenly my phone rang, and it was Iden.

I quickly answered and said, "Iden," but the person on the other end of the line was not Iden. A man answered and said that Iden was at his bar and had passed out. He explained that Iden had left the phone on the bar, so he dialed the last number that he saw. I told him that I was Iden's wife and to please let me know where the bar was and then asked what I should do. He gave me the name and address of the bar, which was located in Brooklyn Heights, not far from Iden's job. I told him to please leave Iden sleeping, and I would come to get him. The girls asked what was going on and all I could say was that I had to go pick up Daddy, but they knew something was very wrong.

I sat for a moment considering what to do. I had the girls and by no means was I taking them with me. I needed to get a plan together quickly. I immediately called my next-door neighbor to ask her if she could watch the girls and I filled her in because she had been not only a good neighbor, but we had also become good friends. Over the years we had become very close, and she was very aware of my issues at home, so I didn't need to explain too much.

I knew that I would need some help, so I asked Iden's friend Marcos to come with me. The girls gathered a few things and I brought them and Mimi over to my neighbor Suzanne's house. I will never forget how Elizabeth took Claudia's hand and said, "Be careful, Mom! I will take care of Claudia." She was an old soul in a young girl's body.

Marcos met me in front of my house and as we started to drive, I explained what was happening. I thanked him for coming, but he knew I wasn't that fond of him because of all the drinking he and Iden did together. He asked me specific questions and I informed him about the events of the day starting with the doctor's appointment up until I received the call from the bartender at the restaurant.

While we were driving, I also called Ron, who over the years had helped me through some difficult moments, providing much-needed advice and support concerning Iden. He suggested that I call Iden's psychiatrist to figure out the best thing to do. I gave the phone to Marcos to find her number and call since I was driving. I left a frantic message and asked her to call me back as soon as possible. We were just exiting the Long Island Expressway when the doctor called. She asked what had happened and I told her I couldn't explain in detail, but that Iden was passed out in a bar in Brooklyn Heights, and I was going there to pick him up. She said that he was experiencing hypomania and that I should take him to Beth Israel Hospital to be evaluated.

We drove around for some time before finding the address given to me. I double-parked while Marcos went in to get Iden. Marcos was 6-foot-2 and very strong, so I knew he could easily pick up Iden without problem. I had my eyes fixed on the front door, waiting. Other cars were beeping because they couldn't pass by, and then I saw Marcos coming out without Iden. He got back into the car saying that Iden had woken up and left the bar.

Marcos had Iden's eyeglasses and tie in his hand. I started to cry hysterically, and Marcos tried to calm me down. I pulled myself together and asked what we should do. He told me that the bartender had said Iden was very drunk and agitated and that he probably couldn't get too far. We decided to find a parking spot. Even though I didn't pray often, I started praying right then and there to Saint Anthony to help me find somewhere to park. I found a spot at the end of the block and quickly parked the car.

Marcos and I looked in every restaurant and bar we could find in a small radius that was near to the one he'd left.

"We just missed him," Marcos said, so he shouldn't be too far away.

Marcos and I went into all the restaurants and bars for about 20 minutes and then Marcos went into an Italian restaurant and came out to me and said Iden was there at the bar drinking. He told me not to go in, but to go and get the car and he would try to lure Iden outside and get him into the car.

I immediately ran to get the car and was so thankful to Marcos that I gave him a big hug and said I was sorry for thinking he wasn't a good friend. He said that he had tried to get Iden help with his drinking, but that he wouldn't listen. I pulled the car around and saw Marcos with Iden leaning against him. Iden was awake, but not coherent. They sat in the back, and I needed to get to the hospital and phone the doctor to let her know we had found Iden and were on our way.

Iden saw me and started talking nonsense and cursing about his boss and his job. He had some bruises on his face and left eye, and his shirt had some blood on it and his hair was all disheveled. The hospital was about 10 minutes away and during the drive Iden fell asleep.

We pulled up to the emergency entrance and I went in and gave them Iden's doctor's information plus the information they asked about Iden. Some orderlies came out to the car and put Iden on a stretcher to bring him into the hospital. Iden woke up and started asking what was going on. The staff explained to him what was happening and then he started yelling at me, so they asked me to go and sit in the waiting area. Iden started to say, "My wife doesn't let me have a few drinks without complaining…"

I didn't want to leave, but the staff said it was best and that they would be in contact with his doctor shortly and then get back to me as soon as they had admitted him, as per the advice of Iden's doctor. Marcos went to park the car, and I called the girls to let them know that their dad was okay, although he needed to be in the hospital for a bit because he'd had too much to drink and needed help. I didn't know what else to say.

After what seemed like hours a doctor came out to talk to me. He said he spoke to Iden's doctor, and he suggested that Iden stay overnight to be evaluated, but that Iden had the right to discharge himself if he wanted. Since Iden had passed out again they would wait until the morning to see what he wanted to do. This news gave me no comfort because I was sure he would want to be released. I asked if I could see him and they said he was sleeping, but they took me to where he was, and it was a very disturbing sight.

A guard stood at the end of the hall, which had many rooms off it. Iden was in one of those rooms, which was no bigger than a large closet. Iden was fast asleep, still with his clothes on and a blanket thrown over him. I stood looking at him through the window and wondering how we had ended up like this

I left the hospital and called his doctor to ask what the next steps were. She said it was late and that she would call me the following day. I lost my cool with her, telling her I was very upset and needed some information. I didn't care what time it was. She said that Iden needed to be evaluated and to accept a hospital stay, and that we'd take it from there. She was as comforting as a bee sting, so I had to take the bite and just wait until morning to know what challenges we would be facing.

Marcos drove home because I was too upset to drive. I called Suzanne and she said the girls were fine and sound asleep, even though they had woken up asking for me a few times. She told me to just head home and get some sleep and that she would bring the girls home in the morning. Thank goodness for good friends. The whole ride home I couldn't talk and just looked out into the dark night. I felt as if my world had just stopped, and I needed to figure out how was I going to get it moving again.

Marcos dropped me off and I entered my home without my family or Mimi being there. It was 2 o'clock in the morning, and the day had held too much. All I could do was sit on the couch and cry.

The next thing I knew the phone rang and it was 8 in the morning. Iden's doctor called and said that Iden was awake and that she'd spoken to him, and that he was being admitted for a psychiatric evaluation. I asked if I could see him, and she said it was not recommended at this time since he was very agitated and needed to be stabilized. I asked what she thought was going on and she evasively replied that she'd be in touch shortly.

I showered and dropped into Dunkin Donuts to buy some donuts, muffins, and coffee before seeing my girls. The girls were up and ran to see me. They had many questions and I thought it best to just tell them the truth in a way they could understand. I also said it was good knowing that Iden was in a safe place and that he was getting all the excellent care he needed to get better. While the girls were having breakfast, Suzanne and I talked, and she gave me a big hug and told me she was here for me whenever I may need her. We stayed and chatted for a little bit and then headed home.

It felt extremely odd not having Iden home, but in a very weird way it was also a relief not to have to worry about him. I was hoping that his stay in the hospital would get him the help he needed so we could be a healthy family again.

Iden was in the hospital for almost a week before I was permitted to see him. I went to the psychiatric ward and had to wait to be buzzed in to enter. As I walked through the halls some of the sights were very disturbing. A young doctor met me and brought me into his office to brief me about Iden. The doctor explained that Iden was bipolar and had been suffering from a severe episode of mania.

The doctor asked me many questions about Iden and his behavior. After he was finished, I asked what the treatment would be. After I had seen a Jane Pauley documentary, I knew something about the illness, but wasn't sure about the treatment. The doctor told me that Iden would need to be hospitalized for a few weeks to stabilize him and to get the right cocktail of medicines. We spoke a little more and then he took me to see Iden. There were nurses and other employees also present in the room along with other patients.

Iden looked clean, but his face looked thin and his eyes huge. When he saw me at first, he seemed happy, but then he started cursing me and told me I had made him lose his job and that I was the one who needed help. The nurses saw how agitated he was and came to calm him down. I told him that I loved him and understood how difficult this was for him. He didn't seem to think anything was wrong, but he also did not want to leave and had agreed to receive treatment, which was a blessing. The doctor suggested I leave and said hopefully the next visit would be better.

I left the hospital and sat in a small park right outside the hospital to smoke a cigarette. I smoked a few a day and I was wondering how Iden was managing not smoking since he usually smoked a pack a day. I just sat there unable to move and tried hard to think about what my next move should be. I called Ron and told him what had happened, and he said that he would go and visit Iden to see if he could help in any way. He also said that we should meet next time I come into the city to have some lunch and talk.

I didn't want to tell my parents because I didn't want them to worry, but I decided to call them as I walked to the train to inform them about Iden's condition. Dad said that he knew something was going on because Iden had asked to borrow a substantial amount of money. I was shocked when I heard this and asked when he had asked for the money and what the loan was for? Dad said Iden had asked to borrow $20,000 and asked him not to tell me. Dad said Iden had been making a payment every month, and was worried about him. I got off the phone and was in complete shock. I felt as if Iden had a secret life that I knew nothing about, and it made me wonder what other secrets he was hiding.

Iden stayed in the hospital for a little over a month, and during that time I only saw him about three times. Although the girls and I missed him very much, we had developed a new norm. We ate our meals without waiting or worrying when Iden would come home from work. We all went to bed at the same time more or less. It was summer so the girls were both working. Claudia had a job as a junior counselor at our community house, and Elizabeth had her job at the Forest Hills Tennis Club. I was grateful for their jobs because it allowed them to go swimming every day and to be with friends and enjoy their summer.

At nights after dinner we would take a walk and sometimes treat ourselves to some of our favorite ice cream at an old-fashioned sweet shop on Metropolitan Avenue. Most nights we would watch a little TV and then go upstairs to read before going to sleep. In the beginning, the girls asked questions about their dad every day, but all I could say was that he was getting better and would be home soon. I spoke to his doctors a few times a week and they told me Iden was receiving therapy and that they were still adjusting his medicines. He was still in a highly agitated mood but talking more reasonably.

The nights Iden was in the hospital I slept very well knowing that he was safe. During those weeks he was in hospital Mom came over and stayed with us a few days every week. We cooked together and did some gardening, and in between she would ask me questions about Iden, especially about why he needed to borrow money from them. She couldn't believe I didn't know anything about it, and now was certainly not the right time to talk to Iden about it.

The summer was coming to an end and Iden was coming home. A few days before he was discharged I went to meet with his doctor to go over Iden's treatment and things that I should know about bipolar disorder. The doctor also informed me as to his medications. Iden was taking lithium and a combination of antidepressants. Beth Israel had a bipolar group meeting and therapy sessions of which Iden was now a part. He needed to see his psychiatrist once a week and to attend therapy and group meetings once a week as part of his recovery program.

After we had finished talking, Iden was brought into the doctor's office and I got up to give him a hug and a kiss, but he was distant, and I felt nervous about going home with him. I had become suddenly afraid of my own husband. Even after all that he had been through, Iden still looked handsome, although he was thin, and his eyes looked at me as if he was seeing a new person.

We walked to the car, and he insisted on driving. I suggested I drive, but he wouldn't allow me to get in the driver's seat.

"You don't think I am capable of driving now?"

He immediately asked for a cigarette, and I gave him one. I said the girls were very happy that he was coming home and had helped to make his favorite dinner of kebabs and rice. He smiled and said that he had missed them very much and that he was happy to be coming home. He told me that he'd had a very difficult time and that he didn't know how all of this had happened. I took hold of his hand and said that we would work it out together and that I knew he would get better.

We arrived home and when the girls saw us pull into the driveway they immediately came running out to meet their dad with hugs and kisses. Iden took both girls in his arms and lifted them up with giant hugs. Once inside, Iden said he wanted to shower and lie down for a little bit before dinner. The girls and I prepared dinner and waited to wake him when dinner was ready. The doctor suggested that Iden should try and keep to a routine schedule of eating meals and sleeping.

We woke Iden up at 6 o'clock, and he came downstairs saying he smelled the food and was hungry. Although he was quiet during dinner, he did engage in conversation, answering the girls' questions. He ate his food with a good appetite and thanked us for making such a lovely meal. Holding back his tears, he said that he had missed us all very much. The girls and Iden headed into the living room after dinner to watch TV while I did the dishes. Elizabeth soon came to tell me that Daddy had fallen asleep. I told the girls that he needed to sleep to get well. The girls became very good nurses by always asking him what he needed and giving him a lot of love.

The new school year began, and I had to get back to work, so I was a little concerned about leaving Iden at home alone all day. Iden had made some phone calls to work and due to HIPPA he did not need to give an explanation as to why he was on medical leave, but I am sure that they had a good understanding as to why.

Iden remained on a leave of absence for six months and while at home, there were many uncertain times. His medication needed adjustments and he had short episodes of mania and depression and some periods of drinking. I continued to talk to his doctor, and Iden and I decided to go to family counseling. Claudia's anxiety had escalated over these past months and her schoolwork became increasingly more difficult for her. We would have homework battles every night.

After a day of teaching I would sit in my car, light up a cigarette, and try to decompress one long workday out of my system with each exhale before heading home. I just never knew what problems I would be facing when I got home. What mood was Iden going to be in? And how was Claudia's day at school going to affect our night?

The days were long and after the girls had gone to sleep, the kitchen was clean, lunches were made, and the dog was walked, I would sit out on the back porch and have my second cigarette to end the day. Iden would sometimes join me, but I would have to ask him. It wasn't like before where we couldn't wait for the girls to go to sleep so we could have a few quiet stolen minutes together at the end of the day.

One night in the early fall, Iden joined me on the deck while the night air was still warm. He told me he was worried about his job and that he had some financial problems. He said that he made some investments that went bad and borrowed money from my parents and that he was paying them back slowly. I had not mentioned to him that I knew about the loan. I told him I thought we were financially solid now because we both had been working and he had made advancements at work. He apologized for using poor judgment with investments. I was upset but didn't want to complain so I didn't show my feelings, but just kept them inside. I didn't want to upset any balance he was holding on to.

There were days where I felt that I was coming undone, but I had to hold it together. I loved Iden and I missed him. I missed us.

CHAPTER SIXTEEN

ACCEPTANCE

'Life is a series of natural and spontaneous changes. Don't resist them; that only creates sorrow. Let reality be reality. Let things naturally flow forward in whatever way they like.'

—LAO TZU

The years passed by, and we learned to live with the ups and downs of Iden's mood swings. Some months were better than others, and some were very, very difficult ones. Looking back, I am not sure how I really held it all together, but I loved Iden, and my family and I tried my best to accept each change in mood.

Events came and went, and to quote John Lennon, "Life is what happens while you are busy making other plans." There were graduations, special birthday parties, weddings, and dinners with friends and family that we had to get through by holding our breath and hoping for the best. Many of these events were held in our home. I loved having company and planning parties, but it also brought anxiety because I was never sure of Iden's mood, and when his mood was elevated, he would sometimes act inappropriately and embarrass my guests and me. At other times, he would be very down and not talk to anyone. So I learned to go ahead with my plans and not fight the reality of the illness because I couldn't make any difference.

On a few family meetings with Iden and his doctor I asked why Iden was struggling with finding a balance, and why his mood fluctuated so often. I had borrowed many books and had read online case studies about people with the disorder to get more information that could help Iden and our family. Many people were stabilized with the right amount of medicine and therapy. Iden's psychiatrist said that Iden's was a complicated case. He suggested Iden attend more therapy sessions and AA meetings.

Iden did not feel the need to do what was prescribed, so he wasn't making the progress that he could have had he been more compliant and followed his doctor's orders. I even suggested that I go to open AA meetings with him, but he didn't want to attend. He considered that he had just had a few episodes of binge-drinking and that he wasn't an alcoholic.

My 50th birthday and Elizabeth's graduation were approaching soon, and I wanted to get away for my birthday, just Iden and me. We hadn't spent time alone in years, and I didn't want to plan my own birthday party. I had a friend who knew someone that owned a beautiful bed and breakfast in Cape Cod, and even though it was just turning spring, the inn was open. So I asked Iden if we could take a drive and spend the weekend there.

My birthday is on March 17th, and temperatures would still be on the cold side, but it would still be nice to walk on the beach, go to restaurants, and walk around the town. Iden agreed and also said it would be nice to get away, even though he was going through a low period. It was early February and feeling excited about our getaway I started to make some plans. I made a reservation in a nice restaurant for my birthday dinner and made arrangements for the girls.

Even though the girls were teenagers they still needed adult supervision. Elizabeth was graduating high school in June, and Claudia was a sophomore. Elizabeth was eagerly awaiting replies from college applications, and Claudia had just spent a few weeks in the hospital recovering from a ruptured appendix, for which she needed an operation and intense intravenous antibiotics to fight a serious infection. She had missed a lot of schoolwork and we had a tutor coming to the house, which helped a lot, although it was a huge expense.

Iden and I both decided to take the Friday off so we could have an early start to our mini getaway. The girls and my mom made me a special dinner and a cake for my birthday the day before we left.

We left for our getaway around 7 o'clock on a beautiful mild and sunny Friday morning. The girls were still sleeping, so I went into their rooms to kiss them goodbye. Of course Elizabeth (Lizzy, her new preferred nickname), said to please stay in touch and to let her know when we arrived. Mom was already up, and I told her to call me if there was any problem. I also reminded her to let the girls take Mimi out for her scheduled walks. She assured me all would be just fine and to go and have a great time. It was great to have her in my life. She never allowed me to have a minute of worry.

The trip to the Cape was around six hours, so we arrived in the early afternoon. Iden loved to drive, especially to new places. He popped in some classical CDs, and we set off to Cape Cod. For the first hour or so we sat in silence just listening to music and then we started to talk about Claudia. We always talked about Claudia because she presented us with many issues, which recently was her ruptured appendix. Iden also talked about his job and how he was beginning to feel very uncomfortable. He said that ever since he returned from leave, they had treated him differently and he thought perhaps he should start looking for another job. I listened but didn't really know how to respond.

Lizzy was about to start college, and although we had a college savings fund for both girls, we had Claudia's private high school tuition and our mortgage and other expenses. I wasn't sure that given Iden's present mental condition that it wise for him to start looking for a new job. I didn't want this weekend to be filled with worries, so I tried my best to let it go and to change the subject. I told him that I had made reservations for dinner on Saturday at an Irish pub for a traditional corned beef dinner and that there would be traditional Irish music. He told me whatever I wanted would be okay with him.

After a few hours he asked to make a stop to use the restroom and to grab a bite before getting back on the road. We arrived at our inn around 3 o'clock in the afternoon. Our hosts greeted us with drinks and snacks and showed us to our room. Our room had a fireplace and faced the ocean, and it was beautifully decorated with antiques and flowers. A basket was left in our room with wine, champagne, and also tea and coffee. I quickly took the bottles away before Iden saw them, thinking it better he not have them in his sight.

Before dinner, we sat in a common area talking a bit to the hosts before retiring to our room. We both wanted to take a shower and a short nap before dinner. We showered and lay in bed, and although I wanted to be intimate with Iden I could tell he felt differently, as he turned his back to me and quickly fell asleep

Not being able to sleep, I got dressed and left our room to sit in the common area looking out onto the ocean. The hostess saw me and came to sit with me, offering me a glass of wine and asking where my husband was. I said he was tired and resting, and that he would be up soon. She sat and talked to me while she lit a fire, and we drank our wine. She told me about the meal that she was preparing for dinner and wanted to know if we had any food preferences.

I politely asked the hostess not to offer alcohol at dinner to us, even though I was drinking with her at that moment. She didn't ask any questions but seemed to understand. I had only known her for a few hours, but it was like I had known her for years. Her husband soon joined us, and we played a few board games and talked a bit before they headed to the kitchen, saying they had to start dinner.

There was only one other couple staying at the inn and they were not having dinner with us, so it would be a quiet meal. I returned to our room to find Iden still asleep. It was almost 6 o'clock and I tried to wake him to get ready for dinner, but he asked to sleep a bit more. I told him dinner was being served at 7 o'clock, and that we were expected to be on time since it was just the two of us. I could tell by his mood that he would rather have slept the night away rather than have to get up and be social with the innkeepers. I was hungry and looked forward to having a meal prepared for me.

Iden eventually got up and dressed and we sat by the fire in the living room and talked before we headed into the dining room, which was decorated with flowers and candles. The host, Sara, and her husband, Michael, asked if they could join us since we were the only guests having dinner. I heartily agreed and looked forward to having company at dinner.

We were served a most amazing shepherd's pie with parsnips and carrots with a homemade apple pie for dessert. During dinner, our hosts talked a little about their life and how they wound up on the cape after years of working in restaurants. They were interesting to talk to, and I enjoyed listening to all the places they had worked as chefs and where they had studied the culinary arts.

All during dinner Iden was quiet and did not engage in conversation, but rather just sat looking uninterested. I on the other hand was engaging in the conversation because I was interested to hear more about their life and how they came to Cape Cod. While having dessert, Iden excused himself to return to our room, saying he was very tired. He thanked the hosts and turned to me and said, "See you later."

I was happy in a way to be left alone and not to feel embarrassed by Iden's silence. I realized that they knew it wasn't out of rudeness, but it still made me quite uncomfortable.

We moved from the dining room table and went to sit in the living room. I happily accepted the offer of wine as we sat comfortably by the fireplace. They had a skylight ceiling and that night the stars were shining brilliantly. We talked for about an hour or more before finally saying goodnight. They asked if we would be having dinner again with them tomorrow and I said that we had made a reservation locally for a traditional corned beef and cabbage meal. Although after spending the first evening with them, I would have enjoyed having my birthday dinner with them, but seeing how Iden was feeling, it was better to go out and have it just be the two of us.

I returned to the room to find Iden was already sound asleep. I'd brought a book with me and read a little because I wasn't able to sleep right away. The room was decorated so beautifully, with our own fireplace, antique furniture, and a large bay window looking out to the sea. What more could two people in love need to make a night romantic? I turned and looked at Iden, thinking how wonderful it would be to make love here and now.

We got up early and showered and went to the dining room where carafes of coffee, hot water for tea, homemade muffins, and fruit on a table greeted us. Our host came out and said that she could make anything we would like for breakfast. The table was set with all types of syrups and jellies, and there was a sizeable platter of cheeses and fruits. What a treat it was. Breakfast was my favorite meal to have out since I never had time to make more than toast or instant oatmeal on a daily basis given our harried morning schedule. I ordered banana walnut pancakes with powdered sugar, and Iden ordered eggs over well with sausage

We were soon served our lovely meals and Iden once again remained silent. After finishing our breakfast, we filled our to-go cups with coffee and headed back to our room to gather a few things before going exploring. Even though it was off- season, there was some information on events as to what was happening around the town of Yarmouth. We picked up a copy and headed out. The first thing I wanted to do was walk on the beach, even though it was still chilly. We found a spot to park the car and walked down the many steps to the beach.

The New England beaches are quite different than those in New York. There are many cliffs and rocks and the waves on that day were fast and furious. The wind, the smell of the ocean, and the sounds were a birthday gift to me. Iden too loved the seaside, and even though he was feeling down I could see how he enjoyed walking on the sand and inhaling all the sights and smells around us. I hoped all he breathed in would lift his spirits.

Iden took my hand as we walked saying he was sorry for not being social or present. I told him that he was now and gave him a big kiss and a hug. We walked a little longer, but the winds were strong and it was cold, even though the sun shone brightly. We decided to head back to the car and head into town to look at some mansions and visit some estate sales.

We came across an estate sale that was in the most majestic house I had even seen. The ocean was their backyard, and the house had many staircases. There were rooms upon rooms, and closets upon closets of clothes, linens, dishes, and everything in between. All had a price tag attached to it. As we walked through the hallways it was hard to believe that all of this once belonged to someone who was no longer living here. I felt in a way that we were invading their home.

We went into a large den and Iden and I looked over some books before I moved on to look at the kitchen. The kitchen alone was the size of my home and was packed with china and crystal. I wanted to buy something to remember this place, so I found a beautiful little Wedgwood dish that I thought I might put on my dresser to hold my jewelry.

Iden soon came to find me and told me he had bought a book about Benjamin Franklin. When he showed it to me there was also a beautiful leather bookmark in it with the initials RM on it. We both left the house with a little treasure. The sun warmed up the day, so we left the car and walked up and down the streets admiring the beautiful homes. We also stopped in some stores that were open even though it was the off-season. We bought some tea and sat in a park to smoke a cigarette and Iden seemed a little happier than he had been since the beginning of the trip. We talked for a while and then walked back and found the restaurant that we were going to be having dinner in later that night.

We arrived back at the inn to find the hosts had prepared a wine and cheese platter with fruit, nuts, homemade cookies, and some wine and juice. I asked Iden if he wanted to have a snack and he said he wasn't hungry and that he preferred to lie down for a little bit and read his book. I told him I would grab something and then join him shortly. I really wanted to sip a glass of wine and sit by the fire to look out at the sea.

I sat by myself thinking of the girls and gave them a call to see how they were doing. I called Elizabeth's cell phone because I knew she would answer immediately. She was happy to hear my voice and immediately asked, "How is Daddy"? I told her we were both good and not to worry. I described the place to her that we were staying in and that I missed them being here with us, suggesting that we should plan a vacation to the Cape all together. I spoke to Mom and Claudia briefly before heading back to our room.

I opened the door thinking perhaps I would also take a little nap. Iden was already fast asleep, snoring away. I got into bed and actually fell asleep not realizing how tired I must have been. I awoke at almost at 5 o'clock and tried waking Iden, but he was still in a deep sleep. Our reservation was for 6 o'clock so I quickly showered and started getting dressed. I kept trying to get Iden up, but he kept resisting. I told him it was getting late, and it probably would be busy since it was St. Patrick's Day because it was an Irish restaurant. He finally got up and dressed and we went out to dinner.

The hosts and the other guests saw us leave and wished us a good night. We arrived at the restaurant a little late, but we were able to get a table in the very crowded restaurant. There was a band playing Irish music and the place was jumping. The smell of beer and cabbage was all around. We were seated and given a menu, but we knew we wanted the corned beef and cabbage, so we didn't even look at the menu.

I looked at the tables with people who had already been served their meals and the portions were huge, so one meal would probably have been enough for both of us given that Iden didn't have much of an appetite these days; but we did order two. The waitress brought rye bread and butter and asked what kind of beer we wanted. I looked over at Iden who suggested I go ahead, so I did. After all it was my birthday and Iden ordered a non-alcoholic beer.

We listened to the music and watched some people who were dancing. Our meals came with a large piece of cabbage, corned beef, and carrots. I had never attempted to make the meal myself, so I was excited and happy to be served such an authentic dish and especially as delicious as this one was. Neither of us could finish the meal, only eating half of the portion and thinking of how much my girls and my mother would love eating here. I felt bad about all the waste. We stayed to hear more music played while we enjoyed some coffee and Irish soda bread. We left full and I was feeling happy, although I would have loved to do the jig!

Upon our return to the inn, the hosts and the other couple staying there were drinking Irish coffee in the living room and asked if we'd like to join them. Iden said he wanted to go back to the room, but added, "Have fun, it's your birthday."

Upon hearing this the hosts said, 'If it's your birthday, then we should all celebrate." Michael brought out a bottle of champagne and popped it open. We drank and talked for an hour or more before returning to our room.

I would have liked to stay longer because they were all so engaging, and we were having a nice time, but I wanted to go back to Iden. I was hoping he wouldn't be sleeping since it was our last night together, but he was sound asleep. I wasn't ready to end my 50th birthday just yet, so I went back out to join the others. They were pleased I had returned. We continued talking well into the night before I finally retired for the night.

The following day I got up early and took a long walk on the beach, reviewing my life and thinking of what I needed and wanted to stay vibrant and able to be the best I could be for my family. I felt lonely and sad because after finally having a few nights away from the girls in a very intimate place with no one to bother us, Iden was not wanting to connect with me physically. I knew this was because he wasn't feeling well, but it still left me feeling a bit sad, although I know that wasn't his intention. As I walked, I thought of the man I fell in love with and who he was without his disorder.

By the time I got back, Iden was up and dressed. I had already packed my bag, so while Iden finished packing his things I noticed a little comment book on the table by the side of the bed asking the guests to write something about their stay. I wrote that we had enjoyed our stay thanks to our wonderful hosts who were friendly and treated us like family with delicious home-cooked meals and hospitality. I also wrote that my stay at the inn would help me remember my 50th birthday with joy because of them.

We had breakfast before heading home, and we thanked our hosts for a wonderful stay. They handed us some pamphlets about summer rates and availability, encouraging us to return. We were on the road by 10 o'clock and were expecting to be home around 3 o'clock in the afternoon, depending on traffic. We sat in silence for a while and then I said, "I had a lovely weekend, but I missed us."

Iden apologized again saying that he was hopeful his depression would lift so he could enjoy everything with me. When I asked him about his therapy and his medicine, all he said was that the doctors were working with him. I then asked if there was any reason why he wasn't able to maintain a baseline without having so many episodes of depression and mania. He said if there was something he could do he would. I didn't want to start arguing, but I suggested he try a new doctor or therapist. I also suggested practicing some self- care, such as joining a gym or going to AA meetings.

When we change things instead of doing the same things over and over there's a better chance there might be some different results. The idea of waiting around for a depression to lift was no way to live, and for me, when his mania set in, I was the one waiting for it to leave. I was trying my best to accept the current state the best way I could, but sometimes I just missed my old friend.

We drove straight through only making a stop at a Wendy's for a small bite and to use the restroom. We arrived home at our expected time, and the girls and Mimi gave us many welcome hugs and kisses. Mom said the girls were good, except Claudia had given her a hard time because she didn't want to study for her test. When Elizabeth offered to help her, she refused.

Iden took Mom home and I got busy putting my things away and doing things around the house before starting work the next day. Mom had made some dinner for us, and the house was all tidied, so I was able to relax and talk to the girls about their day and see what Claudia needed to study. Iden went downstairs to rest, saying he would be up later.

Elizabeth asked me about my weekend and knowing she wanted to hear all the good things I said we'd had a wonderful time, but of course I missed her and Claudia. I asked Claudia to get off her cell phone that she was lately always on, talking to her friends and, recently, boys. I asked what test she had, and she said she had a math test and that after dinner Elizabeth was going to review with her.

I thanked Lizzy and sat on the couch to show her the pretty little dish I bought and the pictures of the estate sale house that I took on my phone. She couldn't believe people actually lived in such an awesome house. We sat together talking about her graduation and her hopes for college acceptance. I knew she wanted to get into NYU and had the test scores and grades to do so, but she was very concerned about the tuition. I told her to wait and see and that we would figure out a way to make things happen. "Don't let worries about money interfere with your dreams." I told her

It was soon near dinnertime. My mother had left a meal for us, which just had to be heated. Lizzy took Mimi for a walk while I set the table and heated up the food. I called down to Iden that dinner would soon be ready and called up to Claudia to come down. I always needed to call the two of them from either up or down.

The following months passed quickly, and it was soon time for Elizabeth's graduation. So I began planning a house party for family and friends. Iden's mood was elevated, although his drinking episodes seemed to be on pause, and I was hoping that he would continue in this mood for her ceremony and the party. Lizzy's graduation was held at Queens College and Mom, Dad, Iden, Claudia, and I attended. There were only a few tickets given per family. Elizabeth graduated in the top 10 in her class of over a thousand students and received awards, and scholarships, and she was in the National Honor Society. It was a very proud day for us all.

After the ceremony Lizzy took pictures with her three best friends, with whom she is close, even to this day. Although Elizabeth was accepted at NYU, she decided to go to Genesco with her three friends. She wanted to study biology and was thinking of premed but wasn't sure. I think she opted for the state school because of the affordable tuition, and I think she wanted to have a bit of distance from her family. Elizabeth is also a bit shy, and I think it was comforting knowing that her good friends would be with her and sharing dorm rooms together.

With the ceremony over, we went to Elizabeth's favorite restaurant. We had a wonderful time, and everyone enjoyed the day. The following day we had planned a small party after our graduation lunch. I started to get busy preparing food items and cleaning up the backyard. I asked Iden to sweep and wash the deck and to clean some chairs and tables with Claudia, which he was very happy to do.

Claudia always loved to be outside, so she happily helped as well. I started to weed and trim some of the plants on the deck and as I was working, I could see Iden working and joking with Claudia, and I noticed that he seemed to have more energy and his mood seemed to be lifting a little more. We worked in the backyard for an hour or so and then I went inside while Iden and Claudia finished up. Elizabeth preferred to help in the kitchen preparing for the party. I had ordered some hero sandwiches and some hot dishes from our local Italian store, but I was also preparing dishes as well.

We stocked the refrigerators, rearranged the furniture, put up decorations, and laid the table. Once finished, all that I wanted to do was relax and watch some TV. The girls were occupied upstairs, and I was in the living room. Iden was in the basement talking on the phone to someone in Farsi. I went downstairs and asked if he wanted to come up and watch some TV with me, but I was really just checking in on his mood. I wanted to have another nice day for Elizabeth. He said he would be up soon and that he was talking to his family about Elizabeth's awards and the graduation. I watched some TV before heading up to bed. Iden finally came up late into the night.

I woke up early to have a quiet cup of coffee to see that Iden was already up. He was sitting on the deck drinking coffee and smoking a cigarette, so I poured a cup and went outside to join him. We sat and talked for a while and he talked about Lizzy and how he wished she was staying close by and attending NYU, and that he hoped she decided not to go because of the expensive tuition. I explained that I had had a long talk with her, and she had made the decision on her own.

Iden loved taking photos and videos when he was feeling well, so on the day of the party he was snapping a lot of photos and taking videos. The guests arrived and soon we were all were having a good time. I noticed that Iden was talking a lot and I kept an eye on him to see if he was drinking any alcohol. I didn't want to spend the day policing him, but I also didn't want a scene. Lizzy's friends were all wonderful girls, and I was so happy knowing that she would have their support while away at college. We ended the party with a big sheet cake, and cookies, and the guests slowly left one by one.

It was back to work the following day, but I didn't have to worry about lesson plans since it was almost the end of June, and my school was preparing for graduation ceremonies. After the party cleanup, Lizzy opened up her cards and gifts. She was very excited about all the money she received and knew it would come in handy to buy a new computer for college.

We decided this would be a good time to give Lizzy our gift to her, which was a brand-new Apple computer. When she opened it, I realized it wasn't the one we had agreed upon buying, but a more expensive model. Iden explained that she would need a good computer, so he bought her the best one.

The summer or 2007 was very quiet for me. Lizzy was working at the hospital and Claudia was a camp counselor at a community house. Iden was working and had been stabilized, having no major depressions, or bouts of mania. He'd also had no drinking binges, so life was good. I was able to have most of my mornings and afternoons alone to do some gardening, cleaning, shopping, and having lunch or a drink with my neighbor for some girl talk.

Claudia was always easier and more relaxed during the summer months without the pressure of schoolwork. Lizzy and I were making plans for the start of her college days. And Iden was busy working and had been routinely arriving home for dinner on time every night. On the weekends we took some trips upstate, and sometimes stayed home and went to the beach. For the first time in a long time I felt I could exhale and not be preoccupied with worries about Iden.

At the beginning of August, we went to our house upstate with my parents to spend a few days just relaxing at the lake, barbequing, and taking walks. Iden had had an argument with his friend John and wasn't talking to him, so we no longer had late-night visits to his home, for which I was very grateful. We had a wonderful few days together that week at the house, but this would be the last time we would all be together at our house in Hunter.

During the next few weeks, Lizzy and I went shopping for sheets and bedding items and some new college clothes. It was as exciting for me as much as it was for her. It's been said that we relive our youth through our children, and it was inspiring to witness my daughter's hopes and dreams. Since Iden and Lizzy worked in the same hospital, they travelled to and from work together. It was a relief knowing that Iden and Lizzy would come home together after work.

One afternoon after working in the garden, I went inside to have something cold to drink and to cool off in the air conditioning due to the extreme heat of the day. I sat on our couch with Mimi on my lap watching TV and must have fallen asleep when I suddenly heard the front door open and saw Lizzy and Iden coming through the door. When I looked at the clock, it was only 3 o'clock. I asked what had happened and Iden looked at me and said that he was laid off from work. When I asked why he sat down and said that work was downsizing, which is why he was let go. He'd called Lizzy and told her what had happened, and she asked to leave work due to a family emergency. When I asked how he felt about it all, Iden said that he was somewhat relieved because ever since returning to work after his leave, they had treated him differently and he never quite felt things were the same.

I worried about our finances, but Iden reassured me that he would be receiving severance pay, and that he would be able to get another job soon. For the next few weeks we tried to just focus on Lizzy getting ready for college. Iden seemed relieved to be at home.

In late August we took Lizzy up to Geneseo College and moved her into the dorm with two of her friends. The girls and I unpacked Lizzy's clothes, made her bed, decorated her room with both new things and items she brought from home. We then headed to Walmart to get some necessary food items to start her college days. We stayed for a few days before it came time to say goodbye. I will never forget that day in front of her dorm. I gave her a big hug, knowing how much I was going to miss her presence at home. She told me she loved me and that she would always keep in touch. Claudia gave her sister a big kiss and Iden also hugged Lizzy and I could see the tears in both their eyes.

"Enjoy your college days, Lizzy: we will all be just fine," I told her.

It was a five-hour trip home and as soon as we were in the car, we already felt the absence of Lizzy in our lives. When we arrived home, I went upstairs to Lizzy's room and lay on her bed. As I lay there staring at her graduation picture, I realized that she might never return home. I was already missing her but was happy knowing that she was starting to carve out a new life for herself.

That night we ordered pizza and sat on the deck quietly eating, each one of us missing our girl. We called her and I tried to sound cheerful. She was also having pizza with her friends and going to a dorm social to meet all her new dormmates. It was good to know that though we were no longer sleeping under one roof, we were still connected in love.

Joel and Lizzy ©

CHAPTER SEVENTEEN

SECRETS

'The irony of loneliness is we all feel it at the same time.'
—RUPI KAUR

With Lizzy gone it was time for me to get used to a new reality. Passing by her bedroom door each morning and not seeing her there reminded me how much I missed her and loved her. Lizzy had also provided company for Claudia, and I could tell that she was missing her sister as well. Iden was still not working and had not made any attempts to look for work but continued to say he would soon. His moods were up and down, but for the most part he seemed very disconnected and far away.

Claudia, now 17, was going to school dances and dating boys, but nothing serious, although her social interests were always greater than her academic interests. Whenever I disapproved of a particular event she wanted to attend, Iden would give in to her and allow her to go. She never wanted to be at home and always wanted to be out somewhere or at a friend's house.

With Lizzy away at college, Claudia out more, and Iden being disengaged I was pretty much on my own. When I put my key into the front door and opened it my daughters and Mimi no longer greeted me. Since Iden began staying home, Mimi was usually in the basement lying on the couch with him, or when he was feeling a bit up, he would be in the garage talking on the phone, with Mimi running around in the backyard. The intense feeling of loneliness I felt as I entered my home without anyone to greet me was like reaching out for a hug without having anyone's arms to put around me.

The months passed by, and a new norm had settled in. Lizzy and I spoke every day, but my missing her was still strong. When we talked, she mostly asked how her dad and Claudia were doing. She also called her dad daily because she could quickly tell what kind of mood he was in just with a two-minute conversation.

We made a few trips to Geneseo in the early months for a weekend visit. Lizzy wasn't homesick because she was still with her good friends, and she was enjoying her studies. With Lizzy home for the holidays and on school breaks the school year seemed to pass quickly, and before we knew it, it was time to pick her up at the end of the school year.

Iden was doing some consulting work at home for some small companies and bringing in a fraction of his usual pay, so I continued to worry about our finances. I often asked him if we were doing okay, and he reassured me we were.

Iden's mood was generally low at this time, but with the summer ahead his mood always seemed to lift. Lizzy was home and again working at the hospital, although she felt a little awkward working there since her dad was no longer an employee. Claudia was now a full-time counselor and preparing to take the SATs since she would be starting her senior year in the fall.

We made a few trips upstate, but with the girls working and wanting to stay home on the weekends to be with their friends we found it difficult to get away. I suggested to Iden that maybe we should consider selling the house in Hunter because we were not making use of it, and although it was all paid for, we still had taxes, landscaping fees, and other expenses. He argued with me and said that we didn't need to downsize and soon he would find full-time employment.

It had already been a year since Iden had been employed full time. When I suggested some jobs I heard about or knew someone that could perhaps help him find one, he always came up with an excuse. Iden was not lazy and had always worked hard, but he was using his disorder as an excuse to not push himself, and he was starting to doubt his ability to work again full time. I didn't want to feel angry, but I was feeling resentful at his lack of responsibility to his family for not seeking full-time employment.

I also thought Iden's staying at home wasn't helping his mental and emotional well-being. It was 2008 and the U.S. was in a recession, so finding employment was difficult and many people who had lost their jobs were selling their homes and declaring bankruptcy. I was hoping that we would not find ourselves in that position.

Although I hadn't mentioned any money concerns to our daughters, they seemed to know what was going on. One day after work Lizzy spoke to me about perhaps taking out a student loan since Iden wasn't working. She also said that she applied for a work-study program at college to help with everyday expenses. She was such a mature and understanding person and was always looking out for her family. I told her we had college savings for her and that she shouldn't worry, but she did worry and so did I.

We were invited to a barbeque on July 4th and we all decided to go since we weren't heading upstate because the weather was unseasonably chilly. I had hesitations about heading over to Marcos' for the barbeque because he was Iden's drinking buddy and I could tell that over the last few days Iden's mood had shifted upward a little and I was concerned.

Lizzy and I prepared a potato and macaroni salad, and we also made a vanilla cake decorated with blueberries and strawberries. Marcos and I had a good relationship now since the event with Iden in Brooklyn. I realized that he wasn't the cause of Iden's drinking, and that it was wrong for me to blame him. Marcos and his wife were generous hosts and had invited other family along as well. It was nice socializing with all of my family together.

I was busy talking to Marcos' wife, Ella, when I noticed Iden heading to a cooler to reach in and grab a beer.

My eyes met his and they said. *Relax, it's a barbeque.*

Lizzy also saw what her dad had in his hands. She walked over to him and said something to him before coming over to me. She told me I needed to do something, but there was nothing I could do. She, like me, was very fearful that he was going to get drunk and perhaps cause a scene. Once again, we allowed Iden to ruin our day.

The food was cooking and although I was hungry, I had soon lost my appetite. Iden was talking to a woman, and I could see him laughing and telling some silly jokes he usually says when drinking. I asked Marcos if he could say something to Iden and he said he already did because he didn't want him to ruin the party. I decided to take some deep breaths and told Lizzy to try and relax. Claudia, on the other hand, didn't seem to even notice what was going on because she was having a conversation with a boy.

I grabbed a plate of food and sat down near Iden and asked him if he wanted me to fix a plate for him. I thought if he ate then perhaps he wouldn't drink as much. He said he wasn't hungry yet and that I shouldn't monitor his every move. So I moved away because he was acting nasty. He then got up and grabbed another beer.

Lizzy was upset and she got a plate of food and took it to him. She also sat next to him thinking she could control his behavior. As I sat watching her, I felt guilty that she had taken on my worries. Iden ate the platter that Lizzy brought to him and then Marcos asked him to play some music along with some other guests who brought their instruments. There was a saxophone player, a guitarist, and a box drummer and they all started to jam together.

As the music started playing Iden was enjoying himself and was no longer drinking. People got up and started to dance and I let go of my fears and grabbed my daughters to dance along with me. After the music stopped, desserts were served with coffee and tea, and I was relieved thinking that there would be no further alcohol being served.

Marcos had a big-screen TV on which he planned to show the New York City fireworks. We all got seated and ready to watch the show. He also handed out sparklers for us all to light while we watched the fireworks. Iden and the girls and I all sat together to watch the show. Before the fireworks started, I turned to talk to Iden, but he was fast asleep. Lizzy suggested I leave him be and wake him when we were ready to go home

We watched the fireworks and then helped with some cleanup. We woke Iden, and he asked what happened, so I told him he had fallen asleep, and he asked why I didn't wake him. I really didn't have an answer that he wanted to hear, but I knew I didn't wake him because I wanted to watch the fireworks and go home without any problems. I told Iden we were leaving, but he wanted to stay and talk to Marcos a little longer since he had fallen asleep. It was late and Iden assured me he would be home soon. Lizzy offered to stay with him, but I said it was not necessary as she had work the next day.

Before I left, I asked Marcos not to offer any alcohol to Iden and he said he wouldn't. The girls and I walked a block back to our home under a beautiful, bright July night sky. It was almost as if the fireworks were still exploding in the sky. I wished Iden was walking home with us, but I tried to not worry and believed he would be home soon.

The girls and I talked for a bit and then went to bed. By midnight Iden was still not home. Lizzy asked if I could call Marcos to see what was going on and why her dad wasn't home yet. I tried calling Marcos, but he didn't answer. Lizzy was very concerned and suggested we walk over to Marcos' house. So we did.

When we arrived, I rang the bell and Marcos opened the door. He told us they were still out back and to please not get upset because Iden was very drunk. I went through the house to the backyard and saw Iden talking to a few guys, each with a can of beer in their hands. When Iden saw Lizzy and me he said the police were here along with a few other obscenities. I asked Marcos what was going on, and he apologized saying Iden had insisted on staying and drinking with the other guys. I asked for help to get Iden home. Marcos told Iden that it was time to get going and helped me walk him home, but the whole time Iden complained about how I always ruined his fun, and that I didn't allow him to have a good time with his friends. Once home, we got Iden downstairs, and he immediately fell asleep. I really didn't want him lying next to me given the state that he was in.

Although he was home safely, I was worried about the next day and what his mood was going to be after a night of drinking. I lay awake until Lizzy came in and asked if she could lie next to me. We both finally feel asleep, and we didn't wake up until we heard water being sprayed against the bedroom windows. I looked out the window to see Iden watering the garden and cleaning the front windows. The clock showed it was 8 o'clock. I couldn't believe he was up so early after such a late night of drinking.

I ran downstairs and opened the front door to see Iden talking to a neighbor, and he waved to me. He said he was cleaning the windows with the hose. I didn't know what to say except thank you. It was apparent that his mood had shifted, and he was no longer depressed. I tried to cajole him back into the house with some coffee and breakfast, but he said he already had coffee and wanted to clean all the windows of the house. The windows did need a power wash, but it was a little too much and a little too early.

The girls were up by then and getting ready for work. Lizzy came down and asked what Dad was doing. When I informed her about the power washing, she asked if Iden was showing signs of mania. I told her he did seem a bit elevated and that I thought I should inform his doctor about the change in his behavior. His doctor so often asked me to notify him when I noticed a change, but I often held off doing so because the doctor would inform Iden of my call. Iden generally got upset with me about talking to his doctor about his behavior. I was literally between a rock and a hard place not knowing what was the best thing to do for Iden and for my family.

After an hour of power washing Iden came in, made a sandwich, and fell asleep on the couch for a few hours. Lizzy called me a few times to inquire about her dad. I informed her that he was sleeping and not to worry. I held back telling her that I had reached out to Iden's doctor because that would involve a disagreement, but I felt the doctor should know about his drinking and his change in mood. Iden slept the afternoon away and when he got up, he made himself some coffee and checked his phone. He had a few missed calls from his doctor, so he listened to the messages before he came looking for me and found me outside in the front yard doing some weeding. He yelled at me and wanted to know why I had called his doctor to notify him about his one night of drinking.

I left all my garden tools and ran inside because there were people walking by and neighbors listening. I felt so embarrassed. I explained that part of the family therapy was to keep in touch with his doctor and to notify him as to any change in behavior or moods. I then said his drinking and his behavior was something very concerning and needed to be reported. I knew he would get angry, but it was necessary. He spoke for a whole hour or so about how horrible I was and that I should mind my own business. I needed to leave the house, so I took Mimi on a long walk and sat in the park for a while. When I returned home, he was gone. I called Marcos and asked if Iden were there. He was and Marcos said that he was trying to get him to calm down, and that Iden wanted to drink. He told me he would try his best to get Iden home soon.

Iden didn't come home that night because he got so drunk that Marcos thought it best to keep him at his home in order not to cause a problem for the girls and me. The girls were very concerned, but I explained that he was at least safe and that his doctor needed to be informed to help him.

The rest of the summer of 2008 was a series of drinking events and shorter and shorter periods of depression and mania. One weekend I asked Mom to come and stay at my house while I escaped with my neighbor Suzanne and her friend for a weekend away at my home in Hunter. The summer was coming to an end, and soon Lizzy would be returning to college and me to work. I hadn't had a break from life at home and was feeling an urgent need to get away.

I prepared meals and made sure the girls plans were all secure, and that Iden was somewhat stable before I left on a two-day holiday. It was approaching late August and the days were still very warm. We were fortunate to have two beautiful sunny, hot days in Hunter to go swimming in the lake and to do some hiking and barbequing.

My friends and I stayed up late talking and enjoying our time together, and for the first time in a long time I wasn't allowing myself to worry about Iden. I needed to enjoy a few days away. I knew Lizzy was home and she was keeping in touch with me. Our last day in Hunter as I walked out the door, I looked at our home, and realized that perhaps I might never be back.

After a lovely weekend I returned home to find out that Claudia was out very late with a boy and apparently was drinking. Iden had visited Marcos to have some man time together, which also led to drinking. Lizzy didn't want to worry me or Mom so she took matters into her own hands by getting Claudia and Iden home safely.

I felt terrible that she was alone with this and that she didn't reach out for my help. She said that there was nothing that I could have done being so far away. I disagreed with her because I could have at least been present emotionally and provided support by talking to her while she was dealing with the drama.

I didn't talk to either Claudia or Iden about all that had happened over the weekend because my mother was still at my home, and I didn't want to her to hear what was happening under her nose while I was away. She would have also been upset with Claudia and Iden. After Mom returned home, I talked to Claudia, and as usual she didn't think what she did was such a big deal because all of her friends stayed out late and had a few drinks. Yes, she was 17, and should be out with friends, however she was irresponsible when she said she would be home at a certain time and didn't show up. She also didn't answer her phone causing Lizzy to worry that something might have happened to her. I reminded her about drinking and driving and about staying safe when with the opposite sex.

Unlike Lizzy, Claudia enjoyed the party scene, and I was afraid that she might have inherited some of her dad's genes for alcoholism. She was receiving therapy for her anxiety and at times she did seem as if she was better at controlling it, but she still had bouts of anger and some mood swings as well. We didn't argue and she did apologize. It was very difficult to remain angry with her because she was still like a child in an adult body not understanding a fraction of life but thinking that she did.

I went to talk to Iden and found him talking on the phone and smoking out on the deck in the backyard. I asked if he could talk to me, and he said he would be off the phone in a few minutes. An hour later he was off the phone and forgot that I wanted to talk to him. I told him I'd had a nice weekend, but I was disappointed to learn about what had happened while I was away.

"What happened"? he asked.

I told him that Lizzy informed me about Claudia's and his drinking. He said that Lizzy was becoming like me and policing them both and that it was okay for me to be away and drinking with my girlfriends, but he couldn't have a few drinks with his friends. I didn't want to have to repeat the same words again and again about his drinking problem and being irresponsible in not coming home at a decent hour, especially while I was away. I told him I was very disappointed with him and left him sitting in the basement without further communication.

The next day the girls went to work, and I was feeling a bit out of sorts, so I decided to go for a run. Running helped me sort things out and shake my feelings and thoughts out that I didn't like to have flowing through my brain. I was out for about an hour and when I returned home, I went into the kitchen to get some water and found Iden sitting by the window looking very sad. I asked him what had happened. He said his sister had called to let him know his dad had passed away the night before. I hugged him and then he started crying. He went on to say how fucked up his life was. He then said it was important for him to go to Iran since his mother was also very sick and he needed to see his family. The first thing I thought was that yes, it is important, but there were many conditions that made it unsafe for him to go to Iran. There were, of course, the political problems between Iran and America and Iden's mental condition and finances. He said he wanted to leave as soon as possible but I suggested we needed to talk about it, but he said he was going no matter what I thought.

Iden left for Iran a week after hearing about his father's death, and the girls and I were not happy with his leaving. Lizzy was very upset because she was afraid that he might drink in Iran and say inappropriate things that could land him in jail. She was afraid we would never see him again. I tried to reassure them that he would be careful, and the few weeks would pass by quickly and that all would be okay. Although we did worry about his safety, life without Iden at home carried on quite peacefully. The flow of the house moved in rhythm differently than when he was present.

We spoke on the phone, and I could tell he was very excited by his fast talking. The weeks turned into a month until he finally returned home to us. He returned looking very tired and no longer sounding energized. He arrived late on a Sunday night saying that he needed to sleep and that he would talk to us in the morning. The girls left for work, and I decided to take the day off feeling the necessity of being home on his first day home.

I gave Iden whatever time he needed to sleep, and he finally awoke around 1 o'clock in the afternoon. I made him a cup of coffee and he said that we needed to talk. I thought he was going to tell me about his family and about his trip to Iran, but I was wrong. He said that he hadn't been honest with me and that we were in trouble financially. He hadn't paid the mortgage in months, and he was paying the mortgage with borrowed money from his family.

Iden had lied about receiving as much severance pay as he said he did and admitted he had huge credit card debt that I knew nothing about. I sat unable to move or say a word. I had a mixture of emotions that ranged from wanting to hate Iden to wanting to hold him and love him and tell him everything would be fine.

I couldn't understand why Iden would allow this to happen, or how he had accrued such a large credit card debt. I had to walk away before I started to say things that were going to lead to an argument or cause endless blame. I went outside and sat on the deck to smoke a cigarette and started to cry. I finally understood the expression of having a rug being pulled out from underneath you. I was clueless and needed to figure out a plan, but all I could do at this moment was keep myself breathing.

Lizzy and Claudia ©

CHAPTER EIGHTEEN

HOLDING ON

'Life is like riding a bicycle. To keep your balance, you must keep moving.'

—ALBERT EINSTEIN

After hearing the news about our financial situation I wondered what I was going to tell my family and friends. I never thought I would be that person who felt embarrassed about things happening in my life, but at that moment I was. I especially thought about Dad's reaction because he was so good with his finances and always asked me if we were doing well, especially since Iden was unemployed.

The truth of the matter was that I was blindsided by the news. I needed time to sit with my thoughts on how to move forward with a plan that involved holding on to my dignity and gathering up enough courage to move forward. I was hoping that if I were brave enough to say goodbye to what was once, life would reward me with a beautiful new hello. There were a lot of changes happening and I needed a plan to feel at least somewhat in control of what seemed like a life spinning out of control.

Lizzy was graduating college and making plans to move to Boston to start a teaching career with Teach for America after deciding that going to medical school wasn't something she truly wanted. She had been dating a young man named Joel since her sophomore year at college, and I was very happy to hear that he would also be joining her in Boston to study law. He was a very sweet and caring young man, and he helped Lizzy deal with her anxiety about all of us while away from home.

As always, I gave Lizzy my full support, although Iden was disappointed in her decision because he came from a family of doctors and he knew Lizzy had the intellect and drive to succeed in medical school. Claudia was now in community college taking classes to perhaps study nursing, however, her grades weren't meeting the standards, so she needed to repeat classes. She was heavily into the dating scene and making friends her priority without much care to her future.

My parents were experiencing some health issues that were concerning me. Mom had episodes of high blood pressure causing dizzy spells, and Dad was having some issues with his heart. I relied on their strength and advice, and the thought of them not being in my life provoked further anxiety on top of my already existing load of worries and family life.

During the next few weeks before taking any action, I sat down with a pen and paper to make a to-do list. I also asked Iden to sit down with me and to please be honest. I wanted to know the extent of our debt, the reasons why it happened, and why he had failed to inform me sooner. Iden was already in a remorseful place, so I didn't want to cause him extra guilt, but I needed to know what happened before moving forward. He explained that his severance pay wasn't very good and that he had taken cash advances to pay the mortgage and tuition payments. He also said that he had made some purchases for his family that he hadn't told me about while he was in Iran.

I asked Iden if he thought we should talk to someone to see if we could work something out with the bank, but he was very adamant about selling the house since we were so far behind in payments and debt. He said that he had already reached out to the sales agent whom we originally bought the house from to have a meeting.

The price of houses in Forest Hills had increased tremendously over the past years so he said that we should be able to pay off the mortgage and all our debt and have a good amount left over. I also knew that he had borrowed some money from my father and wasn't sure if he had finished paying the loan off. I told him I was very upset, and I did not expect to be moving from a house that we had renovated over the years and loved. Thinking of going back to living in an apartment was not something I was looking forward to, but if it meant relieving us of our debt and perhaps allowing Iden to be free of financial worries then I was ready to move on and do what was necessary to move forward in our lives.

We met with the real estate agent and made an appointment to get our house appraised and for photos to be taken. The agent hadn't been inside our home since we made all the renovations and after doing a walk-through, she was very happy with what she saw and said the house should surely sell quickly.

When I told my parents about our plans they were upset and asked if we wanted to move in with them to save some money. They didn't ask any questions, but they were surely confused and knew that it was difficult for me to say goodbye to a house that had brought my family and me much joy.

After we spoke to my parents, I reached out to a few of our neighbors to inform them about the selling of our house without giving too many details. Within a few weeks there was a big for sale sign pitched in our front lawn and soon we had many appointments to show our home. Although Iden was home during the day, many of the showings were held at night because the potential buyers were working, and therefore they usually showed up right before or after dinner. So for the next few weeks I came home from work, made sure the house was all tidied up, prepared dinner, and quickly ate before the appointments. I had made peace with all that was happening and was actually looking forward to finding an apartment with fewer rooms to clean and thinking perhaps I could be more connected to Iden if he didn't have a basement to hide out in. Silly thought, but it did enter my mind.

The girls did not take the news of selling our house badly at all. Lizzy was getting ready to move to Boston and Claudia was hardly ever home what with working and taking classes, and whatever free time she had was spent with her new and latest boyfriend.

Our house was on the market for only about a month when it went into contract. I was happy that a sweet young couple with one young child and another one on the way would soon be living in our home. As I looked at them, I saw Iden and me and the girls as we once were and couldn't believe how quickly the years had passed. I tried not to have any regrets and to look forward to our new adventure.

We went into contract in September and the closing was set for some time in early October. I was happy that Lizzy's move to Boston was scheduled for late August, so we could settle her in and spend some time with her without us having to move as well. We had looked at several apartments and some we loved, but they didn't accept pets, and some were just very pricey.

We hadn't rented in years and couldn't believe the prices of apartments. We finally settled on a lovely two-bedroom apartment with two bathrooms and a large eat-in kitchen that opened into the living room. There was also a large foyer that could be used as a small office. The best feature was that it had a small balcony where I could go and sit with my coffee and have a smoke after a long day at work. I was only smoking a few cigarettes a day, but lately I was feeling the need to smoke more.

We moved Lizzy to Boston, renting a small truck to load items from Lizzy's room, plus some odd pieces of furniture from the basement and with kitchen items that I had no longer used. The truck only had room for two people so Iden and Lizzy rode in the truck and Claudia and I drove our van to Boston.

Lizzy moved into an area called Brighton that was a very pretty, hilly, tree-filled neighborhood resembling Forest Hills. Joel was already in school, so he met us with a few friends to help us with the moving of the furniture and other belongings. While the men were moving the furniture in, Claudia and I helped put things away in her kitchen and set up the bathroom while Lizzy put her clothes away in closets and drawers. Iden was given the responsibility of setting up her computer and TV. Lizzy didn't want him moving furniture because he was not feeling that great and was feeling tired after the long drive.

After the move was complete Lizzy, Joel, and I went to a Whole Foods that was just down the block from her apartment to fill Lizzy's refrigerator with basic food items and to grab some items for dinner for all of us. Claudia wanted to stay behind and talk to her boyfriend, and Iden was taking a nap.

We had a good few days together before dropping off the truck at the U-Haul station and making the trip back to New York City together. Before leaving we went out to a nearby diner for breakfast and took a walk around the neighborhood to familiarize Lizzy with the stores and to learn the nearest stops on the "T," Boston's train system. We stopped by a florist, and I bought Lizzy a bouquet of flowers and told her to buy fresh flowers every week for herself.

We all hugged Lizzy goodbye but I lingered in our hug and whispered in her ear that she needed to take care of herself and to know that I could manage without her, although I would miss her deeply. I looked into her beautiful blue eyes and said, "I am so proud of you, and I love you!" I could see the tears in her eyes. I promised that I would drive up in a minute's notice if she needed me and that we would make weekend visits regularly.

Iden was holding back his tears as well. As we drove off, we kept waving until she was no longer in sight. My phone beeped with a text from Lizzy saying she loved me and to please let her know if I needed her. My heart was heavy and full of love for our amazing daughter.

We drove much of the way in silence making a stop at a Perkins diner before reaching New York City. As I entered our house it already felt like we had said our goodbyes. I didn't want to think of our move or the packing that we needed to do, but it was on my mind. I just wanted to shower and sip some wine and sit on my back deck to smell the last of the honeysuckle.

Our new adventure began with packing and finding a new home for things we could not bring along to our new home. We had a baby grand piano that needed to be sold along with furniture, a two-car garage of tools, bicycles, and deck furniture. We had about three weeks to pack and get our house broom clean. I wanted to have a tag sale, but Iden just wanted to donate the items to charities and give the piano to an old friend. I understood his not wanting to deal with people and negotiating prices of items that we had to let go, but I thought it would be a great opportunity to make some extra money that was now a priority for me.

We had an attic filled with toys, books, Halloween costumes, and holiday decorations that we could not take with us due to lack of space, which was a good thing because all of those things were from a life lived long ago. As I bagged each item memories went along into the bag. Although it was difficult, it was very cathartic and allowed me to say goodbye to my past and make room for new memories. Iden on the other hand had not contributed any help in packing and was feeling very down. I understood how he was feeling, but there was a lot of work to do, and I really needed his help

Our new apartment would be available from October 1st and our closing date was October 15th, so on the weekends, I started taking my clothing to the apartment to hang up in the closets along with kitchen and bathroom items. The apartment had a good feel to it and as I sat there, I envisioned my new life there. I had made peace with my past and was welcoming my new future with an open and positive mind that things would be just fine.

Moving day arrived and we had all our boxes lined up in our living room all marked as to where they would be placed and the contents of each one. Seeing our possessions all packed up in approximately a hundred boxes seemed to make so much less of the life we had.

The last piece of furniture was placed in the moving truck and as it pulled away Iden and I stood by the front door and before closing it we said our goodbyes with tearful eyes. We walked down our front steps hand in hand ready to greet our next challenge in life. As I turned around to take one last look at our house, I noticed the chime hanging by our door and ran back to take it because my mother gave it to us when we had first moved into the house.

Claudia was waiting at the new apartment to let the movers in if they arrived before we did. Since we packed up everything and the refrigerator was empty at our house, we did not have any breakfast, so we picked up some bagels, muffins, and coffee for all of us. The movers arrived at the same time we did and were equally happy to partake in having some breakfast with us. Once the movers had the furniture in place and the boxes properly laid out in each room, I set to work opening each one. Claudia was in her room taking care of her belongings and Iden was getting the computers and other technical things up and running. I had already set up the kitchen and bathrooms, and most of my clothes were already neatly arranged in the closet from previous trips to the apartment.

All the rooms were large and had many windows allowing in much light and giving the apartment a nice airy and peaceful feeling. Most of our boxes were finished by dinnertime and our new place was starting to feel like home soon enough. We hadn't eaten since breakfast and I was too tired to cook so we ordered in some Chinese food and although it was October, the weather was still warm enough to sit outside on our balcony to eat our dinner. The balcony was large enough for our patio set we had brought from the house, so we were all able to sit comfortably and share a meal together.

After dinner I made some tea and took it out to the patio. Claudia and Iden had both gone back into the apartment, but I sat sipping my tea while taking in the new view. Mimi was staying at my neighbors for a few days until we got settled in, and I was thinking how she would like to sit on the balcony. After taking my short break I went back to opening a few more boxes in my bedroom before retiring for the day.

Claudia came and sat on my bed and said she liked the new apartment because her room was bigger than the one at our house and the apartment was closer to the trains and stores. Lizzy hadn't seen the apartment, so I called her and we FaceTimed each other and I showed her the layout of the apartment. She was more interested in her dad's mood and wanted to know how he had handled the move. I told her that everything went well, and we were all settling in just fine.

Claudia's room was large enough to have two beds so Lizzy would have a place to sleep when she came to visit. We talked about her work, Joel, and life in Boston. She seemed very happy although she missed and worried about us very much. After talking with her for a time, I sat on the couch for a while before I found my eyes too heavy to keep open so headed for bed for my first night's sleep in our new apartment.

I took the Monday off from work to do more unpacking, pick up Mimi, and do some grocery shopping. It was nice having the stores so nearby without having to jump in the car or walk so far. Iden was still unemployed and even though we had made some money from the sale of the house there wasn't much left over after we paid off the mortgage, a home equity loan, his debt, and other incidentals. I knew he wanted to work, but he never seemed well enough with his lack of energy when depressed, or his lack of focus when his mood was elevated.

All of the unpacking was completed, and I had even managed to hang up some curtains. As I was lost in thought sitting in the kitchen staring out the window, Iden entered and poured a cup of coffee for himself and sat down next to me. He started to talk saying that he'd decided to drive for a friend who owns a limousine service, saying he could make some decent money and make his own hours. He said he really wasn't up for interviewing and returning to a high-pressured computer job.

Although I was happy to hear that Iden was getting motivated to work, I was a little concerned about his ability to drive long hours and the thought of having a car in his hands troubled me. I didn't really know how to answer him because I was happy he wanted to work, but I also didn't think it wise to let him know my fears. We sat in the kitchen and talked further before he went outside to have a smoke.

Iden started driving a limousine a few weeks after we moved into the new apartment. He was working a few days a week, and his mood slowly started to change. He had more energy, and he was driving more days and longer hours. I spoke to him and suggested that he stick to a routine of a set amount of hours of working each day, but he said he was feeling better and wanted to work. His hours were random, and I never knew when he would be home.

Iden felt good about earning money again and was very proud when he showed me the amount of tips he had made and happily put it all in my hands. He took a lot of pride in always wanting to provide for us, and I was glad to have the extra income, but I was concerned about his need to keep a daily schedule of eating, sleeping, and taking his medicine to help avoid mood swings. Once again, we were playing phone cop trying to keep in touch with him to lure him back home earlier than he wanted while out driving.

One night Iden came home, and I went to kiss him hello, but he ran right to the bathroom saying he needed to go badly. When he came out, I felt he was a little off by the way he was speaking and slurring his words. I didn't want my thoughts to go there but they did; it seemed as if he had been drinking. He went to the kitchen and heated up a plate of food I left for him and then sat in the living room eating while watching TV. I asked him how his day was, but he said he was tired and just wanted to eat and not talk. After eating, he lay down on the couch and promptly fell asleep.

While Iden was asleep I took his work bag into the bedroom and searched inside. I found an empty pint of vodka and a few parking tickets as well. I knew I had to tell him about my discovery as soon as possible because it was dangerous to be driving and drinking. I was so disappointed and really didn't have space for this behavior. This discovery could not be kept a secret.

The next few months were a series of events of Iden going through hypomania and having drinking binges. He would say he was driving, but just go somewhere and start drinking and fall asleep to return home when he could drive. I soon found out that he wasn't making the rent money for the limousine and was using our money to pay for the rent. I demanded that he stop the job and I called his doctor and told him what was happening. The doctor also told me that he wasn't complying with visits nor taking his medication as prescribed.

Once again, the doctor must have called Iden and told him about my call, which I asked him not to. Iden came home very agitated and started yelling and throwing things. Claudia was home and came running out of her room, scared by her dad's behavior. I sent her to her room and asked him to stop yelling, but he continued, and I was getting very nervous. He went out onto the balcony to smoke, and I went into the bedroom thinking what I could do because I was actually very scared, he might hurt one of us or maybe even himself.

Iden came into the bedroom, and I had my phone in my hand because I was going to call my friend Debbie and ask her for advice.

He said, "You better not be calling the fucking doctor."

He then came charging at me and grabbed my phone and threw it on the floor, pushing the computer down as well.

Claudia came in and said, "Dad! What are you doing?"

He continued to curse at us and then he left the apartment slamming the door. Claudia went to the door and was screaming at him to come back. A few of my neighbors opened their doors, and I felt embarrassed. They asked if everything was okay, but I just said I was sorry and immediately closed the door.

Before I could tell Claudia not to call Lizzy she did, which created even more chaos with Lizzy asking what happened and why did I call his doctor. Once again, she thought I caused the problem. I was told by the doctors to inform them of any change in Iden's behavior, especially when it might endanger the lives of others and himself. Driving while drinking was definitely a time for a call to his doctor. Lizzy sounded frantic and put Joel on the phone.

I explained what had happened and he said he would try and call Iden to see if he could calm him down and get him home. I wasn't so sure being home with him was a good idea, but what else could we do.

A few hours later Iden returned home. He had apparently gone somewhere to drink because he was very drunk. I tried to get him to bed, but he pushed me away. I know he wasn't trying to hurt me, but he just didn't want anyone to tell him what to do or to be near him. I thought if I could just get him to sit down that he would quickly fall asleep, but he was even more agitated than before he left and started talking about random things. He was talking nastily about work, Iran, Claudia's boyfriend, my brothers, my father, some friends, and about many other things and people. Lizzy called and I informed her that he was home but intoxicated. She said to make sure I got his car keys and try not to let him leave the house. I was certainly trying my best.

Iden went to use the bathroom and stayed in there for a while, so I thought perhaps he had passed out, so I knocked on the door. He opened it fiercely and walked over to his closet and started throwing his clothes on the floor saying he was looking for something. Claudia asked him if she could help him look for whatever he was looking for, but he told her to go away. Mimi walked up to him and jumped up on his leg, but he pushed her away. He loved Mimi and when I saw him do that, I could tell he was in a very dangerous place for us as well as for himself.

Lizzy was on the phone with Claudia, and she told her that she was on her way home with Joel from Boston. They had left about an hour ago and should be home in a few hours. I was upset with that news because they were both working, and Lizzy was attending graduate school and Joel was in law school. This situation with Iden was interrupting their lives and there really wasn't anything they could do that I wasn't trying to do. Claudia conveyed that message while on the phone with them.

Claudia stayed talking to Lizzy to keep herself calm because she was getting very scared. I should have told her to leave, but I needed her. Iden went into Claudia's bedroom and started looking in her closet as well. We still had no idea what he was looking for and then I said, "Let me fix you something to eat. You must be hungry."

He didn't answer and then he went over to Claudia's desk and started to throw everything on the desk on the floor and threw the computer at me, and that's when I knew we had to leave the apartment.

I didn't know my neighbors that well since we had just moved in, but I did know a young couple that lived a few apartments down the hall from us because we walked our dogs together. I took hold of Claudia, left our apartment, and rang their bell. Thankfully, they were home and let us in. I let them know what was going on. Again I called his doctor and he said I should call the police and notify them that he is bipolar and that he had been drinking. The doctor said they would take him to a nearby hospital to be evaluated and to also give the doctor's his number and Iden's medical condition. It took everything I had to place that call, but I kept hearing the doctor's words over and over in my head that making the call is actually saving him from something worse happening.

The police rang my neighbor's bell first before we went into my apartment hoping to still find Iden there. He was still at home and our apartment looked like thieves had searched for valuables. Clothes, papers, and photos were scattered about the floor, chairs overturned, and music was loudly playing. I had already given the police the necessary information and when Iden saw the police he started cursing me. Thankfully, I'd told Claudia to stay in our neighbor's apartment.

The police officers very calmly told Iden to please go with them so he could get some help. He told them he was fine and to go away. They persisted saying he needed to go right now, but he refused so they grabbed him and put him in handcuffs, and he struggled, trying to break free the whole time. He was a thin man, but his strength at that moment was herculean.

They took Iden by ambulance and told me it was best to meet them at the hospital. I left Claudia with our neighbors and couldn't even imagine calling Lizzy with the news of what had happened. I arrived at Jamaica Hospital and waited outside in the waiting room. Lizzy finally reached me, and I told her what had happened. She was very upset that I had called the police. I didn't even try to explain. I just told her what the doctor said, and I let her know that I was afraid of something seriously horrible happening.

Lizzy and Joel met me at the hospital, and we waited until a doctor came out to talk to us. A psychiatrist explained that he was experiencing mania and that he had been in touch with Iden's doctor. He further explained that Iden was given a sedative to calm him down and he was now resting comfortably. He said that if

Iden agreed to be admitted they would send him to Beth Israel Hospital to be treated by his doctor, however if he decided against treatment he could leave on his own accord. I asked how that was possible.

The doctor proceeded to explain to us that despite having the authority to keep a patient in the hospital, the professional staff cannot treat the person against his or her will, except by court order. Although Iden did not refuse hospitalization the first time he was admitted, I was not so sure he would agree to being admitted this time.

After hearing the doctor talk about the seriousness of his condition, Lizzy and Joel almost begged the doctor to try and get Iden to be admitted. He said he would talk to him, and a doctor would notify us in the morning as to what Iden decided to do. We left the hospital with heavy hearts and drove home in our separate cars. I called Claudia and told her I was on my way home with Lizzy and Joel. I also informed her that her dad was resting comfortably and that we would talk to the doctors in the morning about the next steps we needed to take.

When we entered the apartment Lizzy and Joel could not believe the state it was in. Poor Mimi was hiding somewhere and did not come out for a few minutes. Although we were all tired,we could not go to sleep. We put all the things away the best we could and then even though we were upset, we were hungry since we hadn't eaten any dinner and it was way after midnight. I started making some sandwiches because preparing a meal always brought me comfort, even at a late and difficult hour of the night. I was also shedding tears and didn't want the kids to see me crying.

I took the food into the living room and we all ate quietly. Lizzy was running through the 'what if's' and I told her to stop and that in a few hours we would hear from his doctor.

That night none of us slept well and when I got up around 6 o'clock in the morning Lizzy and Joel were already up drinking coffee. We all prayed and hoped that Iden would agree to being admitted in order to receive the proper care he needed. We waited for the call, but the hours just ticked by.

The days were getting cold now, but I wanted to get out and take a walk to calm my nerves. So I took Mimi out for a long walk and found a sunny bench in the park to sit and breathe and clear my mind, and to try to think positive thoughts before heading home. I closed my eyes for one minute and the phone rang. It was Iden's doctor. He informed me that Iden had a good night and was just up having breakfast and did not want to be admitted.

The doctor further said that he had made an appointment with Iden for the following day and when he saw him, he would talk to him about being admitted for evaluation and treatment. I asked what time I should pick Iden up and he said I should call the hospital and they would give me all the necessary information. I thanked him and immediately went home.

I told the girls what the doctor said, so Lizzy, Joel and I decided to go and pick up Iden as soon as possible. When we arrived at the hospital, we went to the emergency room area and spoke to the nurse telling her we were there to pick up Iden. She looked him up on the computer and said that he was discharged a few minutes ago. I got very upset and asked, "Where did he go?" The nurse looked at me with a pissed-off look and said she didn't know.

We left the hospital and knew he couldn't have gone far, so we started driving up and down all the streets on the way back to our apartment looking for him. All of a sudden, my cell phone rang, and it was Marcos saying that he was on his way to pick Iden up at Starbucks. Apparently Iden didn't want to return home right away and wanted to stay with Marcos for a while. He promised he wouldn't give Iden anything to drink.

I was relieved to know that Iden wasn't walking around the streets after a night in the hospital and in his unstable mental condition. I told Marcos that he had an early-morning doctor's appointment the next day and that it was urgent for Iden to see his doctor. He said he would try to get him home later, and that Iden was angry with me. He suggested that I should probably leave him alone for a while and that he would take care of him and would call me when he was bringing Iden home. I just asked him not to let Iden leave his house if that was possible.

I gave the information to Lizzy, and although she wanted to see how Iden was, she thought perhaps it was best for him to cool down a bit before returning home. Lizzy and Joel said that they had already decided to take a few days off from work and that they would stay until a plan was in place. We returned home and waited for any updates from Marcos.

Iden returned home very early the next day to shower and change his clothes before going into the city for his doctor's appointment. Lizzy and Joel said that they would drive him, but that I couldn't go. He was very angry with me over the whole event, and I understood, but I only did what I thought was necessary and was following his doctor's orders

After his appointment they came home and Iden went into the bedroom and closed the door. Lizzy said that he wasn't going to be hospitalized although the doctor did suggest it, but Iden wouldn't agree to it. The doctor changed his medicine and told him that he needed to attend more individual therapy sessions and group meetings. Iden was still not talking to me, but when he did talk to me it was usually with very harsh and unkind words.

Once again, I tried to adjust life according to Iden's moods. I tried to continue on the best I could with work, spending time with my family, parents and brothers, and friends. By now those who knew me well knew of Iden's condition and didn't ask where he was when he didn't show up when I visited. It was difficult not to have company over since I wasn't sure of his moods. He still wasn't stable and had more rapid cycles of depression and hypomania with very little periods of being midrange. I tried to balance our lives the best way I could to help him. Most days when he was feeling low, he just slept, watched TV or read. When his mood was more elevated, he talked on the phone for hours and stayed up late looking things up on the computer and listening to music.

The months passed by, and another summer was upon us. I was looking forward to vacation because I was struggling to keep all the pieces of my life together. My parents were aging and experiencing more health problems and I also needed to be there for them to take them to doctor appointments and run errands for them. Lizzy and Joel suggested we take a family vacation in New Hampshire with its beautiful hiking trails and lovely scenery. They did some investigating and found a place in Franconia, N.H., and we rented a house with a pool and a nearby riding stable.

I loved the ocean but being near the mountains filled me with an overwhelming sense of being grounded that I so deeply needed. We planned to leave NY in July and take a two-week vacation, first stopping in Boston to pick up Lizzy and Joel and spending a few days in Boston before heading up to NH. Iden had been going to his regular doctor appointments and attending individual and group therapy sessions as well.

By the time vacation time came around, Iden was in a depressed mood and although it wasn't joyful to be around him at least he was quiet, which made the long car ride to Boston and New Hampshire peaceful. Our house was located facing Mount Washington with trees all around the property. We bought Mimi along as well and she loved running around and rolling on the cool grass on the hot summer days. Our house was located near the Franconia Inn where we went for a delicious country breakfast most mornings.

After breakfast, the girls, Joel, and I took hikes, went horseback riding on beautiful trails in the woods, went swimming in lakes, and relaxed in the sunshine. Iden, not feeling well, just wanted to stay inside the house and lie in bed but told us to go and have a good time. Most of the time when we returned home after an outing he was sleeping. Although Iden wasn't present for most of the vacation, at least I was able to relax and not worry about any incidents because when depressed he was quiet.

We returned to the inn for dinner most of the evenings we were there, allowing me a vacation from cooking as well. We did barbeque a few nights and that was fun too because since selling our house we hadn't had a barbeque. Iden loved a good barbequed hot dog, and I remember thinking how awful it must feel to not even enjoy the foods he used to love to eat.

Although I did not know what it felt like to be depressed, I felt a little bit of his pain because there was very little I could do make his world joyful. We left NH feeling rested and physically rejuvenated except for Iden, who couldn't wait to get home and be done with the vacation. We took Lizzy and Joel home and stayed for one night in Boston before leaving the next day for NY.

I filled my summer days with meeting friends for a day out in the city, having my parents over for dinner, and going to the beach early in the morning to enjoy a long quiet walk by the shore. I tried many times to get Iden to come to the beach with me, but he said the sun gave him headaches and it wasn't recommended to sit in the sun with the medicine he was taking. I bought a huge beach umbrella and a big sunhat to cover his whole head, but he just didn't have the energy to leave the house.

A few hours spent in nature always put me in a better place and helped me feel calm. Nature was like a good friend helping me keep from feeling so lonely on days where I wished I had Iden sitting by my side.

Another school year was beginning in a week, and Lizzy and Joel came home for a few days. Claudia was now attending medical assistant school and had just broken up with her boyfriend, so she was cranky and not pleasant to be around.

Iden's depression seemed to have lifted a bit. He had a few good weeks where he had enough energy to be up and around doing things that needed to be done around the apartment, which he hadn't touched since we moved in almost a year ago. The last day before Lizzy and Joel left to return to Boston, we headed to the beach to have a picnic dinner. When the girls were young, we used to have dinner on the beach at least once a week and as we drove there on this last day of summer, they were remembering those days.

Iden and I both wondered where the years had gone and how happy we were then. We both reached out to hold each other's hand. We found a spot near the ocean and laid out a large blanket and some chairs and a small portable table. The kids took a walk and went to put their feet in the water while Iden and I just sat and listened to the waves and inhaled the ocean air. We ate and talked and watched the sunset before returning home. It was a lovely time. I was happy that Lizzy had Joel in her life, and I wished Claudia had a Joel as well.

We arrived home and couldn't remember when we all had had such a beautiful time together. Just as I put my key in our front door my phone rang and it was Mark informing me that Mom had suffered a stroke and fallen in the street. She was taken by ambulance to a hospital in Flushing. I told him I would be there as soon as I could. The girls were very close to Mom so the news frightened them. Lizzy and Joel wanted to come along to the hospital, but I told them I wasn't sure how many people they would allow in the hospital at one time. We decided for Lizzy to come with me and if she weren't allowed in, she would drive back home, and my brother could drive me home later.

When I saw Mom she looked confused and scared. As I sat next to her, a doctor walked in and said she had suffered a mini stroke, called a transient ischemic attack (TIA), which is caused by a lack of blood flow to the brain. They were going to admit her to do a series of tests. I told my brothers I would stay until she got settled into a room. Dad was not in NY because he was spending a few months a year in Florida, but Mom preferred to stay in New York.

After Mom was brought up to a room and settled in, Mark drove me home. I explained what had happened to Mom to Iden and Claudia, and Lizzy decided to stay a few extra days in New York to see her Nanny before heading home. Iden was also very close to Mom, and he took the news badly. The perfect day ended in not such a perfect way.

During that year Mom continued to have more TIAs and Dad was diagnosed with prostate cancer. He also developed heart valve disease. My brothers contributed some time with our parents, but I was the one running to the doctors with them. A few times when Dad was in Florida, I had to run down quickly because he had taken ill and needed to be hospitalized.

During this time, Claudia was having a series of bad relationships that sent her into some wild periods of drinking and hanging out with the wrong crowd. Iden was not able to deal with any of her drama. Although she was 22, she was still living at home, and my waiting and worrying about her return home after a night out was getting very annoying. I couldn't fall asleep until I knew she was home safely, and she wasn't good at being responsible by sending me a text or answering a call. When I tried to talk to her about her responsibility to her family, she got upset and said that she was old enough not to have her mother keeping tabs on her. I also asked Iden to talk to her and he said, as he usually did, to leave her alone.

I was juggling being a daughter to aging and sickly parents, being a mother to one daughter who was acting irresponsibly and a bit recklessly while also worrying about my other daughter who felt overly responsible to her family, and lastly being a wife to a husband whom I loved, but who I no longer could go to for any sort of support or to share my thoughts or worries. The more my life became undone, the more I was holding myself together tighter and tighter trying to make it all okay.

CHAPTER NINETEEN

THE REUNION

'Throughout this journey of life we meet many people along the way. Each one has a purpose in our life no one we meet is ever a coincidence.'

—MIMI NOVIC

After a few weeks in the hospital Mom returned home and required daily care. My brother Mark found a home attendant to help her get back on her feet after her stroke. I tried to visit her every Wednesday after work, and for a few hours each day and on the weekends. She so looked forward to my visits, and even though I was tired from work and dealing with family issues, I never wanted to disappoint her by not showing up.

Mom also needed physical therapy and to have visiting nurse services, so juggling all of her schedules was becoming a full-time job. Iden was not working at all at this point since he was unable to sustain any long periods where he wasn't either depressed or manic. There were some good days and many difficult days. I was learning to accept my life as it was, and to continue on despite the constant problems.

By April 2013, I was once again heading into the last few months of the school year and was very much looking forward to the summer months for a much-needed rest, and possibly a nice vacation. Although with my parents failing health I did not want to venture anywhere too far. I always wanted to take a trip to Italy, but that was an unreasonable thought, so I was resigned to finding a place at the shore or upstate.

Sometime in March, Iden had informed me that someone was trying to get in touch with me in reference to a reunion with people whom I had worked with as a young teenager at Blackhead Mt. Lodge in Cairo, New York. I had always loved the place, so when I was a teenager, I worked two summers there as a waitress. I also visited many times with Iden when we were first dating and then after we were married with my girls. The resort was very special to me because it held many happy memories for me as a young girl and as an adult.

The Catskills during the 60s and 70s were the *Dirty Dancing* years. It was also a time where I experienced my first kiss and my first feeling of being in love. Although I would have loved to get away for a few days to spend some time upstate reconnecting with a place that held such memories, I did not even entertain the thought because leaving my family and parents for a few days was not something I would even consider given the present state of health of Mom and Iden.

After dinner one night the phone rang, and I answered. As soon as I heard the woman's voice say, "Patty…" I knew it was Wally, the owner of Blackhead Mountain Lodge. She had a German accent along with a sweet voice that I was able to identify immediately. I hadn't seen her since we sold our house up in Hunter. She asked after my family and how my parents and I were doing. After a few minutes of catching up, she then asked me if I was planning to attend the reunion. I told her that I had a lot going on and didn't think that I could get away for two days. I didn't want to explain everything that was going on, but just said Mom was having some health issues and I felt I needed to stay at home. I thanked her and said that I often thought of Blackhead and of her and her family, and just before she hung up the phone she said, "By the way, Stephen will be attending the reunion."

When I heard Stephen's name, I became 16 years old again and remained silent for a moment.

"Oh!" I said. "How is he?"

She said that she had spoken to him a few times and that although he'd had some ups and downs, he was now doing well. He was married and had three children and also had a very good job as a project executive in construction. We said our goodbyes and she asked if I would please think about coming since she would love to see me. I hung up the phone and thought how nice it would be to see Wally, Eddie, and Stephen.

Stephen was the first boy I ever kissed during my first summer at Blackhead working as a waitress when I was 16. He was a tall, skinny boy with long dark hair who played the guitar, sang, and made me laugh. He was a bus boy and a dishwasher at the resort. Stephen was two years older than me and was from Williamsburg, Brooklyn. We had a sweet summer romance, taking walks, sitting on the back porch of our cabins and talking, and watching the stars at night. Our romance was just that, nothing more than kissing and holding hands, but he was my first crush and the first time I loved someone other than a family member.

After the summer ended, we had said our goodbyes and we stayed in touch by using pay phones to have more intimate conversations daily. We also saw each other when we were back in the city a few times, but somehow, we lost touch and life went on. We lived our lives never hearing from each other again. Iden had overheard my conversation with Wally. I filled him in on what was said and then he said that he thought I should go. He suggested that he was feeling better, and that I deserved a few days away. He promised he would check in on Mom and with me and keep an eye on Claudia. His assuring words made me believe that perhaps I could get away.

The reunion was set for April 19th, which was just a week away. As I did the dinner dishes, I began thinking of all the things I needed to do if I were to go. After I finished in the kitchen, I took out a pad and paper and wrote all those things on my to-do list. First priority was Mom. I had to check in with my brothers to make sure that they would be in town for those two days. I would also have to ask for that Friday off from work.

The week passed by quickly and I spent a little longer with Mom on Wednesday. She was very happy to hear about my visit to

Blackhead. We sat reminiscing about our summers there and then she told me to take some of the old photo albums out to look at the pictures from our vacations. We enjoyed our time talking and looking through old family photos. I even found a few pictures taken of the waitresses and the dishwashers I worked with, and there was one of Stephen as well. When Mom saw the photo with Stephen in it, she remembered I had liked him. I smiled and said her memory was still working very well. Before I left, I reassured her that if she needed me, I would return home. I also informed her that Mark and Claudia would be visiting her on the weekend and that Iden was home, and he would check in on her as well. We kissed and hugged each other goodbye and before leaving, I looked at her and said, "I love you so very much."

Monday morning, I left for work and was looking forward to a shorter workweek with Friday off to head upstate. As always, I checked in with Mom and sent Lizzy a good morning text. She replied saying she was going to the Boston Marathon to watch Joel's uncle and aunt and a few other friends run in the race. She already knew of my plans for the weekend and told me she would keep in touch with her father, expressing how happy she was that I was allowing myself some time away.

The school day was almost finished when a teacher came into my classroom and informed me that there was a bombing at the Boston Marathon. We had spoken earlier that day and she knew my daughter lived in Boston as well as her son. I took a breath and tried calling Lizzy to find out if she and Joel, and his uncle and aunt were all safe. My call went straight to voicemail.

If Lizzy couldn't answer her phone, she would usually text me right back to let me know when we could talk. I waited for about 10 minutes and still didn't hear from her. I called Iden who had already heard what was happening since he was home and always on his computer watching news or on social media. I told him that I was trying to get in touch with Lizzy but couldn't reach her and was getting nervous. He said that he was sure she was safe and not in danger, and that he would try to get in touch with her and suggested that cell phone service might not be operating because of the bombing. I left work as soon as school was finished and drove home as quickly as possible.

When I arrived home, Iden informed me that Lizzy had gotten in touch with him and that she and Joel were both safe but wanted to come to New York because they were very shaken up by what they had witnessed. The bomber was still loose in the city making them even more anxious to leave Boston as soon as possible. When they arrived, they were tired and hungry, so I made them sandwiches and while they ate, they explained what they witnessed. After a long night of trying to settle their nerves down they finally fell asleep.

The next few days Lizzy and Joel stayed home watching the news for any updates of the capture of the bomber as well as updates on the condition of the injured. I realized that my plans for a weekend getaway were now gone and that I needed to stay home with my family.

After work that evening, I came home and was about to make the call to inform Wally that I could not make the reunion due to the current situation. As soon as I put my key in the front door, Lizzy greeted me with a big hug and a kiss and said that the bombers were found. They were two brothers and during the shootout with police, one brother died and the other one was captured. All of Boston was relieved upon hearing of the arrest of the bomber, however the incident took the lives of three civilians and 264 people were injured.

I had already told my family of my change of plans when Lizzy approached me and said that she thought it would be a good idea for me to attend the reunion. She was feeling better after being home and with the capture of the bomber. I asked Iden what he thought, and he said that I should go as well.

In a way Lizzy and Joel being at home gave me reassurance that they would keep things in order and would inform me if something was wrong. I always walked around anticipating an impending crisis. I sat around thinking on the idea of going and had to make up my mind soon since I was due to leave in a few days.

Lizzy and Joel took Mimi for a walk, so I stepped out onto the balcony to have a smoke. Lizzy absolutely detested my smoking, rightly so, and I knew I had to stop. It was a chilly and bright night and Iden came out to join me. While we were smoking there was an intense stillness and I turned to look at him. It was obvious he wanted to say something, so I asked him, "What's going on?" He said that he was sorry for all that he had put me through these years, and that I should go away and try to not worry about them. When he spoke like this, I remembered the man I fell in love with and once again I felt that pain of missing what I loved and needed.

After the talk with Iden, I decided to take the trip upstate. I already had my bag packed so I was good to go. I left early on Friday, April 19th, not knowing what adventure I was about to enter when leaving that morning.

I had made arrangements to ride up to Blackhead with one of the women that I had worked with at the resort who lived near me. Donna, the woman I was meeting, had worked with me as a chambermaid for two summers back in 1973 and 1974. There is something amazing about making relationships during your youth that even after many years apart when reunited you somehow pick up where you left off. Once we caught up about our families, careers, and other such things we were suddenly like teenagers again at least in spirit, and that was a wonderful feeling.

In less than a three-hour car ride we had become roommates again and I started to feel the tension leave my body. I looked forward to meeting the rest of my coworkers shortly. We stopped at a rest stop along the New York State Thruway to use the restroom and grab a coffee. All of a sudden, her cell phone rang, and it was Paul, a dishwasher who worked with us and with whom she had stayed in touch over the years. She told him that we were on a rest stop, and he asked where. She told him where, and coincidently he was also pulling into the same rest stop.

I hadn't seen Paul since I was 17 years old and when we saw each other we hugged each other tightly. Both Stephen and Paul worked together as dishwashers during my time as a waitress. He too had a romance with one of the waitresses during our summers together at Blackhead. Both Paul and Stephen were childhood friends, growing up together in Williamsburg and keeping in touch over the years. After hugging me, he quickly called Stephen and said, "Guess who is here with me?" After he said a few words, he gave the phone to me and I just said, "Hey! How are you?"

He responded with just a "Hello," but even with that one word his voice was so familiar to me.

Donna and Paul were having a conversation about where they should stop and pick up liquor before reaching Blackhead. All of a sudden, I remembered all the drinking the waitresses, busboys, and dishwashers at Blackhead used to do. I was only 16, yet I had served alcohol at dinnertime to guests, even though the age requirement was 18. Most of the help was already 18 and well into partying with drugs and alcohol.

Many times the boys would start drinking in the early afternoons, sipping alcohol while cleaning the bar in the casino. The girls who were 18 would have a drink in the casino or have beers and smoke pot with the guys in our cabin. Little did I know they were high. I just thought the guys acted silly to entertain us waitresses as a means of flirting.

We arrived at Blackhead a little after 1 o'clock in the afternoon and checked into our assigned rooms. I was looking forward to taking a shower and relaxing a bit before meeting everyone. I had spent some time walking around the grounds and talking to Wally, and even though some things had changed, I saw it as I remembered it from the last time I had been here.

I made a few calls home to check in to see if everyone was doing well. I first called Mom, and she was happy to hear my voice and said she was having physical therapy and that she was feeling better every day. Next, I called Lizzy. Iden was at home reading in the bedroom, Claudia was working, and she and Joel were about to make some dinner for everyone. She also added that they were walking Mimi regularly and not giving her too many treats. She told me to have a good time and that we would talk soon. I took a long hot shower and put on some sweatpants and a tee shirt and put the heat on for a bit, since it was rather chilly.

As I lay in bed, I couldn't remember the last time I was away from my family and lying still was hard to do, especially trying to quiet my mind from all my thoughts. I stared out the window at the beautiful Blackhead Mountains and remembered many vacations with my family as a young child, as a teenager, and as a mother returning with my husband and two daughters. Although I hadn't thought of Blackhead in a while, it was still a very special place because it belonged to a different time, one that I missed.

Before closing my eyes, I tried to remember Stephen and some of the other help and found myself laughing at some of the funny things the guys did that I seemed to have forgotten until now. They would imitate Eddie's German accent, take us for rides in the tractor, and spray us with the dishwashing hose every chance they could get.

While I was taking a trip down memory lane I must have dozed off because the next thing I remember was a loud knock on my cabin door. It was Donna telling me she was walking down to the main house where all the guests were meeting before dinner. I could not believe I had fallen asleep for almost two hours. I told her I had just gotten up from a nap and did not realize the time and apologized for running late, saying that I would meet her as soon as I was dressed. I had already laid out my outfit, so I quickly washed my face and got dressed.

Before leaving my cabin, I checked my phone just to make sure there were no urgent texts to call home, and then I closed my door and walked quickly down the hill to the main house.

As I entered the main house, I heard many voices in the room outside the dining hall. Donna called out my name and I saw about 15 people along with the owners and their family greeting the guests. I was immediately asked if I would like a drink and was handed a glass of champagne. It was fun walking around chatting with Wally's sons and reacquainting myself with former employees. I was scanning the room looking for Stephen, when Paul came over to say that Stephen would be here a little later because he was coming after work from New York City. Paul immediately started to make me laugh, along with his cousin Jimmy, truly making it feel like old times.

We sat and talked as more guests arrived that I didn't know, and then Wally and Eddie gave a little speech about how happy they were to have some of their favorite former employees along with former guests and family members join together for this small and intimate weekend getaway. Just as they were about to finish their speech, Stephen walked through the door and once again I became a 16-year-old girl. I put down my glass and went to hug him and said, "Hey, it is so nice to see you."

He hugged me back, saying, "And it's nice to see you and I'm so glad you could make it."

After that short exchange I seemed to have blocked out the rest of the guests. We walked into the dining room together and were seated at the same table close to each other. Stephen had changed, and I am sure he was thinking the same about me. As a teenager Stephen had thick long hair, now he was completely bald, but sported a well-trimmed goatee. He had more wrinkles than some of us, but he still had his beautiful hazel eyes and a charming smile.

Many of the people I had once worked with had significantly put on weight and were out of shape, but Stephen still had a youthful and toned body. During dinner, I later found out through our conversations that he participated in many marathon and triathlon races. Both Stephen and I also talked with other people sitting close to us at the dinner table, but conversations always seemed to return to us.

Both Stephen and I looked at the food on the menu, commenting on the fact that we currently did not eat that much red meat, but we went along with the festivities. During the meal, our glasses were constantly being refilled with wine and beer and I noticed that Stephen declined all the time, saying water was just fine. I immediately thought back to the days of his drinking and was thinking that he either was taking medicine or was living a sober life. He noticed that I had seen him declining alcohol and he leaned over to me and quietly whispered that he had been clean and sober for almost 30 years.

"Wow!" I said. "Congratulations!"

I immediately felt guilty reaching for my second glass of wine, and he sensed my hesitation and said, "It's okay. I'm totally fine."

I wanted to ask him questions but stopped myself because it was way too personal to ask him questions about his journey to sobriety. In the back of my mind I was thinking of Iden and wishing he had someone like Stephen to talk to. After dinner we left the dining room and went into the room where we had first met all together earlier. We sat and continued conversations about our lives and all the paths we had taken to arrive where we currently were right now. Stephen and I moved around and spoke to other people, but once again found each other and started talking about our lives over the past 40 years.

It wasn't like I wanted to become best friends with Stephen again; it was more like trying to reconnect to the person who I once was, with someone who knew me before I became the person I was now. I met Stephen when I was 16 and living a so called "hippy life," which included practicing yoga, meditating, following a vegetarian diet, and reading spiritual and inspirational literature while trying to find the best path to doing some good in the world. A bit much for a 16-year-old, but that was how I was wired without really thinking too much about it.

And now, after 40 years, we found ourselves looking at each other and looking differently, but we were still able to find that youthful teenager and we began to feel young again. It was a feeling that had long escaped me. As I talked to all the people I knew and to Stephen, I felt as if I was shedding years with each conversation about younger days. Iden had grown up in a different country, and although he was very knowledgeable about life in the United States during the 70s, he didn't have the same connection to the same experiences as I did with the people sitting here at the reunion with me.

After dinner there was entertainment, with music and dancing in the casino. Paul remembered I loved to dance and asked if we could do the famous polka dance. Every Saturday night during the summers in our youth, most resorts had live bands and dancing. Since Blackhead was a German resort there was a mix of American and German songs played in the casino. The hired help would get to the dance floor and have fun dancing the night away and also partner up with guests to help them learn a few steps.

Stephen, Paul, and Jimmy were all sharing a room together since they had remained friends over the years. However, all the girls had single rooms since we had not been in touch for 40 years. Stephen's room was close to mine so when we left the dining area after dinner, he walked me to my cabin. We talked a bit more as we walked trying to fill a 40-year gap of information in some small moments of conversation. Before we left each other we promised that we would talk more later.

For the few hours that I was at dinner, I hadn't even thought of calling my family to check in on them. When I realized the time, I immediately picked up my phone and noticed that I had a few missed calls from Claudia. I called her right away and my first response was thinking something was wrong so when she answered I said, "What's wrong?" She said she just wanted to check in with me and say hello. I found that a little suspicious because she didn't have a history of doing that, so after I hung up, I called Lizzy.

Lizzy reaffirmed that all was well, and that Claudia was actually home early and had helped make dinner and that her boyfriend was at the house as well. She also reported that Iden had eaten dinner with them and was now watching TV in our bedroom. I told her I would be home early Sunday afternoon, but she said that she would probably not wait for my return since she had to get back to Boston. I understood and thanked her for all her help. We said our goodbyes and I went to change my top for a night of dancing in the casino.

Although it was chilly, I changed from wearing a sweater into a dressy blouse that had some flare and added a little more makeup and jewelry. I started to feel a little guilty about feeling happy. Although I didn't have any attraction toward Stephen, talking to him made me feel good. It had been so long since I had enjoyed a conversation with someone who was older than 12 who actually listened.

While I was getting ready, I missed Iden because we used to talk and share all our thoughts and dreams together. Most of our conversations over the years now were a series of questions and answers that revolved around his medicine, doctor appointments, and therapy sessions.

The loneliness I felt was the lack of sharing all that I was feeling for someone who used to always listen. There is a Sicilian saying that goes, "*La lingua va dove il dente*," which translates to, "The tongue goes where the tooth is missing." Whenever I feel the need of something my thoughts and feelings always search for Iden. I've always wanted what I need to be filled by him, and when he isn't present, the missing occurs.

The girls and I met and walked over to the casino together. The sky was brilliantly lit with millions of stars. Living in the city you can forget about looking up at the sky. I stood for a few moments staring and feeling a sense of smallness, but at the same time feeling a sense of grandeur and hope. It is hard to believe that we can forget that we coexist with such beauty every day, and every night. I bought myself back to earth and caught up with the other ladies.

The casino already had a band set up and people were sitting at the bar and tables. The boys combined tables so our group could sit together. Stephen, Paul, and Jimmy had been in touch before the reunion and brought along their instruments thinking perhaps they too might play a few songs at the casino. Stephen was a guitarist, Paul, a drummer, and Jimmy, a bass player.

Stephen was already sitting down so I waved and sat next to him. After the other girls sat down a waitress came and took our drink order. Some of the ladies ordered martinis so I also ordered one, although I had never had one before. Everyone was engaging in conversation, but soon the music started. We listened to a few songs and then the band started playing a polka. Paul turned to me and said, "Come on Patty, let's dance!" He took my hand and we hit the dance floor.

Slowly the dance floor got filled up and I was laughing and dancing at the same time. Wally and Eddie also joined in and midway we changed partners. We stayed on the dance floor for another dance and then returned to our seats. Stephen commented that he could see that I hadn't lost my love of dancing. My martini was waiting for me and after just one sip I realized that I would only be having one. As I sat there, I reached into my bag to check my phone and realized I had left it behind in the cabin. Part of me wanted to go back to get it, but I had to let that thought go and try to just enjoy myself knowing that all was fine at home.

The band took a break, so Wally asked the guys to play a small set of songs. Along with their instruments they also brought along some percussion instruments like tambourines and all kinds of shakers for others to join in and play along too. While they were busy setting up, I stepped outside with a few others to have a cigarette and again as I stood smoking I looked up at the sky and it seemed even more illuminated than an hour ago. We stepped back inside waiting for the music to start. They played a few songs and sounded good, even though they hadn't played together recently. After they played a few more songs, Stephen played by himself, "Fire and Rain" by James Taylor. He sang it so beautifully almost sounding exactly like J. Taylor himself. After Stephen finished playing, he came back to the table and sat down to listen to the other band members play a few solos.

I said, "It seems like you haven't lost your love of playing and singing."

He smiled and said, "I play most every day."

We stayed in the casino till a little after midnight, and then we all met back in the main house and talked a little more before heading to our cabins to call it a night. Stephen said that he was an early riser and wanted to know if I would like to take an early-morning hike with him. I explained that I rise early every day, even on the weekends, and that one of my favorite things to do is hike. We decided to meet around 7 o'clock in front of my cabin. We said good night and went to our cabins. I closed the door and leaned on it, thinking to myself, *what am I doing here?* I did some self-talk and realized it was all okay. I was just allowing myself to reunite with an old friend and to have some much-needed fun.

We met at 7 o'clock and Stephen was already waiting for me with his camera and ready to go. I said good morning and asked if we could stop in the main house to grab a cup of coffee to go because I always needed one to start my day. We got two cups of coffee and headed down the long, winding road away from Blackhead Mountain. As we walked, we talked about everything and nothing and took breaks to just listen to the sounds and observe the beautiful nature around us. I spoke about my family but didn't talk about Iden's condition. I just said that we had our share of good times and disappointments along the way and that we were doing the best we could.

Stephen talked about his alcohol and drug abuse and his road to recovery, which was all inspiring to hear. I was amazed at his honesty and openness to discuss his past with me. He also talked about his marathons, triathlons, his music, and his art. As we walked, Stephen took photos of things that caught his eye and before heading back we sat on the rocks listening to a gushing stream of water. I asked if we could stay for a few minutes because it was so peaceful, which he happily agreed to do.

The night before, we had all decided to visit Shingelkill Falls. Shingelkill Falls was a place that was very memorable for all of us. When we worked at Blackhead, we had one day off a week and, although we were never all off at the same time, we managed to arrange the days off with whom we wanted to spend our time.

After our morning coffee at Blackhead, we just sat around and talked for a bit and planned to meet later to head to the falls around 11 o'clock. Before we left, I called home to check in and was pleased to hear that all was well and I also informed them that I was having a nice time and thanked them for giving me this much-needed break.

We all met as planned and broke into different groups to carpool to the falls. Stephen and I were riding together and happy that it worked out that way so we could continue to catch up on the past 40 years. He turned on the music as we made our way to the falls talking and laughing. I had visited the falls with Iden and my girls over the years but hadn't felt that teenager reappear inside of me as I did now.

We walked down the path to the river and took our shoes and socks off to put our feet in the icy-cold water. The guys commented how ridiculous it was to jump into the falls because the water wasn't that deep below. I said that's why girls are smarter than boys because we never did jump in the falls. That gave everyone a good laugh.

We later decided to head to a favorite Inn for brunch and sat on the porch of the inn until brunch was ready. It was very peaceful, and I felt worry-free. Brunch was served and we were all hungry after our trip to the falls. Staff led us into a beautiful Victorian decorated dining room with tables set with lace tablecloths, bouquets of flowers, and all the place settings had different dishes and glasses. We all sat at one large table and Stephen and I were once again sitting across from each other.

The waitress put out pitchers of homemade ice teas and lemonade and also carafes of coffee and hot water for teas. Our meals were served on lovely plates decorated with edible flowers. Everything was perfect: The food was hot, the toast perfectly toasted with butter and served with homemade jams, and the pancakes were served with hot, pure maple syrup. Stephen and I shared the frittata and pancakes, and we happily enjoyed the combination.

After returning from the falls and our delicious brunch, a few of us sat on the front porch of our cabin to enjoy the lovely mountain view in the warm spring air. Some of the guys started to pass around joints and since it was never my thing, it did not bother me, but it did make Stephen uncomfortable, so he and I decided to move to the porch on the second floor of the cabin. We sat facing the mountains in silence and then he said although he was clean and sober for over 30 years it still bothered him.

I soon found myself opening up to him about the problems in my life and he also started telling me about problems he was having with his second wife. His second wife had informed him that she no longer wanted to be in the marriage, even though she loved him. He hadn't decided what he was going to do after hearing that information, but he knew he needed a change. I also opened up about Iden and his condition, and explained that I loved him very much, but it was a difficult time in our relationship. We were somewhat in a similar position, however I still wanted things to be good with my marriage, but Stephen's wife had basically told him things were over. We also talked about our children and about our parents, although his parents had passed away a few years before. We talked for about an hour then I excused myself as I was feeling a bit tired and wanted to call home and lie down for a while.

I returned to my room and couldn't believe how much I had revealed to Stephen about my life just a couple of days after reuniting. I guess I needed to unload about my troubles, and when I found a person who was willing to listen and to also share some of his life with me, it became easy. I never spoke to anyone like that before other than to Iden. In the past, I had spoken to my mom about everything, but over the years I didn't want to worry her with my problems.

I wanted to take a short nap but before doing so I called Lizzy and we talked for a while. She was getting ready to leave and I already felt sad knowing she would soon be gone when I returned. Having her near me gave me support and didn't make me feel so lonely. I thanked her for giving me a weekend away with no worries knowing that she was at home

I woke around 5 o'clock and had no idea where everyone else was, so I just took my time to leisurely wash up and get dressed for dinner later. I knocked on Donna's door, but no one answered. I heard some music coming from where the guys were staying, so I made my way over to their cabin. The door was ajar, and I peeked in and saw everyone listening to the boys jamming together.

I entered and found an empty spot to sit and listen and even to sing along to some oldies that they were playing. We had to stop the music in order to have our evening meal with the other guests and with Wally and Eddie. Once again Stephen and I found ourselves sitting in the same spots as the night before. Before dinner, Wally and Eddie thanked everyone who came to the reunion, and they also thanked us for sharing stories about our time at Blackhead with everyone. We had another delicious German meal then sat around drinking coffee and eating homemade strudel.

The following day we all wanted to get an early start back to the city since we had work and family waiting for our return. Donna had mentioned that she wanted to leave before breakfast since she was going home first and then heading to Boston to see her son. Stephen overheard her talking to me and offered to drive me home if that was okay with both Donna and me. Donna was relieved because she didn't want to make me leave around 6 o'clock in the morning, and I preferred to have breakfast with everyone and say my goodbyes a bit later. We said goodnight and then Stephen asked if I would like to take another morning walk before breakfast, so we arranged to meet. In a few short days I had felt the loneliness I had been feeling dissipate, and although it felt wonderful, it also scared me. I was so used to feeling a certain way, and I could not understand this new feeling I was experiencing. I sat in my cabin trying to figure out if it was just being away from my everyday life or was it something more.

Stephen and I met in the early morning and the fog was thick and almost touching the ground. We took a walk up the mountain and conveyed our thoughts about how much we enjoyed our time together. Stephen suggested that perhaps we could meet up sometime for dinner in the city. I said that I would like that

We walked back to the main house and since it was still too early for breakfast to be served, we sat with Wally and Eddie and talked over coffee.

Eddie asked, "So whatever happened to you two lovebirds?"

We looked at each other and laughed and said life happened. We talked until the rest of the gang entered the room looking a bit hung over and in need of coffee. We had a light breakfast and a quick conversation and then we exchanged addresses, emails, and phone numbers before saying our goodbyes. I loaded my bag into Stephen's car, and we headed down the New York State Thruway.

We listened to awesome music and talked about anything and everything we wanted to share with each other. We only made one stop on the New York State Thruway to use the restroom and so I could have a smoke. I told Stephen that I only smoked a few a day, but over the past few years I had been smoking more than I wanted to and wanted to stop. He said that he hoped I would and if he could help in any way he would. The three-hour car ride went by quickly and before we knew it, we were back in Queens near my apartment building. Before I got out of the car Stephen asked if we could exchange numbers and I reminded him we had all exchanged numbers at Blackhead already. He said he wasn't sure if he got all of our numbers, so he took out his journal and asked me to write it down for him.

Stephen pulled my luggage from the trunk and then he opened my door. We gave each other a hug and a kiss on the cheek, and I said it was really a pleasure to spend time with him and I expressed how proud I was of his sobriety and other accomplishments in his life. I watched as he drove down Queens Boulevard not knowing if I would ever see him again or even talk to him again. Having had someone be present for me and to listen to my thoughts brought life back to me. I felt satisfied almost like how your stomach feels after eating a delicious meal, but the difference was that it was my heart that was full.

Before heading upstairs to my apartment I sat on one of the benches out front and lit a cigarette to bring myself back to reality to re-enter my life. I took the elevator up to the third floor and heard my phone beep and saw that I had received a text from Stephen saying he totally enjoyed the weekend because of me. I quickly texted him back to thank him. I then deleted our texts, which made me feel somewhat guilty for our exchange of words. I wiped the smile off my face, put the key into my front door, and stepped back into my real world.

CHAPTER TWENTY

GRIEF

'Courage is knowing what not to fear.'

—PLATO

After my weekend getaway my life seemed to become divided between the time before and after reuniting with Stephen. The change had to do with not so much about meeting Stephen, but rather what happened to me during those two days. Over the past 10 years I hadn't had a moment when my thoughts were not filled with worries, mostly about Iden. We had many good times despite the troubles, but I had not felt like I was fully participating in my life. It was difficult to make plans because of Iden's volatile moods as well as the failing health of my parents.

I realized after spending some time alone that I was lonely and lacking a purpose for my life other than taking care of people. Of course, once you become a wife and a mother your life changes, and it is a wonderful change that offers you the most wonderful gift to love and be loved. There is no question that all families have their share of challenges and hard times, however, I think I was losing myself by trying so hard to solve everyone else's problems

Somehow the time I spent with those friends at the reunion and talking to Stephen made me want more time for myself, and yet at the same time, wanting less time feeling so lonely. There was a new conflict growing inside of me that left me feeling a new sense of unsettledness that I have never felt before. I wanted to start living a joyful life again but didn't know how given the life I was living with Iden. He was my husband for better or worse and there was no doubt that I loved him, but we weren't living a life together any longer, and the separateness of our lives was growing more and more with each passing year.

The connection I had made with Stephen sparked a need for more conversation and companionship than I had with Iden. The thought of being in a relationship with Stephen other than as a friend was not something that I was contemplating, however, I did look forward to receiving his texts and calls every now and then.

Another holiday season was nearing, and although it always brought me much joy, I just couldn't seem to work myself up to doing all the preparation and joining in the activities associated with this time of year. In past years, my Christmas tree and house would be all decorated, gifts would all be bought and wrapped, and cards all made out to be mailed. I always attended my school's holiday party but decided not to that year. I just wasn't feeling so joyful.

I was looking forward to my daughter Lizzy returning home for the holidays with Joel. I missed her very much and she always brought me happiness when we spent time together. Mom's declining health was always on my mind as well as Dad's. At this time of year, Iden tended to be in his most depressed state, so he wasn't able to offer much help giving any holiday cheer.

Mark and Kathy, had taken over hosting Christmas, since I no longer had my house. They also knew of my situation at home and knew I could use a break from all that is needed to prepare for a big Italian Christmas Eve celebration.

Claudia was working and no longer attending college. She had received an associate's degree and wanted some time to figure out her next steps. Although she had calmed down a little with her drinking and staying out late, she wasn't much help at home. She wasn't someone who would walk Mimi, make a meal, or run errands, although she worked late hours as a medical receptionist and would spend most of her free time with her boyfriend whom she had been dating for a few years.

It was difficult to walk outside and see the streets and windows glowing with lights and holiday decorations and not feel like smiling or be excited about Christmas. In a way, I couldn't wait for the holidays to end so I could go back to how I was feeling and stop pretending to be happy. I wasn't depressed, but just in a funk, and I knew I needed to make a change. It wasn't as much as needing to make a physical change, but more of needing to make a mental change in the way I was approaching my life and dealing with my family life and all its responsibilities.

Christmas came and went without any major problems. Holiday gatherings were difficult for Iden, and he could swing either way, so I was glad he was quiet, although very noticeably distant. We all enjoyed a delicious Italian Christmas Eve meal with all the trimmings while having an exchange of gifts. We returned home late and while everyone was getting into bed, I didn't feel like going straight to sleep so I headed out to the balcony to have a smoke. As I lit the cigarette, I reminded myself of my New Year's resolution to quit this horrible habit. Although it was Christmas, it did not feel like it for many reasons, but especially because the temperatures were almost in the mid-50s.

Before heading back inside I received a Merry Christmas text from Stephen, which was a special gift since I hadn't heard from him in a while. I returned the text and also wished him and his family a Merry Christmas. He then sent another text asking if we could meet in the new year sometime. I didn't answer right away but waited a few minutes thinking what I wanted to say. I did want to see him but wasn't so sure that was a good idea so I just sent a text saying that it would be nice to see him again. Iden saw me on my phone and asked whom I was texting. I immediately said that I was just checking my messages and responding to my holiday greetings. That was my first lie to Iden, and it made me feel extremely guilty although nothing had happened, but then why was I feeling that way?

Stephen and I continued to text and have quick conversations, either before I started my day when getting off the train and walking to work, or when leaving at the end of the day and on my way home. Once in a while, we would have a quick hello during a lunch break when our schedules allowed. Iden was always home, so talking or texting after 4 o'clock was not something I felt comfortable doing, but every now and then we would send each other a text before going to sleep. His texts and the short conversations we had seemed to give me what I needed to get through the next few difficult months.

The winter had passed along with the cold and snowy days, and I had managed to get through the cycles of Iden's moods, but overall we were living separate lives. Most of the time when I was home, we would be in different rooms, and even at night when he was in a more up mood, he would fall asleep on the living room couch, or when feeling depressed he would retire early to our bedroom alone.

Easter soon arrived, almost a year since I had met Stephen at the reunion, and although we were texting and talking on the phone we still hadn't met because it just didn't feel right. I was planning on having Easter dinner at my apartment with my brothers and their wives and my girls and their boyfriends. I needed to have my family around me as it had been a long time since I had invited anyone to our apartment. I really enjoyed entertaining and cooking, so I was looking forward to having my family gathered together for the holiday.

Easter Sunday was on April 5th in 2014, and it was a life-changing moment for me. I had prepared my parents' favorite meal as well as many appetizers and a pasta dish. Lizzy was home with Joel and helping me in the kitchen and even Claudia offered some help by running to the store for some groceries with her boyfriend. Iden had spent the last few months in a very deep depression and was slowly coming out of it but was still not involved with any family activities nor excited about the upcoming dinner with my family. Easter morning while I was preparing some food, I received a text from Stephen, which was a quote from Bob Marley:

"Only once in your life, I truly believe you find someone who can completely turn your world around. You tell them things that you've never shared with another soul, and they absorb everything you say and actually want to hear more..."'

There was a lot more of the text, so I went to the bathroom to read it and I stayed inside for a few minutes digesting the words. They were intense and intimate words to be sharing and I wanted to shake them off before I walked out of the bathroom and continued cooking Easter dinner. I did not send a response because I wasn't sure how to answer, but I did want Stephen to know that I received the text that was filled with such beautiful sentiment. I just sent him a text saying, "Thank you, and we will talk soon. Busy preparing Easter dinner." He instantly replied and said, "Enjoy, beautiful!"

The whole exchange with Stephen started turning my head upside down and I needed to get my head back into reality and wipe the smile off my face. Those words lingered on my mind throughout the day, and I looked forward to finding an opportunity to either send a text or a have a conversation with him.

I returned to the kitchen trying to stay focused on making dinner but found it difficult to concentrate. Thankfully, my parents arrived with a handful of goodies. I hadn't seen Mom in many months outside of her home and it was nice to see her with some makeup on and not in house clothes but dressed up with slacks and a pretty sweater. Although Mom seemed thin, she still had her beautiful smile, and her eyes still expressed a desire to live and love.

Lizzy, Claudia, and Joel were helping me serve and trying their best to lure Iden out of the bedroom. Dad asked where Iden was, so I went to ask him to please join us since it was almost time to eat and everyone was asking for him. He said he wasn't feeling well and that he would join us later. I told him my parents would like to see him, but he said he just couldn't join us.

I returned to the living room and made up an excuse that Iden had a bad cold and didn't want anyone to catch his germs, but he would come out later to say a quick hello before they left. My parents had gotten use to the many excuses I made over the years, so this one didn't seem to bother them, although it disturbed Lizzy and she got up often during dinner to check on her father.

I was happy to see Mom eat with such a hearty appetite. She hadn't eaten well in many months and Dad didn't complain about any of the food. We enjoyed the meal and when I started to clean up, Iden came out and fixed himself a plate, eating in the kitchen while everyone else went and sat in the living room. I felt like saying how rude it was for him to not join us, but that was just my frustration speaking and I knew he just wasn't capable. Or was he? I just didn't know anymore.

My parents talked to my girls and Joel about work and many other things. It was comforting to see the girls sharing their thoughts and ideas and listening to my parents' advice. I served coffee and tea along with the delicious desserts my parents had brought. We talked more before my parents said they were feeling tired and wanted to go home. I walked them to their car with Mimi and before going in I sat outside on a bench to smoke a cigarette and to think again about Stephen's text. His texts were something that I needed, yet they caused me to feel anxious because it left me wanting more at the same time. It was also causing me to have some mixed feelings that were perhaps wrong.

I woke up very early Monday morning wanting to head into school a bit earlier since I hadn't prepared all I needed for the day because of dinner on Easter Sunday. I had an unsettled feeling, with many thoughts running through my mind. As always, before I started my day, I called Mom for our morning talk. I usually called her at 7 o'clock and we would talk while I walked from the subway to my school for about 10 minutes or so. She would always answer with a happy morning hello. That morning I arrived at school a bit before 7 o'clock and treated myself to a coffee and a muffin at a diner a few blocks away from the school.

While I had my breakfast, I looked over some lesson plans and before leaving I called Mom. The phone rang and kept on ringing. Something was wrong. The aide arrived usually around 9 o'clock, and Mom always answered after the first few rings. My dad had difficulty sleeping so he slept in a separate bedroom from my mother. I thought perhaps she may have been in the bathroom and immediately hung up so she wouldn't rush to answer the phone. I tried again a few minutes later, and still no answer.

Mark had purchased a lifeline to allow a person to alert someone if there was an emergency. It was a special system worn on a person's wrist that could be activated by just pushing a button. I tried a few more times and then called Mark and explained that I thought something had happened. He said the aide lived nearby and he would try and get in touch with her. He would keep calling to try and get Dad up, and to see what was going on. Dad was a heavy sleeper and hard of hearing, and he took out his hearing aids at night before going to sleep.

I couldn't work not knowing what was happening with Mom, so I walked into my principal's office and told her I needed to leave. I explained what was going and she understood, so I left right away and headed to my parents' house, which was about 15 minutes away from my school. While I was walking to the train my brother called me and reported that Mom's aide got to the apartment and found Mom on the floor. She was now awake but must have fallen and may have had a stroke because she wasn't able to talk. The aide called 911 and an ambulance was on its way. I asked what I should do, and Mark said that I should meet him at the hospital since she would be gone if went to her apartment. I asked how Dad was, and he said he was okay but felt terrible that he didn't hear the phone ring nor did he hear Mom fall.

I called home and quickly told Iden what had happened and that I was heading to New York Presbyterian Hospital on Main Street, Flushing. I asked him to please take care of Mimi, and to keep in touch with Claudia, and that I would call Lizzy after she finished work. I said I really needed his help. Mom needs me. I took a cab to the hospital and went to the emergency room, and I saw my brother, the aide, and Dad. Mom was already admitted and being examined by a doctor.

I just wanted to see Mom, and I knew she needed to see me. The doctor came and said that they scheduled some tests and it seemed likely that she had broken her right hip when she fell. The fall may have resulted from a stroke, but they would know more after her tests. I asked how she was and if she was in pain. They said they'd given her pain medicine and that it was difficult for her to talk. We would be allowed to see her after the tests were performed, so we waited and waited. I arrived at the hospital around 10 o'clock in the morning and didn't see Mom until about 2 o'clock in the afternoon. She was sleeping when I saw her, and she looked so small and frail. I kissed her cheek and held her hand and I knew she knew I was there. I stayed with her until she awoke, and she smiled when she saw me. She couldn't speak very well, but we were able to communicate just by looking at each other.

Mark took Dad home and I stayed the night. I called Iden and told him I would be staying over in the hospital so I could speak to the doctors in the morning. He seemed as if he were already sleeping so I just said goodnight and that I would call in the morning. I then called Claudia and she was already home and asked if I needed her to come to the hospital. I suggested she stay at home, and I would let her know if I needed her. I asked her to please take Mimi out early in the morning since Iden always got up so late.

It was after 8 o'clock and I was hungry, so I went down to the cafeteria to grab a bite and a coffee. I sat at a table and called Lizzy to tell her what had happened. She immediately started crying and said she would come home right away. I told her it wasn't necessary and as soon as I talked to the doctors, I would let her know what condition Mom was in and when she should come home. I took a few bites of a turkey and cheese sandwich and couldn't seem to swallow. The coffee was cold, so I ate some chips that came with the sandwich.

I checked my phone and decided to check in with Dad to see how he was doing. He answered the phone this time because Mark had told him not to take out his hearing aids. Dad was having something to eat as well and said that he would see me tomorrow. He sounded sad, and even though my parents were not the closest of couples, I could already sense the loneliness he was feeling on the other side of the phone.

I put the phone down and thought about calling Stephen, but I knew he would be home with his family and that wasn't something I would do or had ever done before, but I decided to send a text saying, "Sorry to bother you, but at the hospital because my mom fell. When you get a chance can you give me a call? I will be sleeping at the hospital tonight. Thanks."

As soon I sent the text my phone rang, and it was Stephen. I was very happy to see his name appear and even happier to hear his voice. I thanked him for calling me right back and that I hoped I wasn't disturbing him with his family. He said he was alone since his kids and his wife were working an event at school.

We spoke for almost 30 minutes, and he was able to steady my nerves just by letting me talk and hear my worries about Mom. He offered to help me in any way he could, and I said he already had by calling me back, so I didn't feel so alone. He asked me to call him at work the following day to let him know how Mom was doing. I promised I would as soon as I talked to a doctor in the morning.

I slept all night in a chair next to Mom, waking as the nurses came in during the night to check her vitals while I sat and thought about many things. Mom and I had a connection that allowed me to feel I wasn't so alone. And soon that very strong life force might be gone.

I looked at Mom lying in the bed with all sorts of tubes and machines hooked up to her and knew that she did not want to end her life this way. She was an exuberant being and I could feel her pain and knew that her end was near but didn't want to allow that thought to enter my mind because of my fear. What would I do without her? Perhaps that was a very selfish motive, but I needed her, and the thought of not having her terrified me and made me feel like a child instead of a grown woman.

At 6:30 in the morning a doctor came in from neurology and explained my mother's condition. She'd had a stroke and broken her hip and they were going to perform a hip replacement. Given her age and her current situation it was a risk, but it had to be taken. I asked again if she was in pain, and I was told they were medicating her well with pain medicine.

The surgery was due to take place around 9 o'clock in the morning, and he said the surgery could go either way. She could have another stroke after the surgery, or she could regain mobility through therapy but would need to be placed in a rehabilitation center to receive the proper treatment and care. My mother awoke and a nurse came in to take her vitals and explained the surgery she was about to have. She was able to understand, and we looked at each other and as I grabbed her hand, we both said we loved each other in the best way we could.

I called my dad and two brothers to let them know what was going on and Mark said he would meet me at the hospital as soon as possible. I checked at home and told Iden the news and he expressed how sorry he was and almost started to cry. He said he would take care of things at home and that Mimi and Claudia were just fine. I started to cry while saying I was very frightened for Mom. Iden listened and said he would say prayers for Mom and that he loved us both very much. Hearing those words helped me calm down.

They took Mom up to surgery, and then she was brought back to an ICU unit. During the surgery she had suffered another massive stroke and her prognosis was very poor. Mark and I waited in the ICU waiting area to talk to a doctor about the next steps for my mother. Mom was paralyzed from her neck down, couldn't talk, but was aware. The hospital was able to keep her for a week or so, but eventually she needed to be moved into hospice care.

There were very important decisions needing to be made and we relied on Mark to make most of them. My older brother Ron loved my mother as much as we did, but he had a different approach and attitude on many things, so we both relinquished our decisions to Mark.

Mom was moved to a nursing home where she lived the last few months of her life. Every day after work I would visit her and spend a few hours with her. She still knew and greeted me with a smile. She was becoming thinner and thinner every day, as she couldn't eat and was just receiving intravenous liquids. Her eyes would meet mine and I could still feel her love. I lay on the bed next to her, to smell her and touch her soft skin, and although she was so frail, she still comforted me

Iden had never visited Mom at the hospice until one day I said Mom was going to die soon, and I thought he should visit her before it was too late. It took all he had in him to visit her. He loved her very much and the minute he saw her he started crying because he wasn't prepared to see her in the condition that she was now in.

Mom would wake every so often and while Iden was visiting she opened her eyes, and they exchanged some love. Iden couldn't stay in the room too long and had to wait in a family room while I continued my visit. On our way home he cried so much. All I could do was to try to comfort him by telling him he was always so good to Mom, which he was. When we arrived home, we sat and talked for a while, probably the most we had in a long time.

After speaking to a palliative care representative, my brothers decided to take Mom off life support because she was now going in and out of a coma. She lasted 11 days and then I received the call at 4:30 on a Sunday morning that she had passed away, I went into the kitchen and stood looking out the window with tears streaming down my face. At that moment I knew I would need to learn to be strong because I had no idea how to exist without her.

Iden and Claudia were sleeping, and I went in to tell Iden about Mom. He embraced me and we cried together. He stayed in bed while I made a cup of coffee and watched the sunrise over Queens Boulevard. Mark called me and we spoke for a bit and said we would talk later about Mom's funeral arrangements. We waited to tell the news to Dad, and my brother decided we should go together to deliver the news.

Mark and I went to see Dad, and when he saw us, he immediately knew that something had happened, and he began to cry. My parents didn't have a loving marriage, but he did love her, and we knew he felt her loss and was in pain. Mark drove me home, but I needed to go for a walk before going in and facing the family. I had delivered the news already to Lizzy, who was now living back in New York, and to Claudia. As to be expected they were very upset, and I needed to be strong for them.

Mark started all the necessary funeral and burial arrangements for Mom. She was a very social person, so the funeral parlor was packed with many friends and family members. Many of my coworkers and friends as well as my brothers' came to pay their respects. After the funeral, we had dinner at my mother's favorite Italian restaurant. Dad was planning on relocating to Florida now, since Mom never wanted to move away from her family, so we were going to make plans for selling their home and helping him move.

During those few weeks I spoke a few times to Stephen and our talks gave me some much- needed comfort. He remembered my mom from the years that we worked at Blackhead and the few times he came to see me in Jackson Heights when we dated. He remembered she had an amazing lively spirit and said that I also seemed to possess that gene as well. He always managed to say things to make me feel better.

I had taken a few days off from work and returned not feeling I was ready, but it actually helped me fight off the sadness. It was early June and there were only a few weeks of school left, so I was trying my best to just sail through the next few weeks.

After school one day I received a text from Stephen asking if I would like to meet for a walk in Central Park some weekend. By now he had moved out of his home and was renting a place still near his family in New Jersey. I texted back saying I would get back to him. I had to really think over my decision and even though I wanted to see him, I wasn't so sure it was the right thing to do. Every now and then I would return to the earlier text that Stephen had sent me with the quote from Bob Marley because it was such a loving and powerful message, especially now since the loss of my mother

When I arrived home, I was thinking of a way that I could possibly meet Stephen. Iden was on the balcony smoking and talking on the phone and I opened the door to let him know I was home. I left my phone on the kitchen counter and went into the bedroom to change. While I was in the bedroom, Stephen sent me a text saying that he hoped I could find a way to meet. When I came out Iden was holding my phone and asked who Stephen was and what was going on? Iden was coming out of another long depression and his mood was slightly elevating every day. I told him exactly who Stephen was and that nothing was going on.

I had explained before to Iden about all the people I had met at the reunion and that Stephen was one of them. I further explained that we had exchanged a few texts over the past year and a few talks. Iden became very upset and started accusing me of many things before he threw my phone on the ground and left the apartment saying he needed to take a walk. He returned soon after and apologized, but he remained quiet for the rest of the night.

For the next few weeks Iden had a cycle of agitation and hypomania along with drinking episodes. I thought certain situations could trigger his mood change, but realized it was more of his mood change that caused his reactions that were unreasonable. At a time when I needed some peace in my life, I was finding it very difficult to deal with Iden's behavior, even though I understood his being upset with Stephen and my text exchange.

I understood that I was texting a man and that I was married, but nothing had happened. I just longed for friendship, understanding, and someone that I could talk to that I didn't have at home other than with my daughters. My friend Annie was visiting from Ottawa, Canada, which she did every year at the end of June. I always had her come and stay with me for a few days and I would also visit her in the city where she rented an Airbnb for a few weeks while she and husband visited family and friends and also did some work.

I started planning a meet-up with Stephen using Annie as an alibi. I spoke to Annie and did want to see her but figured I could meet her during the day and then meet Stephen after work for a quick conversation to finally see each other again after almost a year of just talking and texting. And so a plan was made to see my dear friend Annie in the West Village and then meet Stephen. I discussed my plans with Iden, and he knew Annie very well, so he just said to have a good time. We hardly spoke these days

I met Annie in the West Village and we walked around talking and trying to catch up on our lives. She knew my mom as well I knew hers, so we shared many memories we had visiting each other's homes during our childhood and teenage years. We found a quaint little spot to eat at, which wasn't difficult in the West Village, and had a nice brunch.

We also talked about work, and she talked about her travels and life in Ottawa. She knew me well and even though I only saw her once a year we stayed in touch through emails and calls. She asked about my girls and asked about Iden. She knew his condition, and I opened my heart to her saying that it has been difficult, even more so lately because of the grief I was feeling over the loss of Mom.

My girls weren't much of a part of my everyday life since they were grown adults now working and living their own lives. I explained the overwhelming sense of loneliness I was feeling even though I socialized and always had invitations to go somewhere. It wasn't for the lack of not having something to do, or someone to do it with, but rather a lack of intimacy, emotional intimacy. I missed having someone I loved that I could talk to in my daily life. I knew I could tell Iden what I was feeling, but he rarely had any response to what I was saying. Most of the time I ate, walked Mimi, did errands, watched TV and visited family members alone.

Annie sat and listened and asked me what I was going to do about it?

"You deserve to be happy, Patty," she said.

Then I started talking about the reunion and meeting Stephen and about our texting and talking that had taken away some of the loneliness and sadness that I was feeling. Annie started filling the role of a therapist because she asked me many questions and then finally asked what I would like to see happen with Stephen? I looked at her and said I really didn't know, but that I was meeting him for the first time since the reunion and was hoping to figure out these feelings that didn't seem to go away.

I knew I was opening up a door that might not easily be closed, but I had to do something and then decide how I needed to proceed. I loved Iden, but we had lived like roommates for over 10 years. We had been together for over 30 years, and I had learned to adjust to this life. What was causing me fear was thinking of a life without Iden.

We sat and talked more and then I walked her back to the apartment where she was staying while in New York City. She had an appointment around 3 o'clock, so I had to leave her. We kissed and hugged, and she told me not to be so hard on myself.

"You are a good person and have been a good wife."

We both said, "I love you" at the same time, and then parted ways.

I thought I would be nervous seeing Stephen again after not having seen him in over a year, but I wasn't. When I saw him outside Macy's walking toward me, I hardly recognized him because he was wearing a suit and a tie, and I had never seen him in anything other than jeans and tee shirts. We exchanged a kiss on our cheeks and then sat on the chairs outside Macy's.

There were stands selling drinks, snacks, and food nearby and Stephen asked if I would like something. I said maybe something cold to drink would be nice, so he went and bought two ice-cold lemonades. He talked about his work and how busy he had been. Stephen worked as a project executor for a construction company, and he explained how difficult this business was trying to meet deadlines and to not go over a proposed budget. He also took out a journal that he wrote in everyday and showed me some drawings that he did while riding on New Jersey Transit. He then pulled out a watercolor bookmark with beautiful flowers that he had made for me. I told him how lovely I thought it was and he said he loves to do watercolor paintings. We talked a little more and rather than feeling nervous I felt calm and enjoyed every moment of our conversation.

It was around 6:30 when he said he needed to get home because he heads up an AA meeting at 8 o'clock every Friday. We walked down to the train station where I needed to take the E train back to Forest Hills and he needed to take New Jersey Transit home. We hugged each other and he said he appreciated my effort in meeting him and he hoped we could meet each other again sooner than later. I responded by saying, "Yes that would be nice," and then felt myself blushing a bit. As we walked away, we both turned around to look at each other at the same time. We gave a quick wave and then headed down to our designated trains.

The connection that I had made with Stephen that last day in June separated me even further from Iden. The friendship I had with Stephen was causing me to re-evaluate my life and to think about what I wanted my future to look like since I wasn't happy with my present circumstances. Stephen was already separated, and his wife and he had a very amicable relationship and were planning a divorce. We spoke about this a few times saying that he didn't feel guilty because he wasn't the one who asked to be out of the marriage.

As we talked more, Stephen said that she actually did him a favor because the marriage was not as good as he thought it was and it was a wake-up call for a new direction in his life, and he was now thankful after years of feeling hurt. I explained that Iden and I had been together for many years too and our love for each other was clearly evident, but we had both changed. I worried about him and wanted the best for him, but I believed we could no longer give each other what we needed, or rather he couldn't possibly give me more of what I needed.

Over those summer months Stephen and I found ways to meet. I started a slippery slide of lying and it wasn't something I felt good about. Stephen and I started texting more and I would call him on my walks with Mimi. One day I texted Stephen saying I would call him in a few minutes on my walk after dinner with Mimi. I got distracted with a knock on the door from my neighbor asking if she could borrow some milk, and of course I gave her some, and then went to take Mimi out for a walk.

When I reached for my phone, I realized I had left it at home. I was hoping Stephen wouldn't call nor anyone else because then Iden would hear it and see my calls to Stephen as well as my texts, which were not anything more than friendly exchanges of thoughts and ideas and about our daily plans. After the last time Iden had seen a text from Stephen I knew he would be very upset if he saw all the current texts and calls between us.

I immediately ran back to my apartment and opened the door. And that's when a new chapter in my life was about to begin. Iden had discovered all the texts and calls to Stephen and asked what was going on. I answered honestly saying that we had become good friends and nothing more, although I was by now feeling more than friendship, but hadn't acted upon it. There were a few texts that I hadn't deleted where Stephen had played a part of a song on his guitar and said some thoughtful and loving words to me, but nothing more. Iden was upset and accused me of the worst, carrying on until midnight and for the rest of the days that we remained together.

After a few months of unacceptable behavior, we agreed to separate. One afternoon after I had come home from work Iden informed me that he had found an apartment in Briarwood, and that he would be moving out in about a month. Although the thought of a life without him was something that I could never imagine, I began to feel that it was a turning point in my life. Stephen and I had still been in touch by phone and by texts, and nothing more, even though we did seem to be moving in the direction of needing more.

Iden had reached out to my daughter Lizzy and suggested that I had started an affair with someone and on one of her visits home, she said to me that she understood life with her father was difficult, but I should have waited until we were separated to be involved with someone new. I didn't know how to react to that statement other than that she needed to truly understand the facts and not react. The fact that Iden had reached out to my daughters and suggested that I was involved with someone was very hurtful.

After dinner one night while he was having a smoke on the balcony, I asked him to please reconsider his wanting to move, thinking that perhaps we could have a much-needed conversation. He expressed his need to be separated since I had found someone who offered what he could no longer provide. He spoke with no anger but only expressed regret and sorrow about the need for our separation. His desire to be alone was so much more than my desire to be without him in my life, regardless of the feelings I may have had for Stephen.

A few months later Iden packed his belongings and hired a truck to move him to Briarwood, which was a few minutes away from Forest Hills. After he moved in, we went to Ikea, and he picked out some things he needed and I gladly paid for the purchases. Claudia also was now living with her boyfriend, so I was alone in a large two-bedroom apartment with Mimi.

Dad was still living in Florida, having moved there shortly after Mom died. I visited him during the summer and was now getting ready to start a new school year. Iden had settled into his new apartment, and we had kept up a daily conversation. He said he was doing some consulting work and I could always tell when his mood was elevated or down, but I tried not to be overly concerned, but rather more present in my own life. Now that Stephen and I were living alone we had the ability to meet more and start a relationship that changed my life. I was not prepared for all that would happen, but I allowed myself to fight through the fear to possibly live with more happiness than I had had over many years. It was frightening, but somewhat exciting.

In the second week of school, Dad called me and asked if I could come down to see him since he wasn't feeling well. I immediately made arrangements to leave work to head down to Florida. I reached out to my brothers, but Ron was somewhere in Europe giving a talk and Mark was not able to get away from his job at the Federal Reserve. And so I took a few days off and headed down to Florida to visit Dad, not knowing what to expect.

Stephen and I had now been seeing each other on the weekends and he was very supportive of all that I needed to do and asked if I needed him, as he would gladly come with me. I expressed my gratitude for the offer, but knew it was best for me to go alone.

I arrived in Tampa and took a cab to Dad's home. I had just been there the previous month for a visit, and in the few weeks since I had seen him, he looked very thin and pale. He said he wasn't feeling that great and needed to see his doctor in a few days. He really appreciated my coming back so soon to be with him. He wanted to take me out for dinner, although I suggested I could make one of his favorite meals at home. We walked a few blocks to his favorite restaurant, which was on the dock facing the ocean. We had martinis and a steak dinner with French fries and sat and talked until the sunset. Dad ate all his dinner and even had a second martini, and I couldn't believe he wasn't feeling well. Maybe he just was feeling lonely. Either way I was happy to be there and enjoying this beautiful evening with him.

Dad went to bed when we got home but I stayed up a little longer making calls to check in with Claudia, Lizzy, and Iden. Iden was concerned about Dad and said to give him his love. I could tell his mood was high and he was talking rapidly, but I didn't allow myself to think about it since I had all that I could manage at the moment.

After the calls to my family, I called Stephen and we chatted for a while, and he was able to calm me down and put me in a better place. I went to sleep after midnight only to be awakened around 3 o'clock in the morning by Dad telling me that he wasn't feeling well. I asked him what he wanted me to do, and he suggested that I take him to a hospital in Pasadena.

I had no idea how to get there so I listened to Dad's directions and drove his brand-new black Cadillac to Pasadena. I called Mark to notify him what was going on and he said that I should place a call to Dad's doctor, letting him know that I was taking Dad to the hospital. We arrived at the hospital a little after 4 o'clock, and I took Dad into the emergency unit. It was a very quiet hospital, so Dad was seen right away. I waited for a few hours until Dad was evaluated, and some tests were performed.

A cardiologist came out and said that Dad's heart was having some problems and that they would be admitting him. He suggested I go home and return in the morning, but I wanted to see Dad and said I would wait until he was placed in a room. Sometime after 7 o'clock the next morning I was allowed to see him. He was plugged into all kinds of machines and also had some blood being pumped into him. I sat with him, and he told me he was tired and needed to sleep. I stayed, as I wanted to talk to his doctor.

Around noon I saw the doctor who said that Dad needed to have heart valve surgery, but since he was 93 and had some other compromising issues, it was a dangerous operation. Since living without the surgery was not possible, he suggested we keep him in the hospital to make him ready for the surgery. I called Mark and he said he would try and come down as soon as possible to be with me.

I stayed for a little longer and asked Dad if he wanted anything to eat since he complained that the hospital food was terrible. He wanted a good cup of coffee and some apple pie, so I left the hospital in search of some pie. I figured a diner would have some decent pie and coffee, so I went looking for one in Pasadena. I found a diner that had some pies in stands on the counter and bought two apple pies and two coffees.

I came back and thought about checking with the nurse to see if it was okay to give him pie and coffee but didn't. Dad was sitting in his chair with all the machines attached to him and if pie could bring him some happiness, then so be it. We sat and ate the pie together and then a nurse came in and said he was going to be taken for some tests. She suggested I go home and get some rest and come back later around dinnertime, but shouldn't bring any pie!

I said goodbye to Dad, then left and headed back to St. Petersburg driving the Cadillac. I arrived home a little after 3 o'clock in the afternoon, and made a few calls home to Iden, Claudia, Lizzy, and then to Stephen before closing my eyes to take a much-needed nap before returning to the hospital.

Just before I fell asleep, my cell phone rang, and it was the hospital telling me that I should come immediately since Dad seemed to be unresponsive. I asked what that meant, and she said that he was awake, but not able to communicate. I drove that big black machine down to Pasadena as fast as I could. I arrived at the hospital and didn't even park the car, but just left it by the entrance to the hospital and ran to Dad's room.

Dad was awake and when he saw me, he put his hand out and grabbed it. We looked at each other for a few minutes and then he was gone. He had a massive heart attack right in front of me. It was a vision that I have been replaying over and over in my mind over the years. The sounds of the beeping heart monitor and the nurses running in and pushing me away trying to use a defibrillator machine to get his heart pumping again were images that will remain with me forever. On September 24, 2015, Dad passed away, just three months after my mom's passing.

I sat in a chair outside Dad's room not believing what had just occurred. I placed a call to Mark, and he tried to console me and give me some directions, but I wasn't able to absorb the information. I just felt like throwing up. I sat there for a bit and then a nurse made me sign a form and then she handed me a bag of my dad's belongings. Life over and finished just like that. I sat, unable to move.

I finally made my way to the car. I had left the key in the car, and it was now parked in hospital lot. I informed security that I had left my car when I went running into the hospital like a madwoman. I drove home in a daze.

I entered Dad's home not knowing what I needed to do first. I made calls to Iden and my daughters informing them of Dad's passing and then I called Stephen. I couldn't talk for long, so I had quick conversations, and then closed my eyes because I just couldn't see any longer.

I awoke the following morning feeling somewhat rested, but with a heavy heart because I was faced with making arrangements for Dad's cremation and taking care of things that needed to be done in his apartment. Mark was very good about taking charge and directing on all that needed to be done before I left, so I followed his directions before heading home. I also gave myself a few days to sit by the beach and just gather myself before heading home, even though I wanted to be near my family.

In just a few short months, both of my parents had died, Iden and Claudia had moved out, and Lizzy and I had had some relationship issues because of my involvement with Stephen that had caused a rift in our connection. Around Lizzy, I felt guilty about no longer being with her father even though he was the one who left. It is true that no one can make someone feel guilty, but her not even wanting to talk about my relationship with Stephen nor hear about anything we did together made me feel like my relationship was wrong. It hurt. Although Claudia was difficult in many ways that Lizzy wasn't, Claudia accepted my need to move on and have some happiness with someone else since her father and I no longer could.

I returned home and spent the weekend just regrouping and getting ready to return to work on Monday. Mark had made arrangements for Dad to be cremated and had his ashes sent to New York to be buried with Mom. Mark was also making arrangements to sell Dad's home and would be flying down to Florida to clear out his apartment in a few weeks.

I needed to find the courage to not fear the new life that I was now living without parents, the change in the relationship with Iden, who had been my husband and friend for almost 40 years and adjusting to the changes occurring in my relationship with my daughters. I was also now in a relationship with Stephen and not sure of where that was heading, and I had to ask myself if I were able to fully take a leap of faith and jump into it given all that I was feeling presently.

My dad, Joe 2015

CHAPTER TWENTY-ONE

HEALING

"Plant hope in your heart's wounds."

—ALEXANDRA VASILIU

I was faced with a life without parents, no children living at home, and the end of a 30-plus-year marriage. Even though it was difficult to finally come to that moment of deciding we needed to separate, it was very courageous of Iden to take the first step because I wasn't sure I could have done it. Iden had settled into his new life and Claudia was working and living in the city. Lizzy was living back in New York and more involved in family matters. I had decided to move from my current two-bedroom apartment into a smaller and more affordable place. I also wanted to start with a clean slate. A new place with a new beginning, alone.

I decided to start therapy, and even though I was making an effort to move on, I felt stuck. I needed to reinvent myself and to allow myself to grieve, cry, and be with whoever made me feel happy. I was so lost in my sadness and dysfunction that I didn't believe or think that I was capable of creating a life where I could find some peace. Stepping away from my role as a daughter, a wife, and a full-time mother was indeed a new experience. I never wanted not to be connected to my two daughters, nor no longer to be in touch with Iden but I realized the relationships that had once existed were no longer present. I was no longer able to accept living a life that wasn't offering me what I needed.

My relationship with Stephen was giving me companionship but I still needed more. I needed to find stillness in a place; I needed to be alone. I had never lived alone, never decorated a space that reflected my personality and offered me an acceptance of who I was. I was no longer a wife, a mother, or a daughter. I was just me.

I found a studio apartment in a small building in Forest Hills a few blocks from my current apartment. The building accepted dogs, so it was a good fit for Mimi and me. I didn't want to move too far away from my safe zone where I had a neighborhood with familiar faces and people, but still needed to be in a new place that was mine, with no history from other family members. I had plenty of furniture but wanted to unload things that brought memories from my past. So I bought a new couch, a kitchen table and chairs, and most definitely a new bed!

With the move came some changes in my relationship with Stephen. We had many things in common that we loved to do, which was the main attraction. I also experienced a physical attraction, which brought about much excitement along with guilt and confusion.

The relationship I began with Stephen offered me new insight into who I was and what I really desired as a person and as a woman. Iden however, had offered me his sincere love and I knew he would do anything for my girls. Even now his love was still evident, although his illness prevented him from being present in our lives. I could longer thrive on memories. I could no longer wrap my arms around a past memory or feeling. I needed to love in the present where I felt the things I needed were being met, and to have a life that I wanted to live and that was acceptable to me. I needed to find a peaceful solution. I needed to find a way to leave a life I had once lived and loved to enter into one that would not be known or perfect. I was willing to take the chance, regardless of whatever guilt or fear that I had.

Some of the things Stephen and I have in common are our adventurous nature and our love of travelling. We didn't need to decide too long on a place we wanted to visit. I had always wanted to go to Italy, and without the responsibility of my parents I felt more comfortable about being away for a period of time. Lizzy and Joel were living back in New York City and knowing that they were around also helped. I knew they would check in on both Iden and Claudia if I was away.

Both Stephen and I are planners, so we researched for a few weeks then scheduled a trip to Italy in late September. We had our itinerary set and had purchased online tickets to the Vatican and tickets for a train that ran between the cities we were visiting. Stephen had been to Italy before, but I was beyond excited. We were landing in Rome then going on to Florence, Assisi, and Venice for a total of 12 days. I was planning on retiring in June, so it was my very first autumn vacation.

My last school year was very busy with work and setting up my new place and making it my own. On the weekends, I was spending time with Stephen in New Jersey and making time to see my daughters and check in with Iden as well. Iden was still having his periods of depression and mania due mainly I believe to his not making his scheduled psychiatrist appointments nor taking his medicine correctly. He was also drinking and thought he could hide it, but it was always evident by the way he slurred his speech when he spoke, and by the confusion of his thoughts. I tried very hard to set boundaries. I wanted to be involved in Iden's life, but I didn't want to be involved in his day-to-day activities.

My daughter Lizzy was somewhat like the police. She called Iden many times during the day and would let me know how he sounded. Many times he wouldn't answer his phone and she would have panic attacks thinking something had happened to him. More often than not he was sleeping after a day of drinking, and he would be passed out and not capable of answering the phone.

The only way I was able to stay distant was reminding myself that it was not in my control how he behaved. Somehow, feeling the pain he imposed on my family helped me detach, but when I let go of that pain, I felt extreme sadness and pain for Iden. I also felt guilty for having a life that I was starting to enjoy. I had an apartment that when I entered brought me joy, I had a boyfriend who offered me support and happiness, and I was planning a dream vacation, and was soon to retire.

The swing of my emotions also went up and down. Work always forced me to be in the present, which didn't allow me the time to struggle with my thoughts. At home I would have a mixture of feelings. When making dinner I would often think of Iden, especially if I was making one of his favorite meals. And before going to bed I would wonder if he was home and safe. Sometimes I would check in, but if he didn't sound well or would start talking nastily, I would tell myself not to call again. But of course that never lasted too long.

I decided to find a therapist but was feeling exhausted before even starting to reveal what was going on in my life to a complete stranger, but I knew I needed to talk to someone. I needed to unload what I was feeling in a safe and nonjudgmental forum. I called a few places and wanted to find one that was near to where I lived, and I also thought I would feel more comfortable with a woman therapist.

After the initial intake with a psychiatrist I met with a therapist. The session started by her asking me what brought me into her office today. I sat for a few minutes before responding because there were many reasons. Just thinking of them all I felt a surge in my belly and a pull in my heart and felt for a minute that I would start crying, even before I started to talk. Most of what I was feeling was a sense of loss.

So I started my first therapy session by saying I have huge sadness and grief for the loss of many relationships that are no longer present. The hardest one is grieving for a relationship with a person who is still alive. Living in Forest Hills where I had lived and raised my family for over 30 years brought about constant memories as I walked down almost every street. Some days were harder than others and I knew that in time, I would miss the relationships I had once had less, and the new ones would become my new reality. It was fine to remember the past, but the grieving for relationships that were no longer present needed to be addressed.

Every Tuesday night at 5 o'clock I would start my session with the therapist, finishing at 6 o'clock. I only lived a few blocks from the psychologist's office, but I needed to walk after my session a bit more before returning home. I felt full and needed to let off some post-therapy session emotions. Walking always made me feel better. Stephen always wanted to talk after my session, but I just wasn't capable of talking. I needed a little time to process the session. It was difficult in the beginning because I held back some things I was feeling and thinking. But eventually therapy began to help me reveal my pain, let go of my shame, and share honestly about my life.

Each month that passed by was one month closer to retirement and our trip to Italy. I always loved teaching, but it is a funny human phenomenon that we can do something for most of our lives, but when we reach the point of it coming to an end it can seem somewhat unbearable. By the time May had arrived, every day felt like a week. All teachers feel exhausted at that time of year, but I had a "I am really done" kind of attitude.

My school gave me a beautiful retirement party and I was thrilled to see many teachers who had previously retired attend the event. It was a bittersweet time because I was once again ending another long relationship along with many friendships that I knew I would no longer have after retiring. I was eager to move on, but just not sure how I was going to begin. I was going to give myself a good amount of time off with some downtime. I wasn't sure exactly what that was like since I had been working and taking care of my family and involved with my parents for most of my life. It was exciting, but also challenging. I wanted to carve out a new existence in many ways. I wanted to perhaps get a part-time job, take some cooking and Italian classes, to travel, and perhaps even write a book.

The hot weather of June had arrived along with the end of the school year festivities. I was to give my last graduation speech to the lower grades and didn't think I would have a difficult time delivering the speech. When graduation day came, I was to lead the procession line down the auditorium as the Mistress of Ceremonies.

As "Pomp and Circumstance" began to play and we began to proceed down the aisle, I began to get teary-eyed. I really loved my job and was always so proud of my students' accomplishments that brought much fulfillment to my life as well as to theirs.

After a few opening songs and the Pledge of Allegiance, I started my speech. I wrote the speech and practiced it a few times and had it written out on paper that I held in my hand, but I didn't look at it. The words I wanted to say came from my heart, so I didn't need any help in delivering them. After almost 25 years at the same school I knew the community very well. I had even taught many of the parents of the children now graduating. I managed to get through the speech but was choked up near the end. After my speech I was given a standing ovation and some students walked over with a big bouquet of flowers. Although teachers don't teach for the money or the appreciation, it was a wonderful feeling knowing that perhaps I had touched some lives during my years at the school.

The last few days at work I cleaned up my room and gave away most of my collection of children's literature and many other supplies to the new teachers and to some of my teaching buddies. We had a teacher's luncheon and a cake for my retirement. I returned to my room and waited for the time to leave, then closed the door behind me and said my goodbyes to my classroom. As the saying goes, we close one door and open a new one as we move forward in our life's journey.

I wasn't exactly sure what new doors I was going to open, but I was excited to take a pause before taking any action. Over the past years I had been going at warp speed from one crisis to another and I felt the need to start living at a much slower pace. I wanted to walk my dog leisurely, have a cup of coffee sitting down, take a nap while reading a book, go shopping for nothing in particular, try out new recipes that don't take under 30 minutes to prepare, and spend quality time with friends and family. And of course spend more time with Stephen, not worrying about preparing lesson plans.

Even though we had our fall vacation plan to go to Italy, Stephen and I also decided to rent a house in a quaint little beach town on the Jersey shore called Ocean Grove. I had vacationed there a few times with my family when our girls were young. It was always a pleasant experience. It is a dry town, so it didn't attract loud crowds, but mostly families with young children and couples looking for a peaceful beach experience. Stephen and I left right after school was finished. It was another retirement gift for myself.

Our house was right on the beach, and it was wonderful to wake up and sit on the front porch drinking that first cup of coffee as we watched the sunrise. Both Stephen and I are early-morning risers, and having that companionship made me happy first thing in the morning. I took Mimi on my vacation because I knew she too would also enjoy sitting on the front porch. We took her on walks on the boardwalk and on the beach, although she never liked the sand or the water. After a few hours on the beach and a few swims we would change and take long bike rides and find some small little place for a bite to eat. Asbury Park was nearby, so sometimes we sat and listened to music as well while eating.

I promised myself that I would only check in on things back home once a day and not have my phone present to answer the calls from Claudia that were usually with a problem at work, a boyfriend, or her thinking something was wrong with her health. I really didn't want to check in with Iden at all, since he knew I was with Stephen. Before leaving he said some very unkind things to me that were hurtful, but then he would call and apologize. I understood his hurt, but the drama and hurt didn't have to hurt forever. He was choosing to do so. I wanted it to end.

I was trying to accept the things I couldn't change but was slowly learning to change the things I could no longer accept. It was hard being in a familiar place that I had been with my family and now with Stephen. Guilty feelings passed through me, but I was trying to let those thoughts leave and not hold on to them. I wanted what I was feeling for all of my family. I wanted Claudia to lie on the beach and ride the waves, for Lizzy to sip her iced coffee under a big umbrella and read. I also wished for Iden to find someone to take walks with hand in hand on a beautiful summer night.

I think when you are happy you want to share your happiness with the ones you love. It grows your happiness. Stephen spent about five out of the 10 days with me and then he had to get back to work. Lizzy and Joel were able to come for a weekend too, which made me very happy. We had some nice time on the beach and had some fun cooking dinners while looking out to the sea. Claudia had just started yet another new job and couldn't get away.

I looked forward to having a few days to be by myself before Stephen came to pick me up. I lay on the beach getting browner every day, even knowing it wasn't good for me, but it felt good.

After a day at the beach I sat on my front porch enjoying some refreshing summer cocktails and breathing in the salty air. I felt as if I were like a caterpillar shedding some old skin getting ready to transform into something totally new. My physical life had changed, which was now transforming my inner self. I needed to let go of the life I had, not in a bitter way, but with acceptance of what once was and no longer is. It was my journey. I needed to arrive exactly where I was at this moment, regardless of the lack of approval from those whom I loved. Arriving instead of striving is the best place to be.

After returning from our beach vacation, I spent most of the week at home. On the weekends I went to New Jersey to spend time with Stephen. Sometimes he was playing in a gig, and we would go out and have dinner with his band members and their wives and girlfriends. Or sometimes we would go to hear other bands play, and it was always a fun time. We would also spend the morning lying by the pool in his complex, which was almost empty in the early morning.

Stephen and I were growing closer together and deepening our relationship. He would often ask me to move in with him, but I wasn't ready. Although he was patient, I could tell he really couldn't understand. I still needed to be near my girls, even though they were on their own. They didn't need me as much as I still needed to feel present in their lives. I think I needed to hold on to something or somebody familiar amid all the changes.

The summer quickly flew by, and I didn't have much contact with the girls. Claudia was working, and on the weekends running around with her boyfriend and her friends. She was still in party mode, but somewhat more controlled and knowing that she was with her boyfriend made me feel less concerned about her safety. Lizzy had been promoted to principal after being a teacher and an assistant principal so she needed to work some weeks during the summer.

With just a few weeks left till our departure to Rome, Iden had swung into a full mania and our correspondence through texts and calls had been quite disturbing. Leaving on a vacation with his current state caused me to have more anxiety than I would like before flying across the Atlantic, but all I could do was not react to his calls and reassure my daughters that if they needed me, they could always call me. They also knew they could call my brothers if there was an emergency.

Iden and I were officially divorced over the summer, and to many it was still peculiar that I should still be so concerned about Iden's well-being. I still loved him and cared for him, but I also did not want my daughters to have to be involved in his caretaking. He didn't have any family in America besides some niece living in California and all of his friends, our friends, had lost touch with him due to his bad behavior due to drinking and his illness. There is only so much a friendship can tolerate.

After planning Mimi's care with my pet sitter and meeting the girls for one last time before leaving I was ready to leave for my trip. I made copies of my itinerary along with emergency contact numbers.

I met Stephen at Kennedy Airport. I loved that he was always waiting for me, even if I was always early. His responsibility offered me security that let me know I was loved without words. Airports are a bit anxiety-provoking, but he did all the checking in and kept me busy with conversation while waiting to get through security. Once we were all checked in, we settled into our waiting area. Stephen bought us some coffee and some candy, and we sipped away the time while I read, and he wrote in his journal.

After an eight-hour flight, we arrived in Rome in the early afternoon, tired but very excited. We moved through customs then grabbed a cab and drove through the hectic traffic of Rome toward our hotel. We were very happy to take a shower and rest for a bit before heading out to wander the streets and grab our first meal in Italy. It was amazing to walk down every street and be surrounded by ancient ruins and to see the Colosseum while eating a delicious plate of pasta! We walked everywhere day and night, managing about 30,000 steps a day. We both loved to walk and get lost and then find our way again.

I knew some Italian after studying it in college and hearing it while growing up, which helped us get directions and order food. We spent three days in Rome before heading to beautiful Tuscany. We visited vineyards and ate some of the most delicious foods. We travelled by train and bus, and we were in awe of the beautiful landscape, lush with green trees and mountains. I was also in love with the markets, being a foodie. The vegetables, fruit, cheese, and meats all looked so unbelievably fresh and delicious.

Stephen took hundreds of photos and said he couldn't wait to return home to start a painting from one of his photos. Our last stop was Venice. It was truly magical. Our hotel was decorated in true Venetian style with Venetian glass chandeliers, brocade wallpaper, velvet drapes, and big windows with shutters that opened to the canals. We didn't waste any time heading out to walk over the many thousands of canals, down endless alleys, and eating in restaurants that held no more than 10 people and had no menu. The chefs made whatever seemed to be their fancy for the day. Every bit of Venice was thrilling.

While in Italy we did all the touristy things, including visiting a glass factory and witnessing a glass-blowing demonstration. We bought some necklaces for our daughters made of small multicolored glass charms on leather strings. We ate delicious pasta con vongole, and then took a gondola ride to end our last night in Venice. The whole trip was everything and more than I had ever expected, and we had already started making plans to return.

Stephen, being a romantic, said that perhaps one day we could get married here and then he asked me if I had ever thought about that. He was always thinking ahead in planning our relationship. The past few weeks together were amazing, and we were great travel buddies. I was looking forward to returning home to New York to see my family and Mimi, but I also knew I was going to miss being with him 24/7.

Stephen wanted our relationship to keep moving forward, and part of that was to move in with him, which meant moving to New Jersey. I wasn't sure how to answer him because I didn't feel ready for such a commitment, nor did I want to make him feel that I wasn't taking our relationship as seriously as he was. I answered the best way I could, with honesty, saying that I was not able to at the present time to take such a big step. Stephen responded with, "If you loved me, you would move in with me."

At that point I had started justifying my decision to live alone, and hence on our last night in beautiful Venice we transformed what was a dream vacation into a very bad memory. We had the biggest fight, which was actually our first fight. We didn't talk further or sleep in the same bed that night. We had a room with two twin beds that we had put together while in Venice, but that night we pulled them apart.

We left Venice in the wee hours of the morning in a small boat headed to the airport. There were a few other passengers on the boat and Stephen was talking to them, which was odd since he normally was not that social, but I guess the silence between us was too thick, so it was necessary.

The whole plane ride home we barely spoke. We arrived in New York and got the Uber back to my home where his car was parked in a lot; it was as if we were strangers instead of a couple returning from a wonderful Italian vacation. He always said that I should express what I was feeling, but I felt that meant as long as it was the words he wanted to hear.

I was recently divorced, finally had an apartment on my own for the first time, just retired, and was looking forward to time living on my own. I very much wanted Stephen to be a part of it, but not as much as he wanted me to be part of his life. He was divorced and had been living on his own for a few years and was ready for the next step.

I entered my apartment and opened all the windows and unpacked my suitcase, all the while wondering if I was being unreasonable. I could only do what I felt comfortable doing. I wanted to enjoy my alone time. I needed some time to breathe and allow myself to heal. I know Stephen was eager to have our relationship move on to the next level, but I wasn't ready. As I look back now, I used to think it was fear that held me back, but it wasn't. I just wanted to live alone and find some peace.

A few days later Stephen and I contacted each other again. He sent the first text asking if we could talk. We met and talked things through, resolving to take things as they were and not to bring up things like moving in together or getting married until a later date.

After that first argument about our relationship we seemed to relive it many times thereafter. Sometimes we saw each other every weekend, and then there were weeks that went by that it was difficult to arrange things for me to make it to New Jersey. Stephen was involved in music gigs, art shows, and his AA meetings, along with making time for his children, all of which I understood.

The weekends were sometimes the only time I had to see my girls since they were working full time and usually had things going on during the weekend. When we did get together after long breaks, Stephen would often say if we lived together, we wouldn't have this problem, and he'd make other comments here and there of a similar nature. I didn't want to move to New Jersey, although the town that he lived in was charming and I enjoyed hanging out with many of his friends whom I had gotten to know over the years, but I could not see myself living there. Stephen didn't want to live in Forest Hills. In fact, he very rarely came to visit me at my place.

During the summer, my daughter Elizabeth and her boyfriend Joel presented us with news of their engagement. Her wedding date was to be in June 2019. I was very excited and so happy for her. Joel was a perfect match for her, and he was kind and respectful to our family. Since the wedding was within the year, we began to look for a place for the event, find a gown, and all the other things necessary for a wedding to come together. I love to plan and organize so I was very excited to get my pad and pen ready to make a list and categorize the things we needed to do.

I told Stephen the news and he was excited for me, although he had still not met Lizzy, so it was difficult for him to feel part of the planning. He was always willing, but Lizzy wasn't and that was painful for me because Stephen thought if he were important enough to me, she would have met him. Lizzy had trouble dealing with my relationship with Stephen and there wasn't anything I could do or say differently that could make her change her mind. She didn't dislike him; she just didn't want to know him.

When I talked about all the things I needed to do for the wedding, Stephen wasn't that interested. In fact, a few times he said, "I can't wait for this wedding to be over with."

It upset me to hear him say that. I knew the wedding planning was taking up a lot of my time and therefore I was spending less time with him. I believe he made that remark because he was feeling disconnected from something that was so important in my life. Our relationship was on and off again during that year. Sometimes, I just couldn't handle what I thought was his selfishness and would act indifferent, causing him to think I was pulling back, which I was.

I wanted to enjoy the experience of planning my daughter's wedding and not to feel bad about the time I needed to spend with her. I wasn't sure where we were headed, but I was not thinking of living together or getting married anytime soon.

CHAPTER TWENTY-TWO

THE WEDDING

"When we are in love, we open to all that life has to offer with passion, excitement and acceptance."

— JOHN LENNON

I am a true romantic. I love being in love. As the quote by John Lennon clearly states. Love gives us motivation to want to take a huge bite out of every possibility that life has to offer. In my first years after meeting Iden, it was comforting walking around with a full heart and knowing that there was someone with whom I could talk and make plans with, to be excited about the future with; our future. It also made the hard times of getting through school and walking around with little money in our pockets bearable. We used to bring our tea bags to college and just pay for the hot water that only cost a dime. Sometimes now when I go to Starbucks and order a chai latte and pay $5, that memory comes back to me, and I have to smile at our necessary frugality during those years.

Being in love gives you an excitement to do the simplest of things together, like taking walks, talking, listening to music, or just eating pizza on a park bench. Accepting life on life's terms is so much easier when you have a partner to share your thoughts and dreams with. Iden and I had all that and more. We were good life buddies until we weren't anymore. Love is a noun as well as a verb. I had love for Iden, even after I could no longer participate in loving him. When his illness took over, the man I used to know was gone and it was no longer possible to continue loving him in the manner I had, and that's when a light went out inside of me. A sense of loneliness set in. The excitement for life and dreams were diminished. We were no longer able to nurture each other's emotional well-being as well as our spiritual growth.

As the wedding plans got under way, I witnessed the excitement and passion that both Lizzy and Joel had to begin their life together as husband and wife. Although this brought me great enjoyment, it also brought me sadness as I remembered being a young woman who had felt the same way about Iden. Every new beginning begins from another beginning's ending, so I had to make peace with a life that I had walked away from, a life that I had lived in for so long.

Lizzy and Joel's wedding plans soon took shape and they had decided on a beautiful venue for the event. It was all very exciting, and it brought me great pleasure to spend time with Lizzy and Joel and to see how they made decisions and respected each other's thoughts.

With all the wedding planning I did not see Stephen as much during the winter and spring months before the wedding. Lizzy was working long hours in her new position as principal and was doing her best to get things done on the weekends for her wedding. We spent about six Saturdays running around to bridal stores trying to find the gown she would say yes to. Although it was stressful, we had a lot of fun trying on many different style gowns. Lizzy has a very simple style of dressing, and we laughed a lot when the salespeople made her try on frilly gowns.

After each outing, we usually went out for a cocktail and a small bite somewhere in the city. Sometimes Joel met us, and I really enjoyed these moments of planning and talking. The separation that I had been feeling between Lizzy and myself was slowly disappearing and we even had a few words about Stephen. Just a simple statement as to what I was doing on the weekend with him and her giving a reply made me take a deep breath and to feel good. Although it wasn't necessary for her to accept my relationship with Stephen, it did make me feel that she could finally see me as a person and not just as her mom.

After several weekends of searching Lizzy found a beautiful gown. The moment she saw it and tried it on, she knew it was made for her. All the wedding planning filled my time during the week and on many weekends, but I managed to find time to head out to New Jersey with Stephen. We were getting along just fine with no mention of moving in or commitment conversations. It felt good just as it was, especially with the upcoming wedding. I looked forward to seeing him each weekend, and we always had a good time together whether doing something or doing nothing at all.

Lizzy and I were checking off the things to do on our list for the wedding and the bridal shower. Lizzy, Claudia and I decided to meet in the city to shop for a new outfit for the bridal shower

Over the past few years I usually spent time with either Claudia or Lizzy separately due to work schedules. Claudia and Lizzy had grown apart over the years mainly due to Claudia's choice of boyfriends and lifestyle, which was always causing problems. Lizzy needed to withdraw from too much contact with her to avoid unneeded confrontations. Claudia's moods always caused me concern. Her behavior was volatile, and I worried sometimes that she may have had inherited Iden's genes for mental illness. She was never down, but she did have a quick temper and was often impulsive in her decision making.

The months flew by quickly and as March rolled around, it was hard to believe that both the bridal shower and the wedding would be soon. Stephen surprised me with a trip to the Bahamas for my birthday. It was only for five days, and I was extremely grateful to get a break from the planning and find some much-needed to time to be with him. We had only been spending a day here and there together and had not had the chance to step away from our lives. Stephen had been working hard on many difficult projects and needed a break as well.

It was still cold in New York, and I had to start going through my closets looking for my summer wear. I had about two weeks to get prepared, so when I told Stephen I was already packing he laughed because he did his packing the night before the vacation.

When we arrived in the Bahamas we were greeted with the warm brilliant sun and the smell of the ocean air. We immediately headed down to the beach for a swim and to just relax. A few hours of lying in the sun was plenty and we returned to our room to shower and take a nap. I sat on the balcony making calls to check in with my family while Stephen was showering. When he was finished, he came out onto the balcony, pushed my hair aside and started kissing me on my neck, using his hands to feel my body slowly before he grabbed my hands and led me to our bed.

The time went by quickly and our stay was soon over. As we headed to the airport, we sat close together hand in hand and no longer felt the distance that was perhaps there before we arrived. The obvious reason was because we were on a relaxing vacation spending every minute together, however, it was more than that. We talked about many things that were easier said in person and not on a short one-day visit. On our early-morning walks we talked about family and our plans for the future in complete honesty.

I've always had trouble saying things that perhaps aren't what people want to hear, but in the long run I did more damage by not speaking the truth. Stephen always let me know his intentions and commitment to our relationship. I wanted to be with him and enjoyed our time together, but I still needed to work some things out and I needed to do that on my own terms, even if they were different than what he may have wanted. These types of conversations usually led to some dismay on his part, but the more we spoke about it the more we realized that we were both grateful for finding each other again and having the relationship that we were currently in.

I needed to heal. I needed to forgive myself for some of the hurt that I was carrying around due to my guilt about things with Iden, and even with my daughters. Through therapy I was discovering that I felt all the years that I had been caretaking Iden I had let my attention on other important matters go by. With forgiveness comes a sense of freedom of letting go of the past. I wanted that very much but needed more time living alone.

My friend Debbie and I spent the few weeks prior to the bridal shower ordering balloons, flowers, and making decorations. Our conversations were like a therapy session that always included talking about my daughters, Iden, and Stephen. She always offered simple solutions or suggestions to some of the complications in my life. She has known me for most of my adult life and seen me at my worst. The transformation I had gone through since being with Stephen was obvious to her, and she reminded me of all the good changes she had witnessed.

I was beginning to repair my life by reconnecting to my daughters and being more open and honest with them about my life and my relationship with Stephen. I was reading many self-help books recommended by Stephen and they were helping. I needed to learn to love my "self" in a way that I had never even thought of before meeting Stephen. I thought my purpose was to serve others regardless of what I thought was good for me. My old self would have folded into Stephen's desire to move in with him, but I was able to understand that that wasn't where I was at in this present time.

The day of the shower arrived, and it was a beautiful warm and sunny day in April. After setting up, and before the guests arrived, Debbie, Claudia and I sat at the large wooden bar and had a glass of champagne given to us by the owner. We listened to Italian music being piped in through the walls. The guests soon arrived, and we were all ready. Lizzy knew of the event, but I could tell when Joel walked her through the door that she was extremely surprised at how lovely it looked and at all who were there. It was a beautiful day, and everything went better than I could have ever expected.

That night I called Stephen and told him how happy I was at how the day had turned out. I wanted to tell him all about it, but by his lack of interest I let it rest. Even though I knew how he felt about Lizzy, I thought his behavior was a bit immature and detached, but I wasn't going to let it ruin my day.

After my call to Stephen I called Iden to inform him about his daughter's day. He was happy to know it all went well, but he was in one of his up moods and started to ramble, so I ended the conversation quickly. I felt like I needed to share the day with someone and there really wasn't anyone available. Everyone I talked to had attended the shower, and Stephen and Iden were not up for the conversation for different reasons. My heart ached for my mom. Every time we went to a party or celebrated a holiday, we would talk about everything and everyone in detail. Perhaps it was just a girl thing, but I was feeling a bit lonely and then Lizzy called.

Lizzy and I spoke for almost an hour going over how beautiful the day was. We talked about the food, the gifts, the people and how they looked, and most of all she expressed how thankful she was for everything I did and how she wished that her Nanny was there. I felt so much better and felt even closer to Lizzy than before. We talked about how proud we were of Claudia and how she gave a sweet toast and was helpful at the shower. I went to bed afterward with a big smile on my face.

The next few months flew by, and the hot weather of June moved in, suddenly replacing the chilly, wet spring days. Lizzy was beyond busy with wrapping up the end of the school year with graduations and other administrative duties, as well as finishing up the last few items to be done for the wedding. Joel and Lizzy were going to Italy for their honeymoon for about two weeks, so she was also busy getting her luggage packed. They had both been to Italy many times, but they were going to places to take cooking lessons in Bologna, Puglia, and Radda in Tuscany. I think they were more excited about their vacation than their upcoming wedding.

The summertime was often a time when Iden experienced an elevated mood shift, and we were all concerned that he might not be at his best for the wedding. My conversations with him a few weeks prior to the wedding always ended in some sort of disagreement over the smallest thing I may have said, so I tried my best to only contact him if necessary. I gave Joel money to buy Iden a new suit, shirt, tie, and shoes for the wedding since he hadn't bought anything new in years.

We needed to stay two nights at almost $350 a night. I tried to explain that we all needed our separate rooms and Iden then started to get nasty saying that I probably wished Stephen was spending the night with me in my room. I was used to such belligerent type of talking over the years so I just let it go.

Lizzy made arrangements for Iden to drive up with Joel and she and I were driving up with Martin and Claudia. She didn't want any arguments happening with me while I was driving and if Iden was in the car that might well have happened. I had stopped smoking and really couldn't handle cigarette smoke in the car. Iden did not always respect those wishes while in someone's car or in their home.

The week before the wedding I made appointments for Claudia and me to get manicures, pedicures, haircuts, and blowouts. Lizzy had made arrangements for makeup and hair to be done the day of the wedding for the bridesmaids and me. Claudia was the maid of honor, and she was busily preparing her speech and practicing it on me when we talked on the phone. I found this to be very endearing and it reminded me of the days when she was little and had to memorize her studies and she would ask me to test her. She was difficult but had a very sweet and loveable side to her as well.

Stephen and I had not been seeing each other every weekend as we had in the past due to the wedding, but we talked every day, and I could tell he had that 'I can't wait until the wedding is over' tone to his voice. Although I didn't expect him to have the enthusiasm that I did, however, it did bother me when he said things like, "I know my daughters will never want an expensive and elaborate wedding like Lizzy." These words were hurtful. I responded by saying, "Well maybe one day when your daughters find someone they want to marry, they might feel differently."

The day before the wedding I had my clothes all packed with rehearsal outfits, wedding-day dress with all the accessories, and something to wear for the morning-after brunch given for all guests who stayed at the hotel. I dropped Mimi off at the sitter and then stopped by my friend Debbie's to chat and have a glass of wine to quell my nerves.

I was feeling nervous about Iden's behavior at the wedding and didn't want my daughter's day to be ruined. She reminded me that my two brothers said that they would handle the situation if something should happen. I just wanted him to make it down the aisle and have the father-daughter dance. After that I didn't care what happened. I always felt better after a talk with Debbie. I headed home and made a few calls before trying to get to bed early since I was picking up Martin and Claudia in the city early the next day.

June 5th was a beautiful summer day and as I loaded up my car, I prayed that the next day would be as beautiful for Lizzy and Joel's wedding. I called Stephen to say good morning and talk before the four-hour trip upstate. We exchanged a few words and he wished me a safe trip and said to call whenever I had a spare moment. Our conversation was brief, and I felt the detachment once again. His voice didn't offer any excitement for me, but he was rather neutral as if we were talking on just an ordinary day. I shook it off and started the engine. I rolled down the windows and let the summer air fill the car and clear my mind to fill it with positive thoughts about my daughter's wedding.

I picked up Claudia and Martin and we made a quick stop at Starbucks for coffee. I downloaded some of Stephen's playlist to listen to on our ride. Stephen has excellent taste in music, and he made a playlist with all my favorite folk, country, rock, blues and R&B artists. We made just one other stop along the way to use the restroom and to call Lizzy to check in to see how her trip was going, and to find out her estimated arrival time. Joel was driving, so she could talk, and she informed me that Iden had fallen asleep the minute they started the car. Iden's sleeping could either indicate that he had been up all night and was crashing, or that he was hung over or both. I was just happy that he was quiet for the car ride so the kids could drive peacefully.

We arrived around 1 o'clock in the afternoon. We checked into our rooms to rest up a bit before grabbing a light lunch until the rehearsal around 5, followed by dinner. Joel's mom had arranged to have the rehearsal dinner at an Italian restaurant nearby. Lizzy texted me that she had arrived and was relaxing and said she would meet up with us around 2 for a drink and a bite on the outside porch. I washed up and changed my clothes and headed downstairs to order a drink and sit on the porch in an Adirondack chair looking out at the lake.

With a drink in my hand and a spectacular view I was feeling relaxed, and my mother-of-the- bride jitters were starting to subside until I heard Iden's voice behind me. He was telling the waiter a joke, but I tried not to react. Lizzy, Joel, and Iden, along with Claudia and Martin, all gathered with me, and we moved to a table to have something small to snack on before heading to the rehearsal, which was at the hotel by the lake. We sat and chatted and Iden could only sit for a little bit before he was on the phone taking photos of us and then making calls to Iran. He was clearly excited and wanted to share his happiness with his family in Iran.

The bridal party soon joined us and before the rehearsal Lizzy and Joel spoke with them to go over some wedding plans. As I watched them, I was so proud of the woman Lizzy had become and her friendships with such fine young men and women. Having close relationships with her friends made me happy that she had a good support system.

The wedding rehearsal went well and then we loaded up in our cars and drove to the restaurant for dinner. Everything was delicious and Iden behaved well. I was a little concerned about having all the carafes of wine on the table, but he didn't touch one. Before dessert was served everyone said a few words to Lizzy and Joel, and then Lizzy and Joel also said some words of thanks to their families.

We headed back to the hotel and Lizzy texted me that we were going to meet in the lobby after we got back. She wasn't going to tell her father because there would be drinks and music, and she wanted to enjoy the night with Joel and her friends. Iden was more than happy to go to his room so he could talk on his phone. I asked him to please not smoke in the room since there was a $250 charge if smoking in the room was detected. Each room had a balcony so I was hoping that he would sneak a smoke outside.

All of us met in the hotel bar where Lizzy and Joel had covered drinks for their guests. There was music playing and a dance floor where some of the wedding party was already dancing. Claudia loved to dance so as soon as she heard a song that had a good beat, she hit the floor with Martin. I loved seeing her so free and happy. I stayed for a short time and then bid them good night as we had an early-morning wake-up call for hair and makeup.

I called Debbie, as she was arriving the day of the wedding and I missed having her with me tonight. She immediately asked how Iden was behaving. When I informed her that all was going pretty well, she sighed with relief. We talked for a while and then I needed to get to bed. It had been a long day and the following day was going to be a long and emotional one as well. I took a hot shower and went to bed and thought of Mom who I knew would have loved to be here for Lizzy's wedding. I missed her. Although I was excited and a bit anxious, I soon fell asleep.

Around 5 in the morning I awoke and could no longer sleep. The hotel provided a coffee machine, so I made a cup and took it out to sit and look out over the lake. I closed my eyes trying to visualize the wedding and making positive affirmations for a beautiful day.

It was a perfect wedding day with blue skies and warm temperatures. Since I was up so early, I had a few hours before I had to be in hair and makeup, so I decided to take a walk. Cooperstown is a lovely small town, and while I walked down the tree-lined streets with gardens filled with flowers and houses with front porches it all made me miss my house and my garden I once had.

Every block I walked down was impeccably clean and I started to wonder if I could ever live in a small town such as this. There is a certain time in everyone's life that we start thinking about the next phase of life. I never wanted to live too far from my girls, and I know Stephen feels the same way about his children, but sometimes I think I would like a change from city life.

When I arrived back at the hotel after my walk Lizzy was the only one in the lobby. I gave her a big hug and a kiss, and the embrace lingered for a few minutes. She asked where I had gone, and I told her I took a morning walk and she smiled because she knows that it is something I always do to steady my nerves. We sat and talked while we waited for the other girls to arrive. As soon as we were all assembled, we went downstairs to the room Lizzy had reserved for our breakfast, and our hair and makeup session.

The room had been prepared with a table of breakfast items. We had a toast with a mimosa and filled our plates before we started the beautifying process. After breakfast, Lizzy presented her bridesmaids and her mother-in-law and me with a card and a gift. We all received a necklace from Tiffany's along with a heartfelt message of love and appreciation from sharing this most important day.

With hair and makeup complete, all that was needed to do was to get dressed. We returned to our rooms and had to meet back shortly for photos. When we all gathered in Lizzy's room, and I immediately started to cry when I saw her in her wedding dress. Claudia also looked so beautiful and had arrived earlier to help Lizzy into her dress.

We took many photos and as we were taking the photos outside by the lake the sky was starting to get ominously darker. The wedding director said that a room would be set up inside in case there is a passing thunderstorm at the time of the ceremony, which was an hour or so away.

Surprisingly enough, Lizzy seemed to be calm and said she had seen the room where the ceremony might happen in case of rain. It was beautifully decorated, and she was just fine with whatever needed to happen. I also felt the same, although I knew she would prefer the ceremony to be performed by the lake.

The wedding planner moved the ceremony inside since the storm was heading our way soon. We waited for a little bit and then got into format to walk into the room with me leading the line, and the rest of the wedding party to follow. I saw Iden, and with his new suit and hair cut he looked handsome, and he looked like the proud papa with his daughter on his arm. My heart felt a slight tug and I had to hold back tears that I knew would start flowing soon. The music started and I was signaled to start walking into the room. All my family and friends were standing, and I smiled back to them keeping the tears at bay. Joel stood up front and he was beaming. We looked at each other and gave each other a wink, and then Lizzy and her dad walked in. My tears could no longer be contained. I was watching Joel and when he saw her, I could see his eyes watering as well.

Iden and I were seated next to each other and when he first sat down, he grabbed my hand tightly Expressing how much he loved Lizzy while holding back his tears. Joel's grandfather, who was a minister, performed the ceremony. After shedding a few tears, I was able to control myself, but when I heard Lizzy and Joel exchange their wedding vows, I could no longer hold them back. Their words of a life together expressed a promise to love, to understand, to respect each other in all circumstances that may arise.

As soon as the ceremony was over the rain and thunder stopped and sunbeams came shining in on Lizzy and Joel just as they took their first kiss as husband and wife. Everyone applauded and cheered as we proceeded to the cocktail hour and a photo session. I now had a married daughter!

All of the guests were seated at the reception and the wedding party were introduced and seated. Iden was very talkative, but it was an emotional day, and he was holding it together thus far. Lizzy and Joel's wedding song "Shelter From the Storm," started to play, and they took to the dance floor. Iden was up next for his dance with Lizzy. The music started to play and Iden joined Lizzy on the dance floor. They danced for a few minutes and then he returned to the table. We all applauded his dance, and I could tell he felt very proud and understandably so.

Claudia's speech went over big since it was so sincere and had some humor in it as well. Joel's brother also gave a very entertaining speech. Iden was getting a bit agitated and seemed like he needed a break, so Ron escorted him out for a walk so he could have a smoke and take a breather. I told my brother that if he didn't return it was fine since all that was left was just the cutting of the cake.

With Iden gone I felt a bit more relaxed. Claudia was having a ball dancing, and she was getting everyone up on the floor, and dancing with many guests and with Martin. It was good to see her having such a good time. I was tired since I had been up before dawn and also because of the emotional day.

Ron returned alone and said Iden wanted to stay in his room. He needed to call it a night because he was very tired. Lizzy and Joel had arranged an after-wedding party with a dee jay and some finger foods and drinks in the hotel. Although I was tired, I still wanted to make an appearance. We all retired to our rooms to change into more comfortable clothes and shoes before heading into the party. I hadn't had a chance to talk to Stephen, and I didn't even have my phone on me to take any photos.

When I was finally alone for a minute, I called him. When I called, he asked, "How did it go"? I said we'd had a lovely day and when I started to talk about the day, he said that we would talk about it when we got home. He just wanted to know how Iden behaved, how the weather held out, and if I was doing okay. I answered all of his questions, but my heart was full of many emotions, and I wanted to unload, but I felt the conversation was already finished.

Before we hung up, Stephen proceeded to talk about his day, and I said I needed to go and that we could talk later. In my mind, I wondered if he actually needed to tell me about what he was doing. It was one of the most important days in my life and I didn't want any unpleasant thoughts to take away all the happiness I was feeling. I took off my dress and when I laid it on the bed I wondered if I would ever wear it again, although I really loved it. Claudia and Martin came to room before heading to the party. I told her how proud I was of her and how wonderful her speech went, then we went downstairs to continue the festivities.

The music was playing and some of the guests were already there. Lizzy and Joel had changed into comfortable clothes and were looking for something to eat because they said they didn't have a chance to eat at the reception, which was a shame since the food was absolutely wonderful. Lizzy informed me that Iden wasn't coming down to the party because he was tired, which I was happy to hear knowing he was in for the night.

Since I had eaten well at the wedding, including the cake, I was still full and had no room even for a drink, so I just got a Diet Coke and hung out for a short time. When my friend Debbie and her husband showed up, I went to talk to them, and they commented on how beautiful everything was. I walked around and talked to a few of Lizzy's and Joel's friends whom I didn't have a chance to talk to during the wedding, and then decided to head back to my room since it was now almost 11 o'clock, and my eyes were heavy.

I stopped by Iden's room just to check in on him. When I approached his door, I could smell cigarette smoke and I immediately felt annoyed. I knocked on the door and when he answered he had a cigarette in his hand. I reminded him that there was a no-smoking rule in the hotel and that there was a $250 penalty. He said some unkind words to me, so I walked away. I should have been grateful he was in his room and not drinking, and that perhaps it was worth the $250.

I showered and sat by the window where I had started my day. As I looked out into the darkness I relived the day in my mind, knowing in my heart that Lizzy and Joel would have a blessed marriage. The future was uncertain, but I felt that they would grow old together regardless of the bumps along the way. I checked my messages from friends and family members who couldn't make it to the wedding. I also checked my Facebook and saw that Claudia had already posted photos from the wedding. I sent her a message to send me the photos so I could also post some and send some to Stephen. I knew he would be asleep already but wanted him to see some wedding photos. I lay staring out at the moon before drifting off to a peaceful sleep.

We all met for breakfast in the hotel by 9 o'clock, but when I arrived only Joel's mother, Mark and his wife, and a few other guests were up. I was guessing the wedding party stayed up a bit late and had a bit too many drinks, so I wasn't counting on seeing them anytime soon. Since it was such a beautiful morning, I took my coffee out onto the porch enjoying the view one last time before heading home. We went upstairs to pack and then I headed down to the front desk to pay my bill for the three rooms. When the concierge gave me the bill, I noticed the $250 charge for smoking in the room, and it pissed me off. I didn't say anything, but once again it was Iden doing what Iden felt he needed to do

Finally, ready to hit the road, we said our goodbyes and loaded up the cars. Iden was the last to come down and have breakfast, so Lizzy went to hurry him along. Martin and Claudia had been up late, so they were happy to sleep in the back seat for our drive home to the city. I found a chill-out playlist on Spotify for our drive back to New York City. With the wedding over, much of my time would be free and I started to think about my life in a different way than ever before.

Patricia and Lizzy on Lizzy's wedding day ©2019

CHAPTER TWENTY-THREE

SICILY

"Leap of Faith –yes, but only after reflection."

— SOREN KIERKEGAARD

As with all big, life-changing events, the days immediately following Lizzy's wedding had an anticlimactic effect. I had enjoyed all the months planning with Lizzy because with all the years that she had spent away at college followed by moving to Boston to work, I hadn't had the opportunity to spend much time with her and I missed her. During all the months leading up to the wedding, we had enjoyed our time together and I felt that it brought us closer. Lizzy and Joel were off in Italy on their honeymoon, and they called to inform me that they had arrived safely, and all was well.

I needed to find a new focus in my life, something to direct my energy toward now that the wedding was over. I was also retired, and I was trying very hard to not be so involved in the day-to- day activities of both Iden and Claudia. Stephen mentioned perhaps I could stay with him for a week or so to relax by the pool and visit with some friends I had made in Metuchen, which I had not seen recently since I had been busy with the wedding. I thought it was a good idea, but I wanted some time at home just putting on the brakes and allowing myself to not have an agenda or a to-do list. I decided to take a week after the wedding at home and then told Stephen I would come out to his place for a week or so. He was

287

very happy with the news, and he decided to take a few days off from work.

The summer of July 2019 turned out to be a very hot and humid one, so getting out of the city and going to the New Jersey suburbs with large tree- filled parks, beaches, and swimming pools nearby, and moving at a slower pace were all very welcoming. Before leaving, I checked in with Iden to see how he was getting along. He seemed to still be in an elevated mood after the wedding, and after a few minutes of conversation I said goodbye because it was escalating into something I didn't want to have to deal with before leaving.

I had also seen Claudia the day before I was due to leave and asked if she would like to come out for a weekend visit. Stephen often suggested that Claudia should come and spend a day with us. I already had some clothes at Stephen's, so I just packed a few outfits, bathing suits, and things I needed for Mimi and was ready to go.

Stephen picked me up in Queens at 7 o'clock in the morning. He liked to start the day early and not get stuck in any summer weekend travel. He was always on time and not even a minute late, so I waited out front. I loved his sense of responsibility. There was always music playing in the car as Stephen greeted Mimi and me with welcoming kisses and hellos. Even though I was just going to New Jersey it was a good feeling to take a break from the everyday routine, and I was also excited to spend uninterrupted time with Stephen. We always had so much to say, so we talked the whole hour to New Jersey about everything and nothing in particular.

Stephen was happy to have me stay with him and said many times how thankful he was that we would be together for a whole week. He was planning to work Monday through Wednesday and take off the rest of the week. We thought we would go to the beach before the weekend to avoid the crowds.

Stephen always had something exciting planned to do, and I appreciated the effort he made to make my stay filled with fun activities. We also enjoyed just staying in and doing the things we liked to do. Stephen was always working on a new painting, writing a new song, or reading a good book. I liked to cook, and since there was a Whole Foods just a few blocks from his apartment complex, I ventured out to walk the aisles looking for ideas for dinner. In Queens we didn't have a Whole Foods, so for me it was like being in a candy store. I liked to go by myself because I enjoyed my time strolling through the aisles, whereas Stephen not being a cook, wanted to go in and out and get it over and done with. It was good that we managed to do things both separately and together that we liked.

We spent a lovely week together and for the first time in a very long time I didn't have the aching need to be at home. I wasn't sure if it was due to the fact that my family was more settled, but I did feel a greater sense of peace than I had in a long time. After returning home I even felt a bit lonely.

I turned to my writing since I felt that it was a source of company for me and an opportunity to truly express all that I was feeling. I decided to pull out some chapters of a book that I had started because I felt an aching desire to get my feelings and thoughts down about everything that I had been going through over the past few years.

Without working I needed to develop a daily routine. All my years of being both a teacher and a mother kept me on a strict routine. Although I didn't need to still have such a rigid daily routine, I personally do better having one. I was always an early riser so that was easy to keep, along with my morning coffee and a long walk with Mimi. I no longer needed to go to the gym at night so taking early gym classes was working out fine and it gave me an opportunity to see Debbie and other gym buddies as well.

My afternoon routine was something I now needed to work on, so after a light lunch, I decided to start to write and would try to write for at least two hours a day. After the writing session there would be more dog walks, and calls to family, making dinner and my daily talk with Stephen after his dinner and *Jeopardy*. He loved to watch *Jeopardy!*

At night, after the last walk with Mimi, I liked to read or sometimes do a little binge-watching of a Netflix series to wind down my day before going to sleep. My routine was starting to take shape and in between I had days where I didn't go to the gym or write, I would fill it in with some other activities like shopping, or going into the city to visit a museum, or have lunch with a friend.

With a change in seasons on the way, I thought perhaps I might want to find a part-time job since outdoor activity would be more limited and I wasn't ready to be that retired. I was still young and had a lot of energy, so I started to think about getting a part-time job. I just wanted to do something that allowed me to be of service to people in a creative and non-stressful environment. My daughters thought that maybe I should find a job in a gym or something in a gourmet food store since I love to work out and cook. I passed along the thought of working with Stephen and he wasn't a big fan of the idea. I think now in retrospect it wasn't because he didn't want me to work, but rather knowing that if I found a job in Queens it would limit our time together, and even lessen the possibility of my moving to New Jersey with him.

The summer months were at an end and the bright and hot days were now replaced with cooler temperatures, along with magnificent autumn sunsets. Lizzy had a wonderful honeymoon and was back at work. And Iden was coming down from his mania and would soon enter his long months of depression. Claudia had some relationship issues with Martin, but things seemed to be in a better place, and they had just recently moved to Forest Hills, not far from my apartment. Although I was happy she had moved out of where she was living because she had mentioned that there were some unpleasant things going on, I was a bit concerned about her proximity to me. I loved knowing she was in a safer place and knowing I could perhaps see her more often, but I didn't want to be involved in her personal affairs on a daily basis.

Stephen was working very hard with many new projects, and we rarely saw each other during the week. I was able to keep pretty much to my new routine and was nicely adjusting to my retired life.

One morning as I was walking to the gym, I saw a sign for employment opportunities in a new gym that was soon to open. I took a photo of the information posted on the sign. After my gym workout, I went for coffee with Debbie, and I mentioned the idea of applying for a position at the new gym. She thought it was a good idea so when I got home, I applied online.

I didn't have a resume, so I just wrote a letter outlining my work experience as a teacher, and my personal philosophy about health and fitness and why I thought I would be a good fit for the job. I incorporated my knowledge of the neighborhood and my ability to interact and understand people in my age group. I received a request for an interview the next day and was pleasantly surprised by the quick response. I met the young owner of the gym in a vegan coffee shop on Austin Street a few days after, and immediately had a good connection with her. She asked if I could take a few classes with her at one of the other gyms in Brooklyn to see how I liked the environment. And she was also interested in my thoughts on the workout. The new gym owner picked me up the next day and we talked the whole time we were driving to Brooklyn. The class was an amazing workout and I noticed that there wasn't anyone near my age group in the gym. The trainer was amazed that I'd kept up so well and the gym owner offered me the job. I only wanted to work part time and preferably morning hours and she said that would be excellent since the gym was going to be open from 5 o'clock every morning. The training for the job was going start in about a week or so and the gym was planning to open in October.

I immediately called Lizzy and she said that it was a great opportunity and that she was happy for me. I called Stephen too, but he was at work and couldn't talk saying that he would call me later after he got home. I wanted the job but had to think about how many hours and if the schedule would be a good fit. I didn't want it to become stressful. Stephen later called me, and we chatted for a while, and I told him about my job offer. As I expected, he didn't seem as thrilled as I was with the opportunity. Although he did make some good points about not having had any downtime since retiring and asked if I really wanted to have such early wake-up calls again. Although it wasn't discussed, I felt that perhaps it meant that I would not be as free as I would be if I were not working, which would tie me even more to living in Forest Hills.

After giving it some thought I decided not to take the job. I'm not sure if it was Stephen's influence on my decision, or perhaps allowing myself to just have some time without working or planning any big events. As with most of us when we retire, it may seem difficult to slow down and carve out a new agenda that allows us to feel productive. I had always wanted to take Italian lessons so I started to make a wish list and got started doing the things I could now do since I was retired. I signed up for Italian lessons, and instead of hitting the gym five times a week, I decided to take some yoga classes twice a week along with guided meditation sessions after each one.

On my wish list were cooking lessons, visiting museums, spending more time with friends, and the one thing that I had been procrastinating doing was to do more writing, specifically to write my story. The writing was perhaps not even to share, but it was a burning desire to get what I was feeling out of me and onto paper. I once read about creativity, saying It doesn't matter what we create, but if we have that desire and need to create something from that internal source, then we need to put it into the world, or it will leave us and inhibit another person.

I got busy going into the village for language lessons every Wednesday, and usually after class I would walk around looking in stores and picking up something from a market or a bakery. After a few weeks of classes, I had made a few friends and we would go out for coffee and talk for a while before we headed home. Most of the people in the class were retired, so we had the time to take it slow. They were interesting people, and it was nice listening to their stories and learning about their lives.

I looked forward to my classes and even enjoyed doing the homework. My days now included a mix of gym and yoga classes, taking Mimi on nice long walks now that the summer heat was slowly leaving, and trying to write for at least two hours a day. I also started watching YouTube videos to get ideas for trying new recipes. In between my activities, I was seeing friends and my daughters, and every now and then I would grab a coffee with Iden. I was slowly finding a new rhythm to my life and a heaviness that I had carried around with me for so long was lifting. Stephen and I saw each other on the weekends and sometimes we would meet in the city for dinner during the week.

One day in mid-September, Stephen called me in the early morning and asked if we could meet up that night for dinner. I hadn't seen him the previous week and he said he was missing me. Although I am not a spontaneous person, I was also missing him and was excited to see him, so I agreed. We met at an Italian restaurant located downtown on Gold Street. It was a lovely early fall night and we decided to eat outside. We ordered some of our favorite meals, and while we sat eating, Stephen talked about his job and that he had some good news. He had just finished a very difficult renovation of Saks Fifth Avenue in New York City and was in need of taking a vacation. He asked if I would like to go to Sicily for an early-autumn vacation. We had often talked about going to Sicily and the thought of actually going there was beyond exciting. I immediately said yes, and then the planner that I am had a hundred things running through my mind. I took a sip of my wine and happily inhaled my delicious pasta dish.

By the time we got to dessert, Stephen said to let him know since he wanted to book the trip soon, and to be ready to leave by the end of September early October. I really wanted to go but needed to figure some things out and would definitely let him know within a day. He looked at me and said, "If you want to go that's all that matters. Your family will be just fine." I looked right into his eyes and knew that he was right, but I wanted to share this with my family and take it from there. It wasn't easy for me to make a decision based on my own desires at this present moment in my life, but I was making strides in doing what was best for me.

When I got home, I took Mimi for a walk and thought about what Stephen had just offered me; an all-expenses-paid vacation to Sicily, leaving in a few weeks. My first thought was how to tell Lizzy. She had accepted by now that Stephen wasn't going away, and that her father and I were clearly living separate lives, however, it was difficult for her to share in the joys that I have with him. I decided to think about it, and to talk to Lizzy and the rest of my family in the morning before giving Stephen my answer. That night I took out my laptop and started to gather information, and to look at photos of Sicily. It looked divine. I had always wanted to visit the birthplace of my father's family. I stayed up late that night and went to sleep with the blue Mediterranean Sea on my mind.

I arose early the next morning and after my morning coffee and walk with Mimi, I called Lizzy and informed her about Stephen's offer to go to Sicily. Since Lizzy and Joel had been there, she said it was her favorite place she had visited and encouraged me to go. She also said that she would be around since it was the beginning of the school year and had no travel plans. I was surprised at her response and then I called Claudia to inform her as well. Claudia was happy for me, but then immediately the conversation switched to her problems. I held off on making my decision until I sat for a bit with the idea of it before calling Stephen with my answer. I spoke to my friend Debbie, and she said, "There shouldn't be any hesitation unless you just don't want to go with him, and I presume you do, so just do it!" I wish I could be more like her at times, very pragmatic. I called Stephen and said, "*Andiamo in Sicilia!*"

We bought tickets on Alitalia leaving for Palermo on Oct 1st and returning to NY on Oct 10th. With just a few weeks to plan an itinerary, Stephen and I got busy booking hotels and finding interesting places and things to do for our 10-day trip to Sicily. Since Lizzy had been there with Joel, she gave me a guidebook plus some of her recommendations of places and things to see and do. The few weeks leading up to our trip, Stephen and I had not seen each other because he was very busy at work, and he wanted to have everything in a good place before leaving on vacation.

The seasons were changing in New York City, but it was still hot in Sicily, so I packed some summer clothes along with a few light sweaters and a jacket as well. I knew we would be doing a lot of walking, so I bought a new pair of sneakers. The flight was over nine hours, so I also prepared to wear comfortable clothes and shoes and also take along some good reading material. I didn't want to carry too much so I had to leave my laptop home, therefore my writing would need to be done with pen and paper.

As each day passed and it grew closer to departure time, I remained remarkably calm, which surprised me. In the past whenever I went anywhere, even for a day, I would be a bit jittery, but I was managing to keep the anxiety at bay. The only thing that worried me was leaving my sweet Mimi for almost 12 days with my sitter. She was getting old and since I had retired, she really cherished all the long walks, extra treats, and playtime given to her. Dogs have an uncanny feeling of knowing when something is different, and when Mimi would see me packing, she pouted a bit, and I believe she knew what that meant.

I made hair and nail appointments and went to see my daughters for dinner before leaving. I hadn't seen Iden in several weeks, so I called him asking if he wanted to meet for coffee. He was in an elevated mood, although not agitated. He agreed to meet me the next day at an Italian bakery at 11 o'clock. I asked him to call me if he would be late or decided not to come. I was always early, so I ordered a coffee and waited for him. By 11:30 he had not shown up, so I called. When he answered the phone, he seemed a bit frazzled and said he was on the other line and just hung up on me.

I sat for a while and had another coffee and a small pastry, thinking Iden might call back and say he was on his way, but he never did. I didn't want my daughters to have to deal with his problems alone. Many may wonder why I stayed connected, to care for and communicate with Iden regularly. Even I don't really know why, but perhaps it is because I still love him. Ron once said to me that love is a state of being, and not a condition based on anything. Iden and I were no longer married, but we had a long history together filled with much happiness. He was and still is a good man, but he's not well, and is not capable of sustaining a life with someone, or at least not with me.

I waited to hear from Iden, but he never called so I tried calling him back. I wanted to personally tell him I was leaving the following day for Sicily and when I would be back in New York.

This time he picked up and we talked for a bit before he got a bit agitated saying that he had not been on a vacation and I had been on so many. It was hard to stop him once he began his narration of all that was horrible with his life, with the world, and, of course, with me. I tried to calm him down and to end the call, though not in a bad way, especially since I would be gone for 10 days. I needed to have things in a good place for myself before leaving.

The following day, Stephen came and met me in Queens instead of at the airport. Our flight departed at 8 o'clock at night, so we decided to go out for a relaxing lunch in Forest Hills and leave for the airport around 5 o'clock. We both liked having a stress-free check-in, so the extra time allowed us to do that. I am a big people-watcher, so I enjoyed sitting in the waiting area at the airport to watch all the travelers going by. We bought some coffee after we were checked in, and while I did my people- watching, Stephen pulled out a book and did some reading.

We had about an hour to wait, which went by quickly and we soon boarded the plane. Takeoffs always gave me the jitters and Stephen knew that, so once we settled into our seats, he grabbed my hand and said, "I got you babe!"!

I loved that secure feeling he gave me and often wondered why I needed that so much from a man, but I did. Once up in the air we settled into a routine of talking, reading, writing, and taking breaks when food was being served, although both of us rarely eat the meals that the airlines provide.

We couldn't wait to disembark after being on the plane for almost 10 hours. We had arranged to have a car service waiting for us at the Palermo airport to take us to our hotel. It was around 1 o'clock in the afternoon when we arrived at our hotel and although we very excited to walk around Palermo, we both needed a shower, some food, and a nap. We showered quickly and went out and found a cafe to pick up some sandwiches. We took them back to our room and sat outside on the balcony to enjoy them in the summerlike temperatures still lingering in Sicily.

We made some coffee with the machine provided in our hotel room and then we took a nap. Darkness had set in when we awoke.

It was around 7:30. We had slept for almost four hours, but we really needed it, and now felt ready to take a walk and find a place to have our first real meal in Sicily.

Walking through the streets of Palermo was a food feast. There were small restaurants and booths selling everything from roasted chestnuts to gelato. As well as food markets, there was music playing and sellers' tables set up with handcrafted jewelry, paintings, and many touristy items. It was a sensory overload indeed to taste and smell all the delicious foods and to hear Italian music while walking under the bright lights hung up in arches over the streets.

We didn't want dinner to be anything too complicated because even though we had rested, we were stilling feeling a bit off after the long flight and the time change, so we decided to just find a place to eat a nice Sicilian pie. Nestled among so many larger restaurants, we found a quaint little one with just a few tables and a very small wooden bar. There were candles lit on the tables, with fresh flowers on white tablecloths. The waiter approached us and greeted us with a large smile and said, "*Buonasera!*"

I replied with, "*Buonasera, una tavola per due, per favore.*"

I was impressed with my ability to respond without hesitation. We ordered a pie with fried artichokes and red onions, and I ordered a glass of red wine. While we waited the waiter brought some olives, nuts and panne frito (fried bread).

Our table looked out onto the street, so while we waited for our meal and nibbled what the waiter had brought us, we watched the people strolling by. We were very amused when we discovered that the waiter who took our order had to run across the street to place the order because that's where the food was prepared. The restaurant that we were in was so small that there was no space for a kitchen.

The pies in Italy are small and it was just the perfect size for us. When the waiter came to us with the pie it was almost too beautiful to eat, looking like a little wrapped present. Stephen automatically took a photo of me eating it. It was wonderful having him recording all our experiences with his artistic eye. We stopped at a pastry shop and picked up mini pistachio-filled cannoli and ate them as we walked back to our hotel. After our long day we were happy to sleep and to get ready for our first full day in Palermo.

We spent three days in Palermo walking the streets and observing this beautiful old city with its incredible mix of architectural styles. It was fascinating just walking around observing all the sites. I loved looking at the people and how they were dressed, and listening to the Sicilian language being spoken, which brought back memories of being in my paternal grandparents' home enjoying a family Sunday feast.

Almost every street had statues and fountains and all the buildings had balconies with laundry hanging to be dried. On one of our night walks we stumbled upon La Vucciria, which loosely translated means "voices." It is an outdoor market sectioned off with little booths and tables selling small Sicilian plates of food. All the food was about $5, the wine was about $1 to $2 for a small carafe. We ate some pasta with clams and shared scacce (focaccia-like stuffed bread) and for dessert we had some cucidati (fig cookies) with espresso.

We really enjoyed our time in Palermo and trying some of the delicious food. Thankfully, we walked almost 25,000 steps a day so we would not put on 25 pounds by the end of our 10-day stay.

After leaving Palermo, we made our way to Monreale and visited the Norman Cathedral, famous for its 12th-century Byzantine mosaics.

On our way to Agrigento we visited mountaintop Erice. Erice is a wonderfully preserved medieval town with breathtaking views and a great historical presence. We had lunch on a local farm that served the local delicacies and wine. All the walking up and down the mountain was a plus!

Next, we headed to Cefalu before heading south to Agrigento to visit the area's most celebrated site.

Cefulu is an ancient fishing port but has now become a beachside resort for those seeking sun and sand along the Tyrrhenian coast of Sicily. The wheaten rock-filled sand with its many colorful umbrellas is truly a welcoming site to put down a blanket and simply live the dolce vita for a short time.

We visited the spectacular *duomo* (church) that was a vision of gold and beautiful mosaics. We ended our day by having dinner with a beautiful view of the sea and mountains in an outdoor restaurant, where once again the tables were on one side of the street and the kitchen was on the other side of the street.

After dinner we walked along the road to help digest our meal, while taking in the beauty all around us. We stayed in a small hotel overlooking the sea and went to sleep feeling very content in each other's arms. Before I closed my eyes, I could hardly believe that I had not talked to my family in a few days, yet I was feeling okay with it.

The next day we headed to Agrigento and after breakfast, I decided to check in with everyone back home. I tried to figure out the time difference and knew Lizzy would be finished at work around four o'clock U.S. time, so I called around 9 o'clock at night Italy time. She was happy to hear from me and said that all was going well, and she was happy to hear that I was having such a good time. I asked about Claudia and Iden and she said Claudia was busy working and that Iden was doing okay.

I could tell she sounded a bit hesitant when she was talking about Iden, so I asked again, and she said he was in a very elevated mood. She was staying in touch with him and told me not to worry. After our call I felt myself being transported back to Queens and wondering what was going on with Iden.

I stayed there for a few minutes before Stephen jolted me from my thoughts, saying we needed to get on the bus to Agrigento. The weather was unusually warm and after walking around for a few hours in the heat and viewing the temples we took a break for a light lunch before heading to Giardini Naxos. This city is situated in the city of Messina that is a seaside resort and sits below the stunning mountainside of Taormina.

We spent the next day at the beachside resort simply lazing on the beach and eating delicious food. After a day on the beach we headed to Taormina. There is a song that Stephen loves called

"Lights of Taormina" by Mark Knoffler and my daughter Lizzy got engaged in Taormina, so I was so excited to tour the streets and take in all the beauty I had heard about.

We found a bus that took us from Giardini Naxos to Taormina, which is about 1¼ miles. Although Taormina is a touristy town, we both loved everything it offered. The streets were lined with beautiful stores, and we found so many new treats that we fell in love with. After breakfast we did some shopping and then headed to the beaches on the *funivia* (cable cars). Even though it was the first few days of October, the temperatures were still very hot, and it was exciting to be able to swim in the bay and cool off.

A young man helped us obtain beach chairs and set up a beach umbrella and then asked if we wanted anything to eat or drink. We sat by the bay taking in the warm October sun before we took a few dips in the bay. We stayed for a while and then took the cable car back up to Taormina and did some more walking, site seeing, and shopping.

As we walked around the street, we found something called granita. Granita is a semi-frozen dessert made from sugar, water and various flavorings. It is originally from Sicily and related to sorbet, however, in Sicily it has a creamier and smoother texture. After spending hours at the beach and walking for hours in the summerlike heat it was a welcome treat. We couldn't believe how delicious it was and with each and every bite we commented on its divine taste.

After our granita experience, we took a walk out of town and found a quiet road that lead to a beautiful scenic view of the bay and mountains. We also found a mountain trail with over a hundred steps that lead down to a rocky beach. I was very excited to take a swim with no one else around under the hot Mediterranean sun.

Although I had changed out of my bathing suit I immediately stripped down to my undergarments and plunged into the bay. We lay on the rocky beach for a little bit to dry off before we headed back up the hundred steps to the main road. We walked around for another two hours before we realized how hungry we were and found a restaurant to eat dinner.

I wanted to bring my girls back something special from Sicily, so I found a perfume store and bought my daughters and myself a bottle of a special fragrance unique to Sicily. Stephen also picked up some items to take back to his children.

Before we got on the bus back to our hotel, we decided to grab some pastries and espresso. The cannoli were freshly baked and filled, and they were the best I had ever tasted.

With our bellies full and the sun setting we rode the bus back to our hotel. It was truly a beautiful day. Our next stop was Syracuse, located on the Ionian coast of Sicily. It is a city known for its ancient ruins. We had booked a tour for the day but decided to forgo the tour and stay at the hotel for our last day in Sicily and just relax on the beach and walk around Giardini Naxos.

Our hotel was beautiful with a pool and a view of the Ionian Sea. We had breakfast in the hotel and then took a walk through the town before heading to the beach. We spent time on the beach and then headed to our room for a midafternoon nap and some lovemaking. Our last night in Sicily we both decided to get dressed up to have dinner. I asked the hotel concierge for a good restaurant recommendation in town, and he suggested a place located right on the sea. It was dark already and the restaurant was illuminated with candles and millions of stars shone above us as we sat outside on the terrace overlooking the sea.

It was a perfect evening to end what was a perfect vacation, and then Stephen asked me once again if I was ready to move in with him. He said he loved spending time with me and felt his best when he was with me. We had been dating for several years by now and he wanted this move more than ever. He reached over to take my hands in his and said that he would never disappoint me or hurt me and would always take care of me. I believed every word he said, and I felt so happy when I was with him, but I still wasn't sure if I could take that leap just now. I looked into his eyes and said I believed all he had said and asked if I could I get back to New York and think some things through before committing to the suggested move. He said he wasn't expecting me to move right away but wanted to throw out the idea once again and if we could talk about it more when we got home. We finished our dinner and headed home holding hands, relaxed and happy.

We had an early flight back to New York the following day, so we packed our suitcases in silence after getting back to the hotel. I felt the question he asked me would hover over us like a hot summer sun with no relief until I was able to give an answer. Stephen caught up on some work emails and I looked at some Italian magazines trying to translate as I read.

When I awoke the next day, Stephen was already up and had gone out. I found a note saying that he had gone out for a run and would be back by 6:30 to have breakfast with me. It was around 5:30, so I showered and dressed and finished packing before he returned. We had to be at the airport by 9 for an 11 o'clock flight. Stephen returned at exactly 6:30 and in a good mood. He quickly showered and had already finished packing before his run, so we went down for a quick breakfast before heading to the airport.

We got through customs and security at the airport, and I still had some euros left so I did a little last minute shopping, even though I knew everything was overpriced and unnecessary, but it was still fun.

We boarded the plane with happy memories of our time in Sicily and a question that still needed to be answered soon after landing.

Patricia and Stephen 2019 ©

CHAPTER TWENTY-FOUR

PROMISES

'Fear motivates us. Sometimes it motivates us towards what we want, but sometimes, if we aren't careful, it limits us with what we think will keep us safe."

—JAY SHETTY

As I unpacked my bags and sorted my clothes, I thought about our Sicilian trip with each piece of clothing that I either put into the wash, placed on hangers in my closet, or tucked into a drawer. Wouldn't it be great to sort out life's problems so clean and neatly in an hour or so? I had such an amazing time in Sicily with Stephen, but now with the question that he had proposed it seemed to replace all that joy with anxiety.

Although Stephen and I had been getting along well over the past year, I still wasn't sure if I was ready to move in with him. I needed to really dig deep and figure out my fears were, or if it was something that I wasn't even aware of? Perhaps I didn't really want to confront them. My fears were many, and although I knew that they were mostly unrealistic, they kept me in a safe place, which perhaps was not always the best place.

I knew that living near Claudia did not make her act differently because case in point, when she lived in the city with Martin, she'd had the same issues. I felt that her living near me gave us an opportunity to meet for a coffee or have her and Martin come by for dinner. Having some meetups allowed me talk to her and get into her head to see how she was really doing, which was difficult to do on the phone.

My role as a mother was and always will be at the core of who I am. I need to be connected to my daughters and moving to New Jersey, although not far, made me feel a bit like I might lose that connection. I would once again be trying to fit into someone else's life. Stephen on the other hand would still have his friends and children close by, his open mikes to play music, his neighborhood, and much more.

The funny thing is when I asked Stephen if he ever thought of moving to Forest Hills, he said he would never move there. That response always bothered me because it was as if he was saying I want you to live with me on my terms and conditions. When I was younger, I often thought of what it might be like to move to a quieter town after I retired, but that was when I was still married to Iden and had envisioned a different life.

I was just beginning to find myself again. Although I don't think I was ever lost, but I had just lost a sense of peace and the joy of living. I felt over the past year that I was finding the ability to slow down and appreciate my life with all its complications. I was also diving into my writing that allowed me to revisit my past and get in touch with many feelings that I had stored away. I wasn't so sure that I could continue on this path at this point in my life if I moved in with Stephen.

As much as I enjoyed spending time with Stephen, his life seemed to take priority over mine and I often mentioned this to him when we talked about living together. He explained that if we lived together things would be different because I currently just saw him on the weekends. We spent all our time doing everything together. If we lived together, we would have our time together and alone time too for sure, especially since he left for work at 5:30 in the morning and returned home at 5:30 in the evening. I often thought about the fear I had of not growing old with someone to enjoy that beautiful feeling that comes from a committed relationship of living together.

Stephen was good for me. He pushed me to be the best I could be, and I believed he loved me very much. So what was holding me back?

The weeks went by, and Stephen did not bring up the issue again. Many times when I was with him in New Jersey, he alluded to my moving in by reminding me how convenient it was to just walk across the street to go shopping at Whole Foods, to take a walk, run, or a bike ride on a beautiful Greenway Trail, to sit in many of the coffee shops and listen to music to write or read and many other nice things about Metuchen. I wanted to be totally honest with my answer to Stephen as well as to myself. I needed to do some digging to figure out if my decision to move or not was motivated by my own desire, or was I doing it for someone else? I wanted Stephen to know that my lack of talking about the move wasn't because I wasn't thinking about it, but rather more of my searching and figuring out my own feelings.

Whenever we had a really good time together, I felt like I could easily live with Stephen. Then there were times we were awkwardly silent and somewhat distant, and I felt happy to return home to my own apartment. There were also family issues that came up and I felt the need to be more present and available for them. During my therapy sessions, I often discussed all the things I was thinking and feeling about the move with my therapist. She said that taking my time was essential when making such a big move.

Knowing that I am a writer, list maker, and planner, my therapist suggested I write down the pros and cons of both moving in with Stephen or not. The list should include all aspects including my fears. I took her suggestion seriously since seeing things in writing helps me to understand my thoughts and feelings attached to those thoughts.

One early morning late in November, I decided to go for a run. I was feeling more anxious than usual, and I had made a list and was working on it. After some soul searching, I realized that my fear seemed to center around if I had the ability to love and live with someone again in my life other than Iden. I had not realized how much I'd loved Iden and the feeling of falling in love for the first time at a very young age and being friends, lovers, and then husband and wife had been a journey for almost 40 years. Did I want to live with him again? No! Absolutely not! But was I able to enter into the committed relationship that Stephen wanted and was ready for?

I also thought about my daughter Elizabeth knowing she would be upset that I was moving. She would feel as if I were abandoning her with all the responsibility of taking care of her father and looking out for her sister, even though I would never do that. I also had the fear of our relationship becoming complacent if a decision was not made soon. Stephen was very sure about his intentions and if I remained on the edge too long our relationship would surely suffer. I shared what I was thinking and feeling about the move on many occasions and Stephen being a very good problem-solver would always give me a suggested solution to all my fears. I knew he was being honest, but I felt sometimes his intentions were more self- serving. I knew he loved it when I was at his home for an extended amount of time. This allowed me to cook some of his favorite meals and help him with his chores, but I wasn't so sure I wanted to fill the position of becoming a full-time wife again. I ran for almost an hour and decided I needed to talk to him.

When I got back to my apartment, I texted him and asked if we could meet up for dinner. His desire to always see me was endearing, so he immediately said yes and that he was excited about the unexpected surprise. He mentioned that downtown Manhattan was all decorated for the holidays so suggested I could meet him at his workplace, and we could go and have dinner by the river. I agreed thinking that sounded great and before hanging up he asked if everything was okay. Without any hesitation I reassured him by saying, "I just need to talk to you."

We arranged to meet at 5 o'clock, so I had most of the day to think about how I was going to share all that I was holding inside. If I didn't meet Stephen tonight, I was afraid I would lose that compulsion to get it all out, and it would stay hidden away. I spent most of the day doing much of nothing and decided to head into the city a little earlier to walk around by the South Street Seaport before meeting up with Stephen.

I love walking around in the city, observing the people, the buildings, stores and especially now with holiday decorations up. I walked around the seaport taking in all the festive decorations. I walked along the East River Greenway and found a quiet bench to catch a magnificent sunset. I sat watching until the sky earlier illuminated with a palette of yellow and an orange, turned into night.

My phone rang waking me from my reverie. It was Stephen asking me if I was close by and that he was waiting downstairs in front of his office building. I couldn't believe I lost track of the time and apologized and told him I was down the block and would be there in a few minutes. I felt nervous so I needed to shake that feeling off. I walked fast and took some deep breaths. Stephen held his arms open to give me a big hug saying, "It sure is beautiful down here at sunset with the big open sky," and I agreed

We walked to Battery Park City, which was about a 15-minute walk, passing Zuccotti Park all lit up with Christmas trees, and there were huge wreaths hanging in Brookfield Mall that helped jolt me into wanting to sing, It's beginning to look a lot like Christmas!

We walked over to the Hudson River Esplanade to find our way to a restaurant called Le District. Stephen had lived in Battery Park City when he was first married at the age of 26. He had become clean and sober and used to run every day by the river. He said although he had a difficult marriage, he enjoyed every minute when he was living here. It was the best place that he ever lived, and he was happy to be working close by because it allowed him to visit frequently when he had time, either for lunch or after work in the warmer months.

Although I had lived in New York City most of my life, I had only been to Battery Park City a few times. I came a few times to have lunch with Mark who worked downtown, and a few times with Iden and the girls when they were young to visit the World Trade Center. Before going to the restaurant we walked by the river lit up by the buildings across the way in New Jersey.

Although there were many people jogging, riding bikes, walking with baby carriages and dogs, it wasn't loud, but rather tranquil. I felt a sense of calmness as we walked and inhaled the musky smell of the river and listened to the sound of the waves hitting the pier. I was beginning to understand why he said this place brought him so much happiness. As we walked, Stephen was describing all the changes Battery Park had undergone over the years.

We sat at a table with a window view of the river. The restaurant, river view, and the French music playing made me almost feel like I was on vacation in Paris. Once seated, Stephen grabbed my hands and said, "I love it here and I love you, but what's up?"

I held his hands and looked into his hazel-green eyes and told him that I loved him. I explained that and that I had some things on my mind and in my heart that I need to say and to ask him before I could make a decision about moving in with him. I also told him that I had been doing a lot of self-examination and was trying to figure out what was holding me back, and to understand what was at the root of my fears.

Stephen knew my family situation and my connection to Iden and my daughters, but I needed to know if moving in with him would allow me to be available to them when needed without causing problems between us. I wanted to create some distance from my family both physically and emotionally, but I didn't want to feel that I had to choose between them or him. As sometimes in the past, I felt that my attention to my family had caused disagreements between us.

Stephen let me talk for a bit more then asked if he could speak. He started off by saying that he was happy that I was seriously thinking of moving in with him, and he agreed that in the past he may have done and said things that would lead me to believe he was not able to tolerate all the attention I gave to my family. He continued to say that I have helped him become more understanding, giving, and patient, and that he owed me much appreciation for all I have given him.

Stephen further pointed out that he knew how difficult it was to arrange to come to New Jersey every weekend and still do all the things for my family and Mimi. I told him I was tired of living a double life. I was tired physically of travelling and emotionally not being planted in one place. I needed to get some new roots down and I think I was ready to try after having the courage to reflect honestly as to what was keeping me from making the move. I explained that I had a tremendous amount of guilt feeling so blessed to be healthy, happy, and on a new path of discovery of myself, while Iden was struggling every day just to exist. I know guilt keeps us a prisoner of the past and I no longer wanted to be behind those bars any longer.

I truly felt that I was doing all I could do for Iden and my family, and I was finally accepting the fact that I was entitled to live a joyous life. We talked for almost 30 minutes before we were ready to order dinner. I didn't realize how hungry I was until I looked at the menu with all the delicious entrees. I always like to try something new and since it was a French restaurant, most of the dishes were all new to me.

During dinner, Stephen started talking about his lease and when it was up because even though he had a two-bedroom apartment, he felt he wanted to move into a new place that offered a change for both of us. He wanted us to be able to choose a place together. I told him that I would have to see about my lease and what penalties were for breaking it. I had signed a two-year lease and had only been there for a little over a year. It seemed crazy to be moving yet again, and for a minute I started to go down that slippery slide of fear, so I pulled myself up and ended that thought. I asked Stephen to let us finish our lovely meal and we could do some planning soon since we didn't have a gun to our heads to move, but I guessed that he wanted to jump on the opportunity of my commitment before I reneged on the decision.

We ended our meal with two double espressos and a delicious crème brulee. With a full belly, mind, and heart we left the restaurant and took another walk on the esplanade toward the train. As we walked, Stephen stopped and turned me around kiss and hug me and said, "I love you, Patty, and even if this move doesn't happen, I love you for wanting it to happen."

Those words made me feel so good, because in the past I'd always felt anxious about disappointing him when I had to change our plans.

We got on the train heading uptown. Stephen got off at Penn Station to catch New Jersey Transit, and I stayed on riding the train all the way to Forest Hills. As I rode the train home, I was wondering what it would feel like to no longer live in a neighborhood that I had spent almost 40 years living in. I had moved to Forest Hills when I got married at the age of 24 and I was now almost 62. Even though I had some hesitations, I was the type of person that although I may take a long time to reach a decision, once I have made up my mind, I start making a plan to make it happen. But for now I just wanted to savor the night and not think of anything other than the present moment that was giving me much joy.

My brother Mark and his wife, Kathy, were happy to host our family Christmas Eve dinners. Christmas still had some joy, but it had lost some magic after the loss of my parents, my divorce, and my girls being all grown up. Once I was gathered around with my family at Mark's house and reflecting on Christmases past with them, we had some good laughs and cries. I felt that connection to who we were, and it brought a bit of the holiday magic back to the present. Since Stephen also spent time with his family on Christmas Eve with his former wife and children, we met up on Christmas Day to exchange our gifts and spend a few days together.

After a late night at Mark and Kathy's home, followed by Christmas Eve Mass, I returned home. Although I was tired, I was not able to go right to sleep. I sat on the couch with Mimi in a bit of trance thinking of my mom and missing her. She was like a young child at Christmas. She loved this holiday so very much and I especially enjoyed watching her open up her gifts and saving all the beautiful ribbons and bows to reuse next year. It's funny how we remember certain things about loved ones no longer with us.

I heard my phone ring, and it was Stephen wishing me a Merry Christmas and then he started singing Charlie Brown's Christmas song, "Christmas Time is Here." It was 7 o'clock in the morning, and he wanted to know when he should come over. I told him whenever he wanted and as always, he said, "I am ready now." He always expressed his desire to be with me, especially on Christmas Day.

I'd planned to make us some cranberry waffles for breakfast and then we would open our gifts and take a walk in the freshly fallen snow. He was off for a few days, so we looked forward to our time together. We also planned on watching my favorite seasonal movie, *It's a Wonderful Life.*

After walking Mimi and playing in the snow for a while with her, I showered and dressed and went to make coffee and start preparing the batter for the waffles.

As I sipped my coffee, I called Lizzy and Joel to wish them a Merry Christmas because I knew they would be up early since they were headed up to Syracuse to visit Joel's family for Christmas and spend a few days there. I knew better than to call Claudia and Martin because they were late sleepers, especially after the late night we'd all had. I also didn't call Iden because I knew he would also be sleeping late. I called Mark to thank him for the lovely night and he said that perhaps next year Stephen could join us. Mark and Kathy had dinner a few times with us and had enjoyed their time with Stephen. They told me they liked Stephen very much and they thought he was very good for me. I thanked him for his offer and wished him a wonderful Christmas with his wife's family.

When Stephen arrived, we greeted each other with big hugs and kisses. He warmed up with a cup of coffee and turned on some holiday music from his playlist on Spotify and got the tunes playing on my Bluetooth speaker. His energy and enthusiasm was infectious, and it was hard not to feel happy when around him. He made my apartment feel like home with his love. I didn't feel hungry after last night's big dinner, but when the waffles started cooking my stomach started growling. I made the waffles with cranberries topped with pecans, maple syrup, and served with a dollop of crème fraiche on top.

My sister-in-law had also given me a whole tin of Christmas cookies, so we enjoyed a few honey balls and fig cookies. Everything about Christmas seemed to be so rich, sweet, and colorful. Afterward we moved to the couch and Stephen played me some holiday songs on one of his guitars he had at my apartment. Then we opened our gifts to each other. Stephen is a big reader and journaler and also a watercolorist, so I bought him a big book of his favorite artist, Vincent Van Gogh, and some leather bound journals and watercolor paint. I always bought him some silly stocking stuffers and also made him a card filled with endearing words.

Stephen handed me a small bag filled with a beautiful handmade scarf of cashmere wool, which he purchased at the Bryant Park holiday market, along with a matching hat and gloves. The colors and the design were lovely and the wool so soft. He then handed me an envelope that was covered with flowers painted with watercolors. When I opened it there were only four words written inside and they read, "Come Fly With Me!"

I looked at him thinking it may have been a metaphor for going through life with him and I got nervous thinking of what that might mean. Did my suggestion of moving in with him make him take it a bit further?

Stephen then handed me another envelope and he said, "Open it!"

I opened it and it was tickets to Paris for five days leaving New York on February 10th and returning on February 15th. I was extremely relieved to see plane tickets and especially excited to see tickets to Paris. I had not been to Paris in a very long time and Stephen, and I had wanted to make plans to go there in the new year. He said he'd wanted to go in April, but he was starting a new project, so it would be impossible for him to get away in April and for a few months after until things were set in place. April in Paris would be lovely, but Paris in general anytime of the year is an absolute gift.

Stephen also gave me a bag filled with other surprises like chocolate, perfume, and a book. He even brought Mimi some chew toys. I got up and gave him a big hug and asked why now? He said he received his yearly bonus early and it was a combination of many things. It was a Christmas gift and a way of celebrating a bit early our moving in together. It was just the end of December, and we were planning a July move-in date, so yes, it was an early celebratory gift, but I wasn't complaining.

We talked for a bit about many things then took Mimi out for a walk. Although it had snowed lightly overnight, the sun was now out, and it was comfortable walking. When we returned, I gave Mimi her new chew toys and Stephen and I both felt tired after a late night and a big breakfast, so we needed a nap. We got into bed and lay in each other's embrace before falling asleep. We must have been very tired because when I awoke it was already dusk and Mimi was barking for yet another walk. I let Stephen sleep a little more and dressed to take Mimi out for a quick walk.

While I was out walking, I checked in with Claudia who was on her way to Martin's mom's home, and we talked for a few minutes. I then called Iden to wish him a Merry Christmas. He answered and greeted me with a Merry Christmas and asked how I was and what I was up to? Although he knew quite well that I was with Stephen, I just said I was out walking Mimi and enjoying my leftover cookies from Kathy. He said that Kathy had given him some food and cookies from last night's dinner and that he was just watching a movie. He seemed to be doing okay given the fact that holidays are a difficult time of year for many people, myself included, and especially for those suffering with depression. We said our goodbyes and said we loved each other and that it was good being together on Christmas Eve.

As always when I speak to him, I get a little bit of a tug on my heart, especially since I was spending the day with Stephen and had just received a beautiful gift. I stayed out a bit longer than a quick walk just to shake off what I was feeling before I'd headed back in with Mimi.

When I returned, Stephen was up and asked, "Hey, what are we cooking for dinner?" It was hard to believe, but hungry we were, and I had decided to make some pasta with eggplant and sauce and to forgo the meatballs. Stephen was slowly making his way into a plant-based diet and I also was not a big fan of meat, so pasta alla Norma it was for Christmas dinner.

Stephen began to enjoy cooking, so he helped me cook. My kitchen was a narrow galley kitchen so when we bumped into each other we gave a small kiss here and there and the whole experience of cooking a meal together was very endearing. It made my heart grow a little bigger with love for him. When I added the eggplant to the sauce, I thought about Iden and how much he loved eggplant, thinking that perhaps one day we could all have this dish together. Crazy thought indeed.

I just wanted Iden to be happy and it wasn't anything more than that, perhaps a little bit of guilt for feeling so blessed and

Stephen and Patricia, Halloween 2021©

happy. After dinner was finished, we settled down to watch *It's a Wonderful Life* before taking our books and heading off to bed.

The next day we did some after Christmas shopping and I also stopped in a gourmet market to pick up some fruit and vegetables and a few other items. Stephen was staying for dinner before leaving in order to catch up with work. I decided to make a vegetable chili and some rice for dinner giving my belly a break from the holiday meals. Stephen had a fair amount of work to do so asked if he could answer some emails while I started dinner and that he would join me in the kitchen in a bit. I was in the kitchen dicing and sautéing when I peeked out of the kitchen and saw that he had fallen asleep on the couch with his iPad on his lap. He had been working very hard and I was happy that he was feeling comfortable enough in my place to take an unexpected nap. While he slept, I poured myself a glass of wine and felt a sense of contentment and peace that I had not felt in a long time. With the dinner simmering away on the stove, I took my glass of wine and sat down next to Stephen, opening up a new book and listening to him quietly snoring. It was a wonderful Christmas.

CHAPTER TWENTY-FIVE

FLYING INTO FEAR

"There are two kinds of special events: planned and unplanned."

—LAURIE NADEL

The year 2020 started off quietly with a dinner with some friends at Stephen's place on New Year's Eve, followed with a family dinner at my place on New Year's Day. It was the first time we all had gathered in my apartment to share a meal together, and it was especially nice since Iden had joined us. He was in a good place experiencing neither a high or low, and for a brief moment it almost felt like old times.

As much as I wanted to share what was happening in my life with my family it obviously was not the time to announce my upcoming trip to Paris or my plans for moving in with Stephen sometime over the summer. Each family member would react differently, so I was planning to inform each one separately. Sharing the details of my life with Iden was difficult since he was neither in a relationship nor was he in a position financially to take a trip. I didn't want to make him upset or perhaps to cause an argument, since matters involving Stephen naturally did. I knew I should be able to tell all of them without worrying about their reaction, but it was hard for me because I knew how sensitive Lizzy was and how she relied on me for emotional support to help deal with her father, and at times with Claudia. Besides Iden's illness, hearing about a former wife's plans isn't something a former husband wants to hear. Although I was learning to let go of my feelings of guilt, they still resurged at times when I was experiencing great joy.

The cold winter months were soon upon us, and I was keeping busy and adjusting into my new routine of retired life. I had been habitually writing for two to three hours a day, which was bringing much inner peace, and helping me to work out some feelings that I had been harboring inside for too long. The trip to Paris and my move to Metuchen was also keeping me busy because when I wasn't at the gym, writing, walking Mimi, or doing errands and chores, I was gathering information about places and sights to visit in Paris and searching for apartments in Metuchen.

Paris is so beautiful at any time of the year, and even though we wouldn't be there in April, I was planning a walking tour of as much of the city as possible. Stephen and I love to walk, so we preferred to familiarize ourselves with the city by wandering the different neighborhoods and stopping for a coffee or a bite as we go.

Our hotel was located in Montparnasse, and although it wasn't in the center of Paris, it was near the metros that would take us anywhere. I hadn't been to Paris in many years but remembered its beauty and I was getting excited with each passing day, knowing we would be there soon.

Being the planners that we were, when we got together on the weekends before our trip, we sat in front of the computer jotting down names of restaurants, museums, churches, parks, and many other things we wanted to see and do. When we weren't planning our trip, we would look at apartments in Stephen's complex. He had already notified management that he was planning on moving when his lease expired in July and to please notify him of apartments that would soon be available so we could secure one that we liked. Stephen liked living in his current complex because it was just a block from New Jersey Transit.

The complex was only a few years old and had state-of-the art kitchens and bathrooms along with many amenities. There was a gym, a rooftop deck, a pool, barbequing areas, and each apartment had a terrace, and was equipped with a washer and dryer. Most importantly, his building was pet-friendly and had many dog runs and areas to walk Mimi. I had never lived in a modern building and although it had great features, to me it felt like a hotel, but since Stephen was still working and needed the accessibility to New Jersey Transit it was a practical living situation until he retired, which wouldn't be for several more years.

One day after taking a long morning walk, Stephen and I saw the managing agent, Debbie, flagging us down and she asked if we wanted to see an available apartment that she thought we might like. We agreed and went to see the apartment. It had two bedrooms and two bathrooms and a small den with a large balcony and good sunlight exposure. If we wanted to secure the apartment, we would have to put down a $500 deposit.

After we finished looking at the apartment, Debbie said to please let her know as soon as possible and Stephen said we would. When we entered his apartment, he turned to me and asked what I thought of the other apartment? Before I could answer he told me he loved the layout, view, and all the natural light. I could tell from the enthusiasm with which he was speaking that he wanted to put down the deposit. I said I liked it very much but thought maybe we should look at some other ones before deciding. His thinking was if we both liked it very much then why should we wait and look at other ones?

We were very different in the matter of making decisions. I needed to know my options before making a decision. Stephen said that he would go ahead and put down a deposit and we could continue looking to see if there was one that we liked better, but he would risk losing the deposit. Another thing I hated even more than making a quick decision, was wasting money. But I could tell he was going forward with it, regardless of my hesitations and perhaps one of us needed to be more aggressive in the decision making to get things moving. Before taking a nap, I started to imagine how all of his things and my things would come together in one apartment.

After my nap, we talked for a little bit before I headed back to Queens. Stephen drove me home and for most of the ride home we just sat quietly and listened to music. Just before I reached home, he grabbed my hand and said that he loved me, and he didn't want me to do anything I wasn't ready to do. I knew he meant those words, but he was truly hoping I was ready and not changing my mind. I told him that it was just so sudden and that I am not one that makes decisions so spontaneously, that's all. But was there more to it than that?

I picked up Mimi from my neighbor. I usually took Mimi when I went to Stephens, but sometimes it was nice to have some free time without having to worry about her care. I also wondered if Mimi would adjust to yet another new home, but then again dogs have no problem living in the present, and as long as I was with her that was all the feeling of home she needed.

By the end of January, I finally decided to tell my family about my up-and-coming plans, regardless of what their reactions might be. A good way to start the conversation, my therapist said, is to state that you understand how they may feel, but these are things that I want to do and that bring me happiness. I decided to first inform them about my trip to Paris, which was only about three weeks away. It seemed odd to hold back good news as almost as if it were bad news, but it may have appeared as if I were delivering bad news to them. It is all a matter of perspective, and I was trying my best to understand their feelings, but at the same time to go forward with my life, and to allow myself to do the things I wanted to do whether or not I had my family's approval.

I decided to ask Claudia and Martin over for dinner one night so I could inform them about the trip and my plans to move in with Stephen. Claudia and Martin were not that interested in my life, nor did they take part in the care of Iden, so delivering the news to them would not be difficult.

During dinner we caught up on work and I asked about any plans they may have. They said they were planning to visit Martin's sister who lives in Florida in May. I explained that I also had a trip planned with Stephen at that time. Explaining I was leaving in February for five days to Paris. Claudia reacted by saying,

"Wow, that's great"! Martin also gave a similar response. I asked Claudia if she could remember when we were there. She vaguely remembered, as she was only a young child at the time.

I told Claudia and Martin that I was also thinking of moving in with Stephen in the summer. Claudia, always somewhat self-centered, asked if she and Martin could move into my apartment because it was a nicer apartment than the one they were living in. That would involve a lot of planning so I said we would look into it. We finished the night with some dessert and coffee and when she left, I felt good knowing at least one of my family members was happy with my plans.

Next was to tell Lizzy and Joel. I had no problem telling Joel, for I knew he understood and was very supportive of me. He also knew about my hesitation to tell Lizzy because of her reaction to my doing something that made me not physically present. It had nothing to do with her needing me for herself, but rather feeling the need to have me near in case Iden needed help. I felt a huge amount of guilt because of her role in taking care of her father because over the years I had slowly removed myself from the day-to-day drama of his life.

At some point in my life I realized that Iden would always stay in my heart, but I didn't want him to stay in my life. I needed to disconnect from his moods and his life because it impacted my ability to move on. I would always help him and give him a call to check in on him from time to time, but not in the quantity and quality that Lizzy was doing. I often mentioned to her that she didn't need to be so involved since she now had her life with Joel, a very responsible job, and friends that were all equally just as important, if not more so.

I texted Lizzy the day after Claudia's dinner and asked if she could come by on the weekend for a visit, or possibly dinner. I knew she was busy with work and chores and may have had something already planned, so even a quick visit to have a chat would be perfect. She immediately answered the text with, "Is everything okay?"

324   Flying Into Fear

I replied with, "Yes, just miss you guys and wanted to see you."

She said that perhaps on Sunday she could come by for a morning coffee since she was going to see her dad to drop off some food, which I said would be perfect.

The few days leading up to Lizzy and Joel's visit I was feeling a bit anxious, and I spoke to Stephen many times about it. He suggested to just say it as I felt it, and to know she would be emotional so understand that, but that she would come around. He also reminded me that she loves me very much and just wants me to be happy, but her fear of the unknown with Iden prevents her from sharing my joy. He also commented that it is really beautiful how much she loves her family.

Lizzy and Joel came at 10 o'clock on Sunday morning and I prepared a brunch of her favorites. I hadn't seen either of them in a few weeks, so I was very happy to see them. We chatted before catching up on work and also asked if they had plans. They were planning to head up to Syracuse to visit Joel's parents and to see some good friends that they'd known since college days. I told them that I also had some traveling plans, and I proceeded to tell them about my trip to Paris.

Joel was pleased saying that he would love to return to Paris one day. He had studied abroad in Prague and took many trips to different countries during his six months stay. Lizzy got very nervous and started asking many questions, so I answered as best I could. I told her that I would give her all my flight information and if there was an emergency, she had only to call me, and I would be on the next flight home if need be.

I didn't tell Lizzy about my plan to move in with Stephen because there was only so much she could handle at one time. I wasn't up for that speech, and I didn't know the specifics yet of the move, so until I did, I would wait. We talked a little more and then said our goodbyes. I said that I would personally tell her dad about my trip so there was no need to feel like it was a secret.

After Lizzy left, I decided to give Iden a call and test the waters to see if it were a good time to deliver the news about my upcoming trip. I had not spoken to him in a while, so I was not sure of his current state, but since Lizzy did not bring his name up during brunch, I assumed nothing major was going on. When he answered the phone, I could tell in just a few words that he was in a midrange state, being neither depressed nor manic. We talked for a little bit, and he even asked how Stephen and I were getting along. So I was able to say that things were going well and that we were planning a trip to Paris in a few weeks.

Although Iden didn't respond with words, there was a moment of silence before he spoke again. He said that he was sure that I would enjoy the trip because he remembered how much I loved being in Paris when we were there together. He then started talking about the things we did, his family, and how much he missed them. As I listened, I could hear the loneliness in his voice and all I could do was to listen and every now and then say some kind words of agreement.

After reminiscing, I told Iden when I returned from Paris, we would have another family dinner because the girls and I enjoyed the last one we'd had in the New Year. He also said he would enjoy that, and we said goodbye. After the call I just sat on the couch hearing Iden's words over again in my head and in my heart. I allowed myself to feel them and know that they were just feelings. They were ones that I have felt many times, but this time I allowed myself to accept them, release them, and embrace what I have now in the present.

With just a week before our trip I emailed our itinerary to my girls, finished packing, and had made plans for a manicure and hair appointment. I also made time to meet up with each of my girls for a drink and a small bite in the city before leaving. Stephen had been busy the weeks leading up to the vacation trying to get things in order before leaving, so we had not seen much of each other. I was really looking forward to us being far away from his work so he could relax and have quality time together. I missed him when I did not see him as frequently as we usually did. He brought out the best in me, accepted me with all my complications, and was patient with my emotional struggles dealing with my family.

I could not wait to hold his hand while walking down the Champs-Elysees and sharing it together. Stephen loved taking photos wherever we went, especially of me, which was a wonderful souvenir of our trips together. A few days before I left, I tried to spend as much time with Mimi as I could. Even though I was leaving her in good hands, I knew she didn't get on too well without me now that she was getting so old. I gradually managed to check off all the things on my list to-do list.

On the day of departure, I made all my usual phone calls to my family and was to meet Stephen at Kennedy Airport for our night flight to Paris. I arrived at the airport to find Stephen waiting for me at the Air France terminal. I cannot even describe how happy it made me, always knowing that he would be there waiting for me even though I was early. We checked in, went through security, and found a place to sit at the waiting area before boarding. We both had books to read, and Stephen also had his sketch pad and journal with him to keep him occupied. I got busy doing my people-watching to pass the time. We were soon boarded and settled into our seven-hour flight to Paris.

We arrived at The Pullman Hotel in Montparnasse just before noon. We were tired, but equally excited to get out and walk around Paris. Our hotel was just a few blocks from the train station, but for our first day after a long plane flight we decided to take a quick shower to wash off some jet lag, and then walk around Montparnasse and gather some train information to take us to places we wanted to visit.

Before heading out, we stopped by the hotel desk and asked about places to walk and to grab a bite to eat. All the help at the hotel spoke English and were very helpful with suggestions. They also gave us a map of Paris. Stephen and I were both hungry since we did not eat much on the plane. The concierge suggested we try an area called the Breton that has restaurants specializing in crepes not too far from the hotel.

Although it was mid-February it was not too cold, and the fresh air helped wake us up a bit. We walked for about half an hour admiring all the stores, till we found a spot to eat and ordered some savory crepes minus the ham, since Stephen was now eating a vegetarian diet.

We were a bit tired so didn't venture too far, but explored Avenue du Maine, which turned out to be Montparnasse's artist colony. It is a cobblestone cul de sac covered in greenery, where back in 1900, artist studios were built using salvaged materials from the explosion of Paris. Many of these studios are still in use today.

Being an artist, Stephen said he couldn't imagine what it would be like living and working among artists during that time. As we walked you could almost feel the creative energy still living in the streets. We stopped to have some espresso before heading back to our hotel to have an early night and try to get ourselves acclimated to Paris time.

A good night's sleep allowed us to get up early and enjoy a *petite dejeuner* that was provided by the hotel, which included creamy yogurts, croissants, pain au chocolat, pain aux raisins, assorted fruits, and juice, coffee and tea. We walked to the Gare Montparnasse to head into the right bank to walk on the Avenue des Champs-Elysees.

Our first thing to see was the Arc de Triomphe. As we walked down the avenue, I couldn't help but admire the simplistic designs of clothing store windows and the boulangeries displaying exquisite desserts beautifully on plates with doilies. The weather was quite mild, so we were able to walk along the Seine to the Jardin des Tuileries. We couldn't help but stop and browse through books and magazines at the many booksellers along the Seine. As we walked along the river, we saw sightseeing cruise boats go by and although it was a very touristy thing to do we decided to get the information and take a ride.

The temperatures were in the high 40s and sunny, so we were fortunate to be able to stay outside touring the city. After a brief walk, we found the pier from where the cruise ships dock and boarded the next one. We received headphones in English for audio commentary along the way. We passed the world famous monuments, the Eiffel Tower, and Notre Dame Cathedral. We also passed under historic bridges like the Pont Neuf that we later walked on after disembarking from the boat. After a long day of walking we found our way back on the metro to our hotel to take a brief rest before heading out to dinner.

Our next days were filled with more sightseeing, but how can you go to Paris and not go visit the Eiffel Tower? We found our way there, arriving very early in order to avoid the long lines of tourists. Although we did have to wait a bit before it opened, it was great being the first few people in line. Stephen found a place to grab some coffee and pain au chocolat to have while we waited. I am not a big fan of heights, so I was a bit squeamish about going up in the elevator to the top, but I wasn't going to leave Paris without doing it. The tower is about 1,000 feet tall or about 81 stories, which contain three levels of observation platforms to reach *le sommet* (the top). I had to hold on to Stephen while riding up in the elevators to each level for emotional support, but once we reached the top and could see the spectacular view of Paris on a clear sunny day it was worth it. I felt a bit nauseous going back down, but the fresh air and a walk helped get rid of that feeling.

We found our way to St. Germain de Pres. It was a meeting place for intellectuals, a center of the post-war Jazz Age, and a bohemian hub for artists and writers. Today, St. Germain is a fashionable neighborhood with many designer stores and expensive restaurants. On one of the streets called Rue Bonaparte is one of six Laduree stores across Paris where they sell over 15,000 of their signature macaroons a day. We just had to buy some to munch happily along our way.

We stopped in perfume shops, boutiques, and we stopped at Café de Flore and had some onion soup, which was memorable. We sat by a window, and it was so lovely to look out onto the people walking by as we ate and talked. When we had finished eating, Stephen pulled out a little white box and handed it to me. Inside was a Wedgwood pin with a silver antique angel on top. He said while I was shopping in one of the stores, he found a jewelry store called Gloria. He found an angel pin that he thought I would love because my mother's name was Gloria and she loved angels. His thoughtfulness moved me, and I felt a tug on my heart. I reached over the table to grab his hand and gave it a big squeeze.

We walked more and then headed back to the hotel. When we got back to the hotel, we planned to spend the next day at the Musee d'Orsay because both Stephen and I wanted see the paintings of Vincent Van Gogh.

We took the train to the Luxenberg Gardens before arriving at the museum with our coffee and a buttered baguette, finding a bench to sit on to have our breakfast. Many of the benches were full of people having their morning coffee as well and for a moment I went back in time sitting in the same gardens with my girls while they sailed some toy boats in the pond. It was a very long time ago and it seemed like a distant past, and a different life.

We arrived at the museum early to find there was already a line, but once again we were fortunate to have surprisingly warmer temperatures than usual in February, so waiting for about 30 minutes or so was not a problem. Once inside, we had a guide book and besides wanting to see the work of Van Gogh we also wanted to see paintings by Renoir, Degas, and Monet. We took our time and finished our visit with viewing the Van Gogh paintings. We entered the exhibit and as we walked by each one, I could see Stephen's eyes watering up with much emotion.

When we got to Van Gogh's self-portrait we both stood still for a long time taking in this work of art. We had seen other paintings at the Metropolitan Museum of Art in New York City, but we had never seen his self-portrait. It was truly a very moving experience, and we left the museum feeling much different than when we entered.

We were not far from the Champs-Elysees so once again we went walking and talking and to find a place to sit and enjoy all that Paris had to offer. It certainly wasn't difficult finding a café in Paris to leisurely sip a coffee and to spend some time. After sitting for an hour or so and having a bite we decided to visit Montmartre since we were not too far away.

Montmartre is a city located on a large hill and well known for its white-domed Basilica of the Sacre-Coeur on its summit. We took the funicular to the summit, and since it is one of highest points in Paris, the view was spectacular, although I was not happy taking the lift to the top. It is a very busy area, so after arriving we walked around a bit where we saw artists and all kinds of street performers from music to mime. After leaving the crowds we went back down to the main street, Rue Lamarck, to find a quiet place to eat. We only had one more day in Paris, so we decided to have a quiet night in Montparnasse before our Versailles adventure began the next day.

The Palace of Versailles is located about 12½ miles to the west of Paris within the Ile de France area. When we first laid our eyes on the palace, we could not believe all the gold on the building and its magnitude. The day we arrived it had gotten considerably colder and there was already a long line waiting to get in, but we enjoyed doing our people-watching and talking. The Palace of Versailles was the principal royal residence of France from 1682, under Louis XIV, until the start of the French Revolution in 1789. Once we entered it was overwhelming to see such opulence. The construction of the palace was a representation of great wealth and power. Once inside we toured the palace walking through all the different chambers and climbing many winding staircases.

Some of the amazing sites we saw were The Hall of Mirrors with over 350 mirrors, and Le Grand Perspective that was said to be the best view in Versailles. We also viewed Marie Antoinette's bedroom, and the art collection that depicts important events in French history. As we walked through the halls into different chambers, we enjoyed viewing the rooms, but we were fascinated by the large windows with brass handles in so many shapes and sizes, a work of art indeed. Although we both loved museums and historical sites such as the palace, after a few hours we'd had enough and needed to take a break.

We had heard about a restaurant in Versailles called Angelina's, so decided to take a break there and try their famous hot chocolate and their well-known exceptional pastries. When we arrived it was a bit crowded, but it was a tourist spot and so we were prepared to wait. The line moved quickly, and we enjoyed looking around, especially watching the large machine that melted chocolate into their famous hot chocolate. The hot chocolate was so thick that straws were needed to drink it. When it was our turn, we could not resist ordering two different éclairs, one filled with chocolate, and one filled with custard crème. We found two seats by a window looking out into a courtyard and enjoyed our very sweet treats.

After a rest we walked around the grounds and then decided to walk around in the city of Versailles. Although the day started out cloudy and chilly, by the time we finished at the palace, the sun had come out and it warmed up a bit. We had fun walking around the city.

Some flea markets were set up and we strolled around looking at everything. I bought a beautiful pair of jeans for 5 euros that I absolutely loved and still wear at least once a week. We also went into a few food markets and were intoxicated over the freshness and display of the fruits, vegetables, and meats. We then headed to the train and back to Montparnasse. We were leaving the next day, so we wanted to have an early dinner and get all packed and ready to check out by 11 o'clock. We arrived back at our hotel and took a nap and then had dinner at our hotel before retiring. It was a wonderful time, and we were both so in love with Paris and seemingly with each other.

We arrived back in New York and soon heard news about a virus that was spreading into Europe from Wuhan City, China. It was not something causing much alarm, although it was not yet in the states. A few days after getting back from Paris, I bumped into a neighbor who had just returned from China and was wearing a mask. She informed me that China was experiencing an outbreak of a pneumonia that was linked to Wuhan's Huanan Seafood Wholesale Market, a wholesale seafood and live animal market. I didn't think too much of it, but by the beginning of March, Italy and France were issuing strict social distancing measures. By mid-March COVID 19 was declared a pandemic and the reports of people dying all over the world were constantly being reported. It seemed that life for everyone soon became very different than anything we had ever experienced.

In a matter of a week all news was centered on the virus and we were constantly glued to the TV trying to understand what we needed to do to stay safe. Businesses, schools, government agencies were closing along with retail stores, gyms, restaurants, and limited services on public transportation, and significant restrictions on domestic and international traveling.

By the time I was ready to celebrate my birthday on March 17th, 2020, there was orders for people to work from home allowing only 25 percent of a firm's workforce into the office. Governor Cuomo ordered all nonessential businesses closed statewide. By March 29th more than 30,000 New York residents died from the virus and the numbers newly infected were rising. Everyone watched the news and tried to adapt to learning how to live with the new restrictions of shopping and obtaining essential items such as toilet paper and hand sanitizer.

Along with the outbreak of this unexpected virus came the plans that needed to be changed or put on hold. Many wedding plans, vacations, and moves all of sudden needed to be rescheduled or cancelled.

When we arrived home from France, I only saw Stephen once or twice before the pandemic was announced and traveling to and from New Jersey was out of the question on public transportation and even by car, since we were both afraid of contracting COVID and we needed to stay isolated in our own place. Lizzy was working from home, but Claudia, who worked as a medical assistant, went in everyday and we were very nervous for her safety. It was surprising given the fact that she stresses over so many things, yet she was able to handle herself very well during these difficult times. I think she felt very proud working in a profession that offered help to those in need.

Stephen was also working from home and recently his son had moved in with him since he had just relocated from Florida after graduating and did not yet have a job. We would not be seeing each other for some time due to COVID. He seemed to be fine with this restriction of visitations more than I was, which got me questioning many things once again.

We were supposed to start looking at apartments in June, but with the pandemic many of our plans were put on hold. Although I wasn't working, I was keeping busy with my writing, dog walking, working out at home, family involvement, and daily chores. I missed seeing Stephen and we talked frequently about when we thought it might be safe to see each other again. He was concerned because I saw Claudia often and she was working in a medical office for cardiac patients and was testing patients for COVID every day.

Even though my family and I were being careful by wearing masks and keeping a social distance, it was understandable for him to be concerned. The time spent apart from each other was starting to affect our relationship. Our phone conversations were somewhat awkward, and it was difficult for me to feel the connection I usually had with him. I had many things I felt I wanted to say, but at times I just couldn't find a way to express my thoughts because he seemed either not interested or had too much he wanted to say. Either way, things were a bit tense, and we decided we needed to see each other to figure out our next steps.

About two months into COVID, Stephen and I decided to meet at the beginning of May. Stephen drove to Forest Hills to spend the day. The death rate from COVID was about 80,000 in the U.S., and Dr. Fauci reported that a vaccine would not be ready for at least another year. COVID testing was being done, but there was still a limited supply. I was pretty much self-quarantined. My daughter Lizzy was ordering groceries to be delivered to my apartment and I hardly went out except to walk Mimi. Stephen was still working from home and his son had gotten a job working from home as well. We both felt safe to see each other, and it was becoming necessary because the physical distance was creating an emotional distance, even though just a few short months ago we could not have imagined spending more than a week apart.

When Stephen arrived, we embraced each other and gave a brief kiss. I made some coffee and we sat and talked. We slowly started to relax and felt more at ease with each other. We talked about many things before finally discussing my move to Metuchen. I brought up the topic by saying it is a very trying uncertain time and moving now was not the best thing to be doing. I explained that I needed to feel close to my family and wasn't able to choose an apartment virtually. Realtors were not able to show apartments in person and I did not feel comfortable making a decision right now.

I could tell that he was getting angry, and he said, "So are you backing out of your decision to move in with me?"

I responded by saying, "I just don't think it is the best time right now, and besides your son is living with you."

"Where is he going to go?"

He said that his son, Julian, had found a studio apartment in Manhattan in the Wall Street area and was planning on moving in a month with his girlfriend when she comes up from Florida. So now it seemed to be all on me. He still wanted to make the move and was not happy with what I was saying.

With so much going on I needed to be planted where I was. It was not a good time to move, even though it was something we had planned to do. Stephen does not like to have things go differently than expected and it was making our time together very tense. I had prepared some lunch for us, but he said he wasn't hungry and wanted to leave soon. I told him it wasn't as if I was telling him I didn't want to live with him, but rather I didn't think it was a good time given the present circumstances of what was going on in the world.

Stephen left soon after he arrived. We continued to talk on the phone over the course of May and we saw each other here and there with very little discussion of moving in together. It was very much like having the elephant in the room most of the time. With the warmer temperatures moving in slowly, it was becoming more difficult to stay at home, but even more necessary. The numbers of people becoming infected with COVID and dying was growing every day. Hospitals did not have enough beds for the seriously ill patients with COVID, and makeshift emergency units were being set up around the city. Nurses and doctors were flying in from other places to help with the shortages in New York City. It was a very uncertain time, and it was difficult to think beyond the day with trying to stay safe from contracting the virus.

During these months Iden had been very depressed and had been doing some heavy drinking, even though he thought we were unaware of it. Sometime around the end of May his mood was swinging up and by the time summer had arrived he was in full manic mode. He was calling me often and many times did not make any sense. Often his words became belligerent, and I had to hang up on him. There were many episodes where he went missing. At times he refused to answer his phone because he had been drinking and did not want us to know. Since the bars were closed, he would sometimes drink in a park. This was concerning because when drunk and manic, problems could arise and so over the next few months my girls and I were fearful for his safety.

By late May, outdoor dining was set up in New York City. Restaurants were creating outdoor seating with partitions and many streets and sidewalks were being taken over to provide this service to help keep businesses open, and to offer some relief to people who had been staying at home for many months. I was not comfortable with the idea of eating out in restaurants. A vaccine was being worked on, yet no one was completely protected from the virus unless you stayed home.

Stephen and I had started to see each other more since we both had been getting tested regularly for the COVID virus and had been pretty much isolating the whole time. One weekend he came to pick me up and he brought up the topic of moving, but this time he only spoke of his moving. He said that he was very tired of commuting from New Jersey to New York City and since he had been working from home, he realized how much better he felt without having to do the two-hour-plus commute each day. He was seriously considering moving into New York City.

Stephen was particularly thinking of Battery Park City since he would only have about a 10- minute walk to his office and he absolutely loved that part of the city. When I heard him talk, I was waiting to hear if he was also going to ask me to move in with him. He explained how difficult it was to set up apartment viewing and that many real estate agents were only doing either virtual appointments or scheduling only a few in person showings a week. He then turned to ask me what I thought.

My first reaction was that I thought it was wonderful since the distance between us would be so much less and, we could do so many more things we loved to do that the city offered. Metuchen was a small town and has many wonderful restaurants, shopping and parks, but obviously nothing could compare to what New York City could offer. The commute was a lot for Stephen.

When I finally spoke, I said I thought it might be a good idea, but then I asked him how he would feel about giving up playing at the open mics and attending his weekly AA meetings that he had being going to for many years. I also asked how he felt about not being as physically close to his family if he moved to the city? He responded by saying that his band was slowly coming undone, and he no longer really enjoyed the open mics.

Stephen would miss his home group AA meetings, but New York City has many and he could easily find one. He hesitated when responding to the question about moving away from his family. I guess he never realized what that might mean, and perhaps what that might also mean for me as well when he asked me to move to Metuchen. He said that his son, Julian, was already living in the city and his oldest daughter, Hannah, was most probably going to be looking for an apartment as well in the city. His youngest daughter, Maya, was almost finished with college and still living at home and that he would schedule time to see them all.

We talked a little more about moving to the city and then he asked if I would consider moving into the city at some time with him? The thought of moving into the city was exciting and I could very well see myself living there. It would also be good living close to my family making it easier to see them than if I were living in New Jersey.

We had not been as close as we had during the past few months because of COVID, and I needed to have time to get back to where we left off, which was on a very good high after our time in Paris. He understood and said that there was no rush as long as it was something I might want to do in the future. He suggested that maybe we could spend a day walking around Battery Park to just look at some buildings, to feel the neighborhood out, and then look online at apartments and perhaps view some virtually or set up appointments to view them in person when that opportunity came.

I had no idea how much apartments were going for at this time, since many people had been moving out of the city during the pandemic and prices were lowering so there were more apartments available than ever. We didn't have anywhere to go or anything to do this weekend, so he suggested that maybe after a nice walk in Roosevelt Park in New Jersey we could make some dinner and then look at some apartments to get an idea.

With all that in mind we made a plan that weekend for a walk in the park followed by dinner and searching New York City apartments in Battery City Park. It was now spring and it felt so wonderful to feel, see, and smell all of this beautiful season waking to life. We walked around the lake a few times then sat on a bench to catch some rays on our winter-quarantine complexion. Stephen reached over to take my hand and said, "I miss you Baby! It's good to be here with you!"

I squeezed his hand and said, "Yes, it is!" We walked back to the car and rode home with music playing and with our eyes looking brighter than before. We certainly did not know what would happen, but it was good to be connected again and perhaps thinking of a new plan.

CHAPTER TWENTY-SIX

TO AND FRO

"Yesterday is but a dream. Tomorrow is only a vision. But today well lived makes every yesterday a dream of happiness, and every tomorrow a vision of hope."

—KALISDASA (SANSKRIT WRITER)

After our talk about plans of moving into the city I started searching for available apartments in Battery Park City. I had never lived in the city nor looked for apartments, so I had no idea about the average rent of a two-bedroom apartment. We were now moving into late May and although COVID cases had started to decline, there was expressed concern about the spread of the virus after the George Floyd protest via the crowded events. This was certainly a trying time, and although moving into the city was exciting, it was also creating some apprehension.

By the beginning of June, New York City began the first phase of its reopening plan. I found many available apartments, since many young people had returned home to live with their parents because they were working from home, and it was unnecessary to be stuck in an apartment paying high rent. I was shocked at the price of the rent, but Battery Park City is one of the highest rent areas in New York City. There were a few apartments that I took a virtual tour of, and a few I was able make an appointment to visit in person.

Although there was much fear and sadness in the world, I was feeling hopeful that things would get better for everyone. The time I had spent staying at home allowed me to refocus and get some of my priorities in order. My writing also helped me heal and, in a way, to put my past to rest and move on. Understanding your feelings gives you freedom.

I needed to let go of my insecurities to finally become secure, instead of using my insecurities to search for security. My decision to move in with Stephen created a stronger commitment to each other that I was apparently now ready to step into.

I made two appointments in early June to see apartments in Battery Park City. Stephen's lease was coming to end, and he was anxious to find something. I informed him about the apartments I found, and he asked if I could view them by myself first since he was busy at work. If I liked one, we could arrange to see it again together later.

Since COVID I had not travelled into the city, so I suited up with a mask and gloves and headed downtown to meet the broker. It was a beautiful summer afternoon and the cool breeze ever present in this part of the city made it even nicer. When I arrived at the first showing the broker was waiting for me. He introduced himself and gave me the necessary information on the apartment before we headed in to see it

I entered the lobby and filled out the required COVID information forms before seeing the apartment. The lobby was very impressive with fresh flowers on the front desk, marble floors shining like mirrors, and very friendly concierges. We took the elevator up to the eighth floor and there were only about seven apartments on the floor. Jonathan, my real estate broker, opened the door of the apartment that led into a long foyer with closets to the left side and on to the right was an entrance to a galley kitchen.

The bedroom had a full wall of closets on one side and a full side of windows that gave lots of natural light. The living room also had a full side of windows with a view of the river that let in the afternoon sun. Both the kitchen and the bathroom were recently renovated with all modern tiles, fixtures, and appliances.

I asked if I could sit down for a moment to feel the energy and to try and picture myself in the apartment and visualize where all my things, as well as Stephen's belongings would fit. The apartment was a good size, but since rent for a one-bedroom was very high, a two-bedroom at this time wasn't a consideration. Before going to the next apartment, Jonathan showed me the outdoor patio. The whole building had a very homey feeling and I immediately fell in love with it.

The next apartment was a few blocks away and I was not at all impressed with either the building or the layout. After we were finished looking, the realtor walked with me, giving me information about the neighborhood. Before heading home, I walked through Brookfield Mall to grab a coffee and went to sit on a bench by the river. I tried to envision living here and I felt a sense of peace. I know that no specific place can give that to you. It has to come from inside but living in an environment that can offer you help in finding serenity is a big plus.

After sitting for a few minutes I gave Stephen a call because I knew he would be waiting to hear from me to inform him about the apartments I had seen today. He answered right away, and I told him that I saw one I didn't like and one that I liked very much. I explained the details of the apartment and then he asked me for the address. I told him its location and apartment number and just as I was about to say more, he said, "What?" in a very loud voice. I asked him what was wrong, and he responded by telling me that it was the exact building and apartment where he and his first wife had lived before they got divorced.

"No fuckin' way! That's too weird!" I said.

Stephen asked if I really liked the apartment and if so, would it be too crazy to want to rent it? I really didn't mind since it was such a long time ago, as long as he didn't feel uncomfortable with it. He said he would like to see it and then he could determine how he felt. He asked if I could contact the agent to make another appointment as soon as possible. He continued to ask more questions about the apartment and apparently there had been some major renovations done over the years.

We ended the call, and I contacted the agent asking if I could see the apartment again with Stephen, and I made an appointment for the next day at 3 o'clock. The realtor also said he could show me a few other apartments, which I said would be great. Before heading home, I took a walk along the Esplanade enjoying the views of Lady Liberty, the sailboats, and the people walking by. I then headed home to Forest Hills feeling excited but not fearful.

I had arrived early for our appointment the next day, so I took a walk by the river. I wasn't sure how Stephen was going to react to seeing his old apartment, but either way I believed we would be living in Battery Park City. I met Stephen at the building and waited a few minutes for Jonathan. We took the elevator up to the eighth floor and I watched Stephen's reactions. He was revisiting his past with each step he took, and he wasn't entirely sure what he was going to see.

I let Stephen go in to look around since I had already seen the apartment. He spoke to the agent about what it was like living in Battery Park City over 30 years ago. He walked through the apartment quickly pointing out all the changes that had been done, and he seemed to like them all. He even remembered where he had certain pieces of furniture and other items throughout the apartment.

Stephen finished touring the apartment, and then we all sat on the few chairs that remained in the apartment to discuss the lease and other building information. We didn't agree upon anything yet because we were interested to see the other apartments. After seeing a few more apartments, we informed Jonathan that we would get back to him and let him know our decision.

By the time we'd finished, it was getting close to dinner time, so we headed to a restaurant nearby. We sat outside and talked over our thoughts. Stephen started by saying how weird it was to step into an apartment from the past. He said all the renovations were beautifully done and I believed him, given all his years in the construction business. He said he'd always loved the view, layout, and the building. I told him that I also liked his old apartment better than any others I had seen. I also asked if he wanted to view the other apartments and if he would feel uncomfortable living in his old place? He said that it would not bother him at all. He was still in disbelief given all the possible apartments that were available, that we would somehow come across this one.

We finished our meal and continued to talk and make plans. Stephen's lease was finished by mid-July so that gave him a month to make his move. My lease was not over until September so there would be a month between our moves. We decided to go forward with the move and that he would contact the realtor to let him know.

We headed home feeling joyful, and before he got off the train at Penn station he said, "Wouldn't it be nice if one day we wouldn't have a train ride separating us?" We kissed each other goodbye and then the doors opened, and he disappeared into the crowd.

I arrived back in Forest Hills and walked the few blocks from the train to my apartment. As I walked the streets to my home, I imagined what it would be like walking down unfamiliar streets, looking at unfamiliar places, and seeing unfamiliar people that held no past memories. Forest Hills had been my home for almost 40 years. Familiarity brought a sense of comfort, but it also held the yesterdays that I no longer wanted to be reminded of.

The thought of moving to the city offered a sense of a new beginning for myself and for both Stephen and me. I thought it odd that Stephen did not have any qualms about moving into an apartment that he had shared with his former wife. He explained that it was over such a long time ago and he really had no feelings either way for her, so he did not have any attachment issues he had to work through. As I opened the door, Mimi came running to greet me with a bunch of belly rolls and kisses. I wondered how she would take to yet another move.

The next few days I had a mixture of both excitement and fear. I read somewhere that the only way to overcome insecurity is to take a risk. I was definitely a person who needed security. I needed to know what was going to happen at every given moment, and in the future with my life and with everyone I loved. That was a very unrealistic way of thinking and a really a big burden. I was so looking forward to letting all that go and stepping into my life in a different dimension than I had ever done before.

I was not taking a risk without thought and examination of my feelings, but I needed to step out of my comfort zone. I was only a short train ride away from any given family member if there was an emergency, or if they wanted to visit. I would miss seeing my friends, but the few that were very dear to me I would still manage to keep close to for sure. So I decided to make a plan to tell my family about my decision to move, arrange for movers, and to start a new chapter in Stephen's life and mine.

I don't know why, but for someone who usually takes a long time to make a decision about a major event in my life, I managed to inform my family about my move, contact movers, inform my building manager that I was terminating my lease, all within a few days. Something inside of me seemed to all of a sudden let go of my fears, perhaps wanting to have more joyful yesterdays and more hopeful tomorrows. I felt closer to Stephen than I ever had, and I was able to talk to him without holding back, which was a huge accomplishment. I always filtered what I wanted to say to everyone thinking about how they needed to hear things, other than what I needed to say.

Since I had moved around a few times over the years I didn't have too much of anything. I had gotten rid of many items that I no longer needed, wanted, or that no longer brought me joy. I let go of clothes, books, household items, photos and many other things that locked me into past memories. All that I really had a lot of were my kitchen items and books, which were a large part of who I was and that brought me much happiness.

Stephen didn't have much furniture or household items, but he did have a lot of guitars, art supplies, and books. We discussed items we would bring and since I had recently purchased some new furniture, I would be taking that to the new apartment. I made a list of where I had to send notification of my address change and actually got excited writing my new Manhattan address. First time I would no longer be a Queens girl!

In the past, each move brought about some sadness, but I packed eagerly this time and without much remorse. My girls also seemed to be happy for me and this made my decision of moving even more joyful. Because my lease was not up until September, I had some time to pack and move my things out slowly. However, Stephen had only a few weeks to arrange all his moving plans. He was working full time and his hours were long, so I offered to help him, and besides, I was getting really good at moving. Stephen had arranged to take a few days off and he set his move in date for July 29th. All our moving plans were going well, but trouble was brewing with Iden, which was causing my girls and I much concern.

The summer months always seemed to provoke a heightened mood for Iden. Perhaps it was all the sunlight or just his cycling pattern, but he was clearly no longer depressed, and he was doing some heavy drinking. I tried my best not to call or engage with him when he was manic, but when he called, I did my best to listen. When I spoke to him, I could tell he was not focused, his speech was slurred, and he would get easily agitated. Lizzy called me often sounding extremely nervous about her father's mental state and about his drinking. There was very little I could do except listen, and to let her know that I would be available if she needed me. I suggested she call his doctor since I was no longer allowed to. Iden did not allow me to talk to his psychiatrist after we were divorced, which is fair enough. He had been very noncompliant with attending his scheduled appointments, and it was difficult to know if he was taking his medicine properly, especially when he was drinking.

Since it was COVID, we knew he wasn't in bars drinking. Outdoor dining had started, and in order to have alcohol you had to order food. Since Iden preferred to only drink in bars, we knew he wouldn't be frequenting the restaurants to have a drink and would much rather drink in his apartment.

Lizzy called me over the first few weeks in July very upset when he would not answer his phone and when he did, he had clearly been drinking. Claudia was still going through relationship issues with Martin and mentioned that she might want to leave him. So although I was about to embark on a new joyful adventure with Stephen, my heart was pulling some of that joy away with the present mental state of Iden and with Claudia's boyfriend problems.

Stephen's moving day arrived and I went to the New York City apartment, while he met his movers in New Jersey. I arrived a few hours before the movers to get some food items into the refrigerator. I had also bought some daisies and put them in a plastic cup. I brought a book with me to read, but since it was a beautiful day and I had some time before the movers came, I decided to sit by the river and get some sun.

I had spoken to Stephen around 8:30 in the morning to let him know I was already in the apartment. He didn't have many boxes and said that the movers and he should be there by 11:30. He was driving over in his car carrying his guitars and other fragile items. It was a warm sunny day, but there was always a cool breeze in Battery Park City, so I was enjoying my little respite before the chore of unpacking began. In about two weeks I would be moving in too, and I was seriously hoping nothing interfered with my move, but in all honesty, I knew that it was all in control.

Stephen's move went well. We had all of his 30-plus boxes unpacked, and his clothes hung up and put in his drawers by the end of the day. We worked up until 8 o'clock and took a short break to get some pizza from across the street. There were still a few boxes that held paintings, and other decorative items that would eventually find a place in the apartment, but as long as there was a coffee pot waiting to brew morning coffee, a bed with clean sheets, and some towels hung in the bathroom, the move in was complete.

My apartment was completely packed up and Stephen was taking the day to help me with my move in. The night before my move, my daughters stopped by along with Joel and Martin, and we ordered some Chinese food and had a good talk. I was feeling better that Claudia and Martin seemed to have worked through some of their problems. We talked a little about Iden and were all worried about him. I made it very clear to my girls that we are a family and would always take care of each other, and that I would be available whenever needed, whether we are living two blocks, two miles, or two states away.

I gave each of my girls a bag filled with photos from the time they were born until recently. There were photos of my parents, friends, vacations, and holidays. I kept a few of my favorites but did not need all the albums we had acquired over the years. When we sold the house, I did not have the time to go through them all, and did not have the emotional strength either, but now I did, which was a good process of detaching. In *Think Like a Monk*, Jay Shetty says, "Detachment is not that you own nothing, but that nothing should own you." The attachment I had to the past brought me much joy, but also much pain. When I looked at the photos, I felt love and joy, but it was also overshadowed by sadness. Our family was so different today than it was then, and we are each different as well.

Our visit ended, and Joel helped me drop Mimi off at my friend's home, where she would stay until after the move. Iden knew I was moving in with Stephen but had not reached out to wish me good luck or to say anything at all, which was understandable.

Moving day arrived and I was up early because of the anticipation of the move. Since I had everything all packed and was not able to make breakfast, I went out to grab a coffee and a bagel. I called Stephen as I walked because I knew he would already be up. He was an early riser, even on days he wasn't working. He started his day at 5 o'clock with some inspirational reading, meditation, and journaling. Even though he took the day off to help me with my move, he was already answering emails from work when I called. He seemed to be as excited as I was. He'd been up since 4 o'clock, and he couldn't believe this day had finally come. He said my moving in had made him very happy and that he would do everything he could to make me happy as well. Hearing those words made me smile and helped take away some of my jitters.

I returned to my apartment to enjoy breakfast sitting on one of my chairs and resting my coffee and bagel on a cardboard box.

It is a funny feeling looking at your life all packed up in boxes and bags. This was the first move where I was taking only things I really needed with no extra baggage. I also felt for the first time that I was leaving behind my emotional baggage that I just couldn't carry with me anymore. I was not sure what my future would be like living with Stephen, but I was trying to stay in the present and feeling that at this given moment that all was good.

The movers arrived by 8:30, and loaded up, and headed into the city. I was taking an Uber, but I knew Stephen was at the apartment, so I was in no rush. Before I left, I stood by the door and said goodbye to the apartment, and also to Queens. I felt a bit teary, but I eagerly walked forward to a new door opening before me.

I arrived at the new apartment about the same time as the movers. Stephen was already downstairs telling the movers where they could park. We gave each other a big hug and a kiss, and we went up to the apartment. Within two hours the movers had everything in. Stephen had made a fresh pot of coffee, so before we started to unpack, we had a cup with some yummy vegan cookies and talked. I told him that I was fine to be left alone to unpack and actually preferred it. I knew if he were there, we would be opening up too many boxes at one time making it difficult to put things away, so he agreed. He helped lay down the carpets and fix the layout of some furniture before leaving.

I knew I would not get through all the boxes that day, but there was no rush. By the time Stephen came home from work I had finished hanging up most of my clothes and had many of the kitchen items unpacked, but there was still about half of the boxes to be opened. I had managed to put some little items out on the bookcases and on my dresser and when he saw them, he said, "It's beginning to feel and look like a home."

We ordered dinner in and continued to open more boxes after dinner together. By 10 o'clock we stopped and went to bed exhausted, but happy. Although I was tired, I had a hard time falling asleep because the sounds from the cars passing on West Street were louder and the lights shining in our bedroom from the tall buildings nearby were so much brighter than I was used to in Forest Hills. It was just different sights and sounds, but ones I gladly listened to and watched before I fell asleep next to Stephen.

By the end of October, New York City was in Phase 4 of reopening that included museums, gyms, and gardens and intermediate and high schools would stay closed until 2021, but elementary schools would reopen in December. I had settled into my new apartment and life with Stephen, and I making Battery Park City my new home. The shopping was a very different experience than in Forest Hills, but I adjusted to grocery shopping at large stores like Whole Foods and Trader Joe's very easily. I started to recognize people in the neighborhood walking their dogs when out on walks with Mimi. Stephen was still working, so most of my day from 7 o'clock to about 5 o'clock I spent alone, but I filled up the time as I had done while living in Forest Hills by myself. I worked out, did chores, walked Mimi, read books, wrote, and made dinner most nights.

At least once a week we would find a new place to eat and, on the weekends, we usually found a place to have brunch. We started to use Citi bikes to get around everywhere and besides being fun, I was getting into my best shape ever. We went everywhere either by bike or by foot from downtown to Riverside Drive exploring all the sights I had never seen. Since it was early fall it was still lovely to sit by the river and do a nightly walk with Mimi after dinner. I was allowing myself to accept the love and care that Stephen was giving me, and to embrace this new sense of peace that had eluded me for most of my adult life.

Just when I was finding peace, Iden's mental health was becoming a very serious concern and Lizzy was afraid for his safety. Although we talked every day, there were issues with him that she was not sharing since I had made it very clear that I did not really want to know his day-to-day affairs, but if she needed my help I would be there in a heartbeat.

One particular day she called me in tears and informed me that Iden had been having more and more episodes of binge-drinking and he had been skipping his psychiatrist appointments. She had been in touch with his doctor and because of COVID he hadn't seen him in person, and he hadn't been signing into his Zoom meetings. I had made a few calls to Iden during the months I had been living with Stephen, and I could tell he wasn't too well by the way he was talking. A few times he got very nasty with me, so I ended the conversation. I asked Lizzy what she wanted me to do to help, but she sounded like she was coming undone between her difficult job of running a school virtually during the pandemic and taking care of her father. I couldn't help but allow myself to start having feelings of guilt a few minutes after our talk.

When Stephen got home from work, he noticed I was a bit distracted and immediately asked if I was okay. I was going to talk to him about my talk with Lizzy after dinner, but since he'd asked, I told him what was going on. He listened and as he often did, said, that Iden was probably misdiagnosed and was not on the right medication. He clearly was bipolar, but all the doctors we had seen said he had a very complicated case.

Even back in the early days when Iden was first hospitalized at Beth Israel Hospital, almost fifteen years ago, his doctor said that Iden's was a difficult case because of a mixture of his comorbid issues and his personality. He was in extreme denial that he was an alcoholic, bipolar, and that he needed to have a therapist in addition to a psychiatrist. Stephen listened while I spoke and offered to talk to Iden since he was also a recovering alcoholic and had bouts of depression. I appreciated the offer, but given the state Iden was in, I didn't think Iden would be receptive to talking to him.

That night Stephen took the nightly walk to the river with Mimi alone because I felt incapable of moving. I had that sick feeling that something awful was going to happen. When Stephen returned from his walk, we made some tea and talked and he tried to make me feel less nervous by assuring me if something should happen, we would deal with it, and that he would help me in any way he possibly could. Having a partner who helped quell my anxiety and was supportive was indeed a blessing, and that night I went to bed still worried, but surer than ever that my decision to live with Stephen was the best thing for me.

Around 10 o'clock Stephen woke me up and handed me my phone saying Lizzy was calling. Since I knew she gets up at around up around 5 o'clock in the morning she usually is in bed by 9 so I automatically knew something was wrong. As soon as I heard her voice, I knew there was a problem. Lizzy said that she always called her dad to say goodnight and that he had not answered his phone since dinner time around 6 o'clock. She knew something was very wrong. The last time she spoke to him he said he was going to get some groceries and that he would talk to her later, but he never called back or answered any of her calls.

I tried to calm her down because we have been down that road before, but this time she said she felt something was terribly wrong because when she last spoke to him, he sounded like he had been drinking. She was going to go to his apartment to see if he may have fallen asleep. I told her to give him some time and that I would continue to call. Before hanging up I remembered she had a neighbor's number and I told her to call and to see if she could knock on his door to see if he were at home. She said she would and that she would call me back if she heard anything. Lizzy called back saying the neighbor went to his apartment and knocked on the door, but he did not answer, so now Lizzy was very upset and said that she and Joel were going to his apartment because they thought that maybe he had fallen or had passed out from drinking. When she got to his apartment, she would call me.

By now Stephen was up and he asked me what was going on and I explained. He also asked what I thought may have happened. At the best I was hoping he just drank too much and might just be in a heavy sleep. If he wasn't home, given his current mental instability, I was afraid for his safety, especially if he were drinking.

Around midnight, Lizzy called me from Iden's apartment crying, saying he was not home and feared he might be hurt or in trouble. New York City was again facing spikes in COVID cases, so restaurants and bars had to be closed by 10 o'clock. Looking for Iden now would be difficult because he would no longer be at his favorite drinking hole, which we knew.

Lizzy was going to look in some parks where she knew he liked to sit and said she would call me if she found anything. I asked if I should come, but Stephen suggested I wait at home until either we get in touch with him or find him, and then decide what needed to be done. There was not much more we could do. I told Lizzy to be careful since searching in the dark for someone is not only difficult, but dangerous as well. After some time searching for him, Lizzy called and said she was going back to his apartment to wait to either hear from him by phone or to see him when he returned.

I couldn't sleep, so Stephen made some coffee and we just waited. Around 1 o'clock in the morning I received a call from a woman saying that she was with Iden, and he'd asked to call me. Apparently, he had been beaten up in a bodega and the owner had called an ambulance for him. She said he was being taken to Elmhurst Hospital and then she gave the phone to Iden. He was crying, saying that he he'd been beaten up and that he needed me. I told him that I would be at the hospital soon and that I was so sorry.

I could tell he had been drinking and I was sure he was not totally innocent as far as the altercation. Before calling Lizzy, I told Stephen what had happened and conferred with him as to what should be my next steps. He suggested I call Joel and tell him what had happened because Lizzy would be very upset.

Since I did not have permission to talk to Iden's doctor, Stephen also suggested that after informing Lizzy as to what happened she should call Iden's doctor to update him about his condition and predicament. I made the call, and I knew it was going to be a difficult one. Lizzy immediately started to cry hysterically upon hearing the news and demanded to talk to me thinking I could tell her more than I shared with Joel. She asked me many questions and all I could do was repeat what I knew. I told her to please place a call to Iden's doctor and to take some deep breaths. We were grateful that he was alive, and we would do whatever we needed to do to get through this together.

After hanging up I changed into some sweatpants and a sweatshirt and took along some water and a few snacks, knowing it was going to be a long night. Besides being upset with the news of Iden's situation, I was not pleased to be heading to Elmhurst Hospital where there was a large number of COVID patients. Stephen promised me that he would take good care of Mimi and asked to please keep him informed as soon as I knew something. He called an Uber for me, and I was on my way at 2 o'clock in the morning to yet another crisis in Iden's and my family's lives.

I got to the hospital and after a series of routine COVID questions and checking in, I was led to the emergency area to see Iden. A nurse took me to where Iden was waiting. He was already admitted, and some machines were attached to him. When I saw his face, he was almost unrecognizable. His left face was the color of an eggplant, a bluish black, and his left eye was all bloodshot and swollen. When Iden saw me, he grabbed my hand and started to cry, and all that I could do was cry along with him as well.

How he ended up on that gurney was not significant, but rather that he was hurting and in pain was what needed to be addressed. He started to explain what happened, but by the smell of his breath he had been drinking. He explained that he was home and needed cigarettes, so he went to his local bodega where he engaged in a conversation in Arabic with the owner of the store. Apparently, he said that there was another guy in the store who said some racial slurs to both of them and Iden, I am sure being inebriated, answered back equally with some harsh words. After a few minutes of being with him I reassured him that I would help him and encouraged him to rest.

The nurse informed me that my daughter was in the waiting area and only one person at a time was allowed to be with Iden. I told Iden that I would be in the waiting room because Lizzy wanted to see him. He didn't want her to see him as he was, but I suggested she would be more upset if she didn't see him. When I went back to the waiting area, I informed them of what happened and how he looked. I also said that I had not spoken to any doctors or nurses yet, but they would contact us as soon as possible.

Lizzy went in to see Iden and came out crying, feeling completely overwhelmed as to what to do. I repeated the fact that we had to remain calm, and we'd talk to a doctor to see what he says after they'd evaluated him. We decided that I would wait with Iden, since Lizzy was way too emotional, and she needed to be near Joel to help keep her calm. I went back into the emergency room and waited with Iden to talk to the doctors.

The hospital staff must have given him something for pain and to calm him because he was now sleeping. About half an hour later, a doctor came and introduced himself to me and asked who I was. He then started to tell me about Iden's condition based on a brief examination. Apparently, the doctor had noted that Iden had been drinking and that he was in a fight where he received some nasty blows to his eye. He said that Iden may need surgery, but they would need to do some CAT scans and further tests, but it looked like he had a detached lens.

He then started to ask me some questions about his background health. I explained his mental condition and the doctor said they'd have a psychiatrist talk to him and then decide his best placement. He also said that they gave him some medicine to calm him down because he wanted to leave and was very agitated.

After talking to the doctor I went back to the waiting area and told Lizzy and Joel what the doctor had said about his eye and the needed tests and psychiatric evaluation. It was going to be a long time before we knew where Iden would be placed so I suggested that Lizzy and Joel should go home. I said I would stay at the hospital for there was no reason for all of us to be here, but they didn't want to leave. Joel found a nearby Dunkin Donuts to keep us awake at 4 o'clock in the morning.

Iden was asking for us when he awoke, so I went in to see him and he was clearly very unhappy and giving the nurses a hard time. He said he wanted to leave, but I told him that couldn't happen since they needed to do tests on his eye to determine what needed to be done. He asked why a psychiatrist needed to talk to him and why they'd asked if he had a drinking problem. He then proceeded to start screaming at me asking why I had said he was an alcoholic, and other profanities in between. So the staff suggested I leave.

As soon as I returned to the waiting area, I saw Lizzy and Joel talking to a doctor, who was taking down information on a clipboard. He was a resident psychiatrist and was asking about the medicines that Iden was taking, along with relevant background information. Some of the information Lizzy knew better, such as the names of his medicines and his current doctor names and numbers so I let her talk, but as far as his past history went, I knew it better. So when it came time for answering those questions, I did the talking. The doctor said he was going to talk to his team and decide on the best placement for Iden.

We waited until morning turned into afternoon and we quietly sat and ate the snacks I brought from home. Around noon, a young female psychiatrist came out to meet us and said they had now placed Iden in the emergency psychiatric ward because his behavior was deemed dangerous. He needed supervision, which could not be given in the general emergency ward. Lizzy was very upset and asked many questions. The doctor patiently answered them all.

The doctor permitted one of us to go in to see Iden, warning us that many of the patients were not complying with wearing face masks and their behavior may be disturbing to see. I said I would go in and talk to Iden. When Iden saw me approaching him, he started yelling saying that I was responsible for putting him here. He was very agitated and understandably so as it was not a good place to be under any circumstance.

A doctor came and said as soon as a bed opened up Iden would be brought upstairs, and that the staff would update us when he was moved. I returned to Lizzy and Joel, sat them down, and said that although it was upsetting to see him in this environment, maybe he would get the help he needed. Perhaps this was his rock bottom.

We stayed there well into the next day until Iden was finally moved up to the psychiatric ward. We were not allowed to visit at all because of COVID, but even if it hadn't been for COVID, it was ill-advised to see him now since he was still in an elevated and very agitated state. We got details of the social worker, doctor information, and the number of the ward that he was on in order to get updates on the results of his eye tests and his general mental condition.

During the time I was at the hospital I had been in touch with Stephen, updating him on Iden's condition. Since all of this happened on the weekend, Stephen was at home and able to take care of Mimi for me, so I did not have to worry about her care. Although we could not visit Iden at the hospital it was still necessary to go there to talk to doctors and to get updates. I was thinking it would be easier for me to arrange for Mimi to stay with me at Lizzy's for a few days until more information was received and the next steps were in place. It had been a long few days, and I was happy to return home and take a shower, eat a meal, and to see Stephen and Mimi.

After a few weeks we realized that Iden needed to be in the hospital for some time, even though he now seemed to be no longer manic and hostile but was feeling very depressed. Lizzy was in touch with the social worker since Iden now refused to share his status with me since he felt I put him in the psychiatric ward based on the information I gave the doctors. He continued to say that he did not have a drinking problem. Once again, he wasn't accepting any responsibility for his actions. Lizzy had to talk to so many doctors while still working, but Iden refused to let them call me. He did, however, call me daily to let me know how he felt, and all I could do was listen, but when he got nasty I hung up knowing that he would get even more upset.

Iden stayed at Elmhurst Hospital during the month of November and was released with a whole new medication regime and scheduled psychiatrist, therapist, and AA Zoom meetings. We arranged to have a visiting nurse, a cleaning woman once a week, and some meals dropped off by family and food services. It took a team to do all that was needed since he seemed incapable and had entered into a very dark depression after leaving the hospital. He rarely showered and had lost a lot of weight, which he didn't have much to lose to start with, and his appearance was a frightening sight.

Although Claudia wanted to see him, he didn't want to see her, and he hardly wanted to talk to anyone. He only wanted to see Lizzy and Joel and occasionally he agreed to see me. I was beginning to feel very frustrated because he wasn't making progress. We were now entering the holiday season and he was sinking deeper and deeper into his depression. I became alarmingly worried about Lizzy's involvement with her father's illness because her well-being was directly connected to his well-being.

A vaccine had now been introduced and Lizzy, being an educator and Claudia, being in health care, could now get vaccinated. Since being in the hospital Iden was diagnosed with a mild case of diabetes, so he could also soon be vaccinated as well.

I was going into Queens at least twice a week to see my daughters and to drop off food I was making for Iden. My presence and mood was different back home with Stephen. I did not have the same spark of energy or desire to do the things we usually liked to do and in a way was feeling a bit depressed myself. My therapist said sometimes after a crisis we feel that way because we put so much effort into fixing the problem and worrying that when things begin to calm down, we allow ourselves to break down a little bit. Although Stephen was very supportive, I could tell he missed my normal presence.

The holidays arrived and although we were not permitted the usual family gatherings due to COVID, we still were able to enjoy seeing the city lit up and feel the excitement of this time of year. It was a struggle for me to delight in these pleasures and I could not wait until it was all over.

With the New Year, came hope as well as the issuing of the vaccine for the COVID virus, but hope seemed to elude Iden since he was still in a very dark place, and I began to feel that he would never be well again. I was feeling like I was living two separate lives and not particularly doing a good job at either one of them. I was withdrawing from Stephen and not having the patience for his exuberance for life. It was becoming more difficult with each passing day to try and fake an interest in doing things with him when my mind was elsewhere. I was finally getting the knack of being totally honest with Stephen, but I felt as though he thought I could change gears and put all that was going on with Iden aside and dive right back into where we were before this event happened.

I also felt that I was not present enough in my daughters' lives with the caretaking of their father and felt that they were struggling with so much on their plate. I was especially worried about Lizzy because she seemed to have put her life on hold since Iden's hospitalization and was in a bit of a funk herself. It wasn't easy to have all of those concerns going on in my head and to still wanting to plan enjoyable activities with Stephen.

Iden's depression lingered like the long, cold, bleak days of winter. I was splitting my time between my home in Battery Park City and Queens, and with each trip I was picking up more anxiety, fear, and confusion. When I was in the city, I felt I needed to be in Queens helping more with my family, and when I was in Queens, I felt that I should be at home spending more time with Stephen.

I had put aside doing the things that were important to me, especially my writing. The pull I felt to be full time in Queens was getting stronger. My identity first was being a mother, a good mother, and since I felt my girls were hurting, I needed to be more present. Was it a logical feeling? Perhaps not, but the feeling of not being comfortable living with Stephen was presenting me with much confusion. Stephen was being as understanding as he could be, but I could tell his patience was running low with my absence of mind, body, and spirit. Our relationship was suffering.

By March, more and more people were getting vaccinated and along with the coming of spring came hope. I was trying my best to balance my life between my family and Stephen, and it was wearing me down, although Lizzy was doing much of the caretaking herself by taking Iden to doctor's appointments, making sure his medicines were delivered as well as ensuring food deliveries and home care services were carried out.

I was physically not making many trips to Queens, but my mind surely was. Claudia was also struggling once again with relationship issues with Martin. One night a friend of Claudia's called me to inform me that certain things were going on between

Claudia and Martin and said Claudia wanted to leave him. She was currently staying at a friend's house due to a huge fight they'd had and was feeling ashamed to tell me. After hearing this news, I reached out to Claudia, but she did not answer her phone, so I left a voice mail simply stating that I missed her and to please call. Perhaps we could meet for dinner after work one day.

A few days later I received a call around 10 o'clock at night. Stephen had already gone to bed, and I was still wide awake so I was watching some Netflix when Claudia called. As soon as I saw her name pop up on my phone, I knew something was up. When I answered the phone, she said a few brief words before she started to cry. When she calmed down, she said she was very upset with Martin and didn't know what to do but did not share any details as to what had happened. She said she was thinking of leaving him but didn't know where to go. Claudia was fearful of living alone, plus her salary would just about get her a very small studio with very little left over for anything else.

Claudia's safety and well-being were the most important, so I suggested she come right over to my apartment so we could talk about making a plan. She didn't want to, so I suggested she ask her sister if she could stay with her until things settled and she had some time to think matters over. I told her I was proud of her for not staying in a situation that she did not feel was right. She said she was staying at a friend's house for a while and that she would figure things out and get back to me about what she was planning to do.

As soon as I hung up the phone, I thought about calling Lizzy, but it was late, and I knew she would be sleeping and I shouldn't disturb her. Plus, Claudia said she would contact her sister herself, but I was worried and had no one to talk to. I couldn't call her father because he wasn't capable of taking care of himself, I didn't want to wake Stephen and talk about more family problems, especially since there had been so much going on already.

I shut off the TV because I couldn't concentrate on the show thinking about Claudia. All I could think about was that if I were living alone, she would be able to come back to my apartment. My anxiety level just grew a bit more that night and all I could do was sit on the couch and think about what I could do to help her. I never made it back to bed and when I opened my eyes, I saw Stephen standing over me saying, "Good morning. What's going on?"

It was only 5, and I did not feel like talking, so all I said was that I had a hard time sleeping and then I pulled the throw over my face and went back to sleep. Before he left for work, he said goodbye and I answered with, "Have a good day."

At that moment I wished I wasn't here and that I did not have to be feel bad for feeling upset. I wanted to tell Stephen what had happened, but I just couldn't because I didn't want to hear his reaction. Most of the time when I talked about Claudia's issues with her boyfriend he would not respond, or he'd just say that she would figure it out. Yes, she was an adult and would eventually figure things out, but the way he dismissed my problems sometimes bothered me. I made some coffee and got dressed to walk Mimi.

Just as I was leaving for my walk with Mimi, Stephen called and said once again, "What's going on?"

It bothered me very much because when he asked that question it was more to find out what was going on with him and me rather than what was going on with me. I am not saying I am better than him or anyone else, however, I am wired a bit differently and if someone seemed to have a bad night, I would be more inclined to ask what was wrong with them than worrying how and what they are feeling would affect me.

His lack of empathy was mostly what our arguments in the past had always been about. I told him about Claudia and his response was, "Okay, I have to get back to work."

After hearing his words, I got a very uneasy feeling, which I hadn't had in a very long time. That feeling made me doubt if I had made the right decision to move in with him.

For the rest of the day I felt unsettled because of the combination of worrying about Claudia and my brief conversation with Stephen. I was having a hard time remaining still, so I took Mimi on a lot of walks by the river trying to get my anxiety under control. Since going to therapy I realize that my anxiety occurs only when I feel

I that I have to make a decision that may be best for me, but not for others. I had only been living with Stephen for several months, but the last few weeks had been very challenging due to my family issues and the way I chose to be involved.

After my last walk with Mimi and before Stephen came home, I sat on the couch and poured myself a glass of wine. I usually started to cook dinner around 5 o'clock. I enjoyed having some wine while I cooked, but tonight I did not feel like cooking, but just felt like having the wine. As I sat looking out the living room window, I noticed dark clouds starting to form and within a few minutes there was a huge downpour. I listened to the rain and thought about how like the weather our lives can seemingly go from calm to stormy. I knew when Stephen got home, I had to be honest with him and tell him how I was feeling because I could not keep it contained.

I heard the door unlock and Stephen came in drenched from the rain. He hung up his coat and went into the bedroom to change into some dry clothes. I heard him complaining how he had five umbrellas at home and never had one in the office when he needed one. He usually came home and went straight to the gym for a workout and then we would eat dinner, but tonight he said he was not going and then asked what we were doing for dinner since he saw that I wasn't in the kitchen preparing food. By the expression on my face he knew something was going on and I said, "I think we need to talk."

He had been sitting on a chair in the living room, but immediately after hearing my words he got up and moved to the couch to sit next to me. I started by saying that I had been having a lot of anxiety about my family and more recently about Claudia. I continued to say that it had been difficult for me, not so much physically, but more so emotionally, not feeling that I am in the best place for myself.

Before I could say another word, he asked, "So what do you want to do, Patty?"

I told him I was not sure, but if Claudia needed to leave and had nowhere to go, I might have to help her find a place and perhaps be in Queens for a while.

After hearing those words Stephen stood up and said he couldn't believe what he'd just heard. He continued to say that he thought I was happy living here with him, and that he did his best to make sure I had everything I needed.

I told him it wasn't about not having something, but rather my need to be where I had to be at this time. I was a mother first. It was not that I did not love him and want to be with him, but I just couldn't play two roles in two places at the same time. I had made progress in distinguishing what was good for me and this decision was not so much based on my family needs, but more on my own need.

He got very angry and said, "Well just leave now. Go ahead and just get the fuck out."

I looked out the window and said, "It's pouring out and I don't have anywhere to go." With that he put on his coat and left the apartment. When he left, I realized I had not made any plan as to where I would go or what I would do, but all of a sudden, the anxiety I was previously feeling seemed to dissipate, even though I had no idea what I was going to do.

I quickly made up my mind to call Debbie. She was my best friend, and I did not need to give her details, but just told her that I needed to spend a few days at her home until I figured out my next move.

As I look back on that night, I feel it may have looked like a very impulsive action, but at that time it was something that I just needed to do. Debbie automatically said to come now, but I said I had to gather some things together for myself and Mimi and that I would more than likely be at her place sometime the next day. I was so grateful to have such a good friend. I thought about calling Lizzy and asking her if I could go to her place, but I needed to think things through before unloading more drama upon her shoulders. All of a sudden Claudia and I were seemingly in the same predicament.

Stephen returned home after a few hours, and I had already taken a blanket and a pillow from the bedroom and made my bed on the couch for the night. He didn't say a word to me, but just went into the bedroom and closed the door.

The next day he was up earlier than usual. He dressed and came over to where I was lying and said that he was leaving for work and said goodbye. I answered with a simple goodbye.

As soon as he left, I got busy throwing some essential belongings into my small suitcase along with Mimi's medicine, food, treats, and toys. I really had no idea what I was doing, but I just knew I could not stay. I was not sure if it was for days, weeks, months, or for good, but I needed to move forward to keep my sense of balance.

CHAPTER TWENTY-SEVEN

AFTER THE ENDING

'Celebrate endings – for they precede new beginnings.'
— JONATHAN LOCKWOOD HUIE

With a small suitcase, a backpack, and Mimi, I left Battery Park City on a windy but beautiful and sunny morning in mid-March. The doorman, Tony, asked if I was leaving town. I said I was just visiting a friend for a while. Given the short time I had lived there, I had acquired a special relationship with a few of the doorman, especially Tony. He seemed to be able to read the sadness on my face.

I was heading back into Queens, to my friend Debbie's house for a day or so, until I could gather my wits about me and decide what my next steps would be. I had not texted or called Stephen, and I really did not feel the need to give him any information based on his behavior the previous night. I totally understood that he was upset, however, his response was way out of line and did not allow me to have a conversation with him to help me figure out what would be my best solution.

Acting from my gut, I decided to leave because the hurt I felt from his reaction was driving me forward. As I sat in the Uber with Mimi on my lap, I watched the Brooklyn Bridge go by, the Manhattan Bridge, and the Williamsburg Bridge, trying not to become emotional, but it was not possible.

The short time that I had lived with Stephen brought me much happiness and allowed me to experience a separation from my life in Queens. Just as Iden was struggling to find a balance, I too was attempting to find a balance of meeting the needs of my family and my relationship with Stephen. Packing my bag and heading back to Queens was indeed impulsive, but it was what I felt I had to do at that moment. I couldn't continue trying to work through my current challenges feeling the way I was living with Stephen. It was necessary to find a new way to stand without falling over.

My friend Debbie opened her door and her arms to me without question. Upon my arrival she had a table prepared with muffins and bagels, and I could smell the freshly brewed coffee. She showed me to her guest bedroom where I laid down my belongings and I filled bowls with water and food for Mimi and then Debbie and I sat down to breakfast before we even started to talk.

A few bites into a bagel and a few sips of coffee, I was ready to explain what had occurred the night before. Debbie listened and did not offer any judgment or advice. She did say that I was welcome to stay as long as I needed and that she understood what I was feeling.

After breakfast we sat on the couch, and I just broke down saying that I could no longer continue living the way I was. I was finding it difficult to enjoy my happiness knowing my family was struggling. Learning how to maintain a healthy equilibrium between my relationship with Stephen and my family was an enigma for me: it appeared that I was able to focus on only one relationship at a time. Was it right or wrong wasn't the issue, but rather it was necessary to do what I felt was right to do at this given time.

Stephen's reaction made me aware that he was not able to share my involvement with my family, and, therefore, I felt somewhat disappointed in him and extremely overwhelmed trying to figure out how to help my family. Stephen had been someone I went to for advice and support. I felt that his patience had worn thin over the last few months to a point where the atmosphere of trust we seemed to have of speaking honestly was difficult.

Debbie continued to listen and then offered her thoughts, which I needed to hear. She and I were the same as far as being committed to our family's needs and she had seen me through some of the worst times in my life. She was happy that I was able to move on and start a new life with someone while still being present for my family. The current circumstances of Iden and Claudia were upsetting, as well as Stephen's reaction last night, but Debbie suggested I take some time to think things through before doing anything drastic. I told her I was planning on informing Lizzy but wanted to figure out what I was going to do before asking if I could stay with her. I still hadn't messaged Stephen, nor did he contact me.

After throwing some ideas back and forth between us, I needed to lie down for a bit since I did not sleep at all the night before and was feeling the effects of an emotional hangover. Claudia woke me up early to inform me that she was doing okay, although was confused and upset with her situation with Martin.

When I could no longer stay in bed, I got up to find Debbie in the living room. I let her know that I thought it best that I return to Queens for now. I really did not know exactly what that meant or what that would look like down the road. I could not see myself returning to live with Stephen, not because of our fight the previous night, but due to the need to be planted in a place that I felt I could stand up and manage my life in a healthy manner.

Would I miss living in Battery Park City with Stephen? Of course I would but living with him right now did not allow me to be what I needed to be the most. I needed to be honest with who and what I needed to be for myself first and then to my family and Stephen as well. Debbie thought I was a very strong person and offered to help me in any way possible. She asked how I would inform Stephen of my decision and what I would do if he decided he never wanted to see me again.

My decision to stay in Queens was not to end things with Stephen, but to be in a place that my heart needed to be. After our talk, I told Debbie that I would call Lizzy to ask if I could stay with her until I was able to figure out what needed to be done. Debbie reiterated that I was welcome to stay with her as long as I needed. I was and will always be grateful for our friendship.

I called Lizzy the following morning before she went to work, and I briefly explained what had transpired over the last few days. Even though Lizzy had not always welcomed Stephen into her life with open arms, she communicated that she thought I should give my decision making some thought in regard to my next move. I told her I would, but I felt I needed to be back in Queens. She told me that I was more than welcome to stay with her for however long was necessary, and that we would talk when we were looking at each other later that night.

My next call was to Stephen, and since I had not heard from him, I decided to be the one to make the call. It was around 7 o'clock in the morning and he was already at his desk working and I could hear the voices of other employees. He answered in a very matter-of-fact manner by just saying, "Hey"!

I replied, "Good morning!" I was waiting for him to say something and since there was silence, I started to speak. I had only planned to inform him that I was currently at Debbie's home and that I would be going to Lizzy's that night.

Without giving any more information I thought Stephen might have asked a few questions, but he remained quiet and just said, "Okay, keep me posted."

Although I felt a bit annoyed at his lack of communication, I understood. I really did not want to have an involved conversation since I did not know what I was doing or where I was going.

Debbie drove me to my daughter's house in Long Island City. She gave me a big hug and told me to keep her posted and to take some time to reflect because there was no rush. I watched her as she pulled away and before going up, I sat on Lizzy's front steps trying to hold it all together. Joel was still working from home, so Lizzy said it was fine to come over whenever I wanted to. I wanted to arrive earlier so I could settle in with Mimi and get some thoughts together before talking to Lizzy. I also needed to talk to Claudia and inform her what was going on, and to find out what her plans might be as well.

When Joel opened the door, he was very welcoming and did not ask any questions. He asked if I wanted something to eat or drink and I asked him if it was too early for a martini. We both laughed, and he said that we would definitely have one later when Lizzy got home after work.

I made myself at home in the small guest bedroom and unpacked a few of my belongings. I took Mimi out for a walk, and although we were house hopping, she was adjusting well.

When we returned, I checked in with Joel asking what Lizzy's favorite meal was and if I could make dinner. As a child Lizzy loved any pasta dish, and over the years it had remained the same. Joel said there was no need to do any grocery shopping since they had just gone to Trader Joe's and had everything I would need. Being in the kitchen was a good distraction to all that was going on in my mind.

While Joel continued to work, I called Claudia and informed her that I was at Lizzy's and might be here for a while because I needed some space from Stephen. I didn't want to go into too much detail until I knew my plans. She accepted the news very easily and just asked if I was okay. She was working and promised she would call me when she finished work.

I had my laptop with me, so I began a search of apartments in Forest Hills. As I started my search, I could not believe that this would be my fourth move in under two years. Something inside me was directing my decision and it felt as if I had very little control over what I was doing. Just a little over six months ago I was looking for apartments in Battery Park City with as much commitment as I was today looking for apartments back in Queens. I saw a few apartments that I liked and sent a message to ask for a showing.

After an hour or so I made a cup of tea. Joel was busy working in the study and I went in to ask if he would like a cup as well and he did, so he joined me in the kitchen for a quick chat. Joel is a super sweet, nonintrusive kind of guy and all he asked me was if I was doing okay. He was an excellent listener and that made me feel I could trust him with my thoughts and feelings. I tried to explain the best way I could in a short amount of time knowing that he was working. I also didn't want to include too much of Claudia's issues since she had not informed her sister about her current living situation. Joel listened and said he was sorry.

Before dinner, Mimi needed another walk. We passed by a park and sat on a bench to watch the young children playing. Seeing children at play was a joyful experience and it always brought back memories of my girls. I noticed an elderly couple sitting close by in the late-afternoon sun. They were sitting close together holding hands while talking and laughing. They seemed to be very much still in love, and I couldn't help but continue watching them. Observing both the very young and the very old on that day brought to me a feeling of exuberance for living and loving.

Joel was finished working by the time I got back and asked if I needed help with dinner. He offered me a cocktail while I cooked and I answered with an emphatic, "Yes"!

He made me a negroni. I had never had one before, but the combination of gin, Compari, and vermouth was delicious along with a twist of orange. Joel kept me company in the kitchen while I prepared dinner, asking questions here and there, including what I was thinking of making. I told him that while I was out walking Mimi I had passed a fruit and vegetable stand, so I bought some asparagus remembering that Lizzy loved my mom's dish of pasta with peas, asparagus, and mushrooms. He said he'd never had that dish and looked forward to trying it. We talked a bit more and then he said he had a few errands to do before Lizzy came home from work. He checked to see if I would be okay alone and of course I said, "Yes!"

I actually looked forward to spending some time by myself to think things through..

Lizzy had a nice big kitchen and, as always, cooking made me feel calm and therefore helped me to think more clearly. I was having conversations in my mind going back and forth with should I do this, or should I do that kind of nonsense, but the voice that kept speaking the loudest was to do what I was feeling in my heart. I knew my place for now was to be back in Queens, regardless of the happiness I'd felt living in the city with Stephen. I wasn't denying all that goodness, nor feeling ungrateful for all we had, but I presently could not conduct my life the way I wanted to while living there.

With our meal cooking I sat down and finished my drink along with some cheese and crackers that Joel had thoughtfully laid out on a plate for me before leaving. Mimi was lying by my feet, and she picked up her head to look at me and it seemed as if she were asking me, "Where to next, Mama?"

Joel and Lizzy arrived home almost at the same time. When they walked in, they immediately said, "Something smells delicious."

I had not cooked for Lizzy in a long time, and it felt good to have a meal ready for her when she came home from work, although Joel had become a great cook during the months working from home due to COVID. In between his meetings and teaching law classes at Columbia University he was usually able to start dinner.

We exchanged small talk while we ate and then Joel did the dishes while Lizzy and I went out for a walk with Mimi. As we walked, we caught up about what was going on in more detail. She suspected Claudia was having issues with Martin because of some of the calls she had received from her needing money and not sounding too happy.

Lizzy said that she thought Stephen was good for me and that I should reconsider such a move. She also explained that Iden was doing a little better and that although it was a lot of maintenance on her part, keeping up with his doctor appointments and providing care for his daily needs, she was able to take care of it all with the help of Joel.

I appreciated her kindness in wanting me to put myself first and for recognizing all the good that my relationship with Stephen had given me, but I felt I could not continue putting in so much effort into the two lives I was living at the same time.

Did it make any sense? Perhaps not, but it did not mean the end to everything if I moved back to Queens. Stephen and I were not in a good place right now, but I knew we would figure things out if we were meant to have a future together.

We took a long walk and when we returned home Joel had some espresso waiting for us. It was wonderful to witness how caring and respectful their relationship was, and this brought me much happiness.

I thought of Claudia and wished she could find someone who could offer her the same care. And then my mind went to my relationship with Stephen. He was caring and respectful, but I just felt that I could not properly allow myself to exhibit the way I was feeling without his getting upset. I knew he wanted me to detach from my family in a healthy manner, but his way was a bit different than the way I felt was able to do.

The weekend arrived and Lizzy and I planned to see the apartments that I had scheduled with the brokers. We headed into Forest Hills and stopped off at our favorite coffee spot, Le Boulangerie, to have breakfast. The croissants, crepes, and coffee were delicious, and it was difficult not to smell the butter in the air as you walked down the block of the bakery. This place had always been a favorite place for Lizzy and me to grab a coffee when she was still living at home, so it was a bit nostalgic to be going there with her once again.

We ordered chocolate croissants and coffee and found a table outside among the long lines of people already lined up on a Saturday morning. We didn't say a word while we inhaled our croissants, which only took a matter of minutes. As we started to talk, once again Lizzy asked me if I thought I was doing the right thing by moving. I tried to put into words exactly what I was feeling. Every action has consequences, and I needed to decide which consequence I could live with. I chose to move back to Forest Hills with the risk of jeopardizing my relationship with Stephen.

The pull to be near my family at this time was very important to me. I knew Stephen was capable of taking care of himself and to self-preserve. I needed to be free to do what I felt was necessary, even if it meant that Stephen and I would need to separate and go our own ways.

After finishing our coffee we headed to meet the real estate agent who was going to show us two apartments, and then later meet up with another agent to see three more apartments. It was going to take a few hours and I expressed to Lizzy how grateful I was for her time and understanding.

All the apartments were within a few blocks of each other. The first one we stepped into I knew was a definite no, just because it was very small and had only two closets. The second apartment was a little better, but it didn't have good lighting and it was on the first floor. We had about half an hour before we saw the next apartment, so we did some grocery shopping for dinner that night. We walked over to the last apartment and right away it felt right. The building was very clean and had well-manicured gardens beautifully arranged. There was also a small sitting area out back with benches and an enclosed area for Mimi to run around in. We met the agent, and he took us up to the 6th floor. Just as I knew immediately that the first apartment was not for me, as soon as I stepped into this one, I knew it was perfect.

The apartment was large, with six closets and a newly renovated kitchen and bathroom. It also had an eat-in kitchen plus a small dining area, a large foyer, which could serve as an office, and a dressing area outside the bathroom. The price was right, it allowed pets, and it was available immediately. I told the broker I wanted it and he gave me his card and took my information to send me the application to file online. He took me on a small tour of the building before we left.

Lizzy suggested we see some other apartments just to make sure this one was the best. But I liked this one and was going ahead with renting it. We stopped to have a drink before we headed home to talk over my move once again and to make sure I was doing the right thing. I told her that I would talk to Stephen before signing the lease, although I knew in my heart what I needed to do. I just felt a conversation was necessary before my decision was made.

We sat sipping our drinks and discussed my move and Claudia. Lizzy believed that Claudia's moving in with me was not the best idea, but, if necessary, perhaps Claudia could stay until she was able to stand on her own two feet. She said that Claudia had an on-and-off relationship with Martin and making a move based on her needs was not something she would recommend. I agreed with her that if that was the only reason that I was considering moving it would not be a wise decision. However, there were a few more factors provoking my decision, especially something unsettling in my relationship with Stephen.

As soon as we arrived home, I planned to take Mimi out for a nice long walk and give Stephen a call. It was a lovely spring day, so Joel said that he felt like going for a run in Astoria Park and asked if I would like to join him. He would drive us there and I could enjoy the park with Mimi and have my conversation with Stephen. I thought that was a wonderful idea, so we headed to the park and left Lizzy at home doing some of her weekend chores. She said she was going to cook dinner, even though I'd wanted to take them out for dinner that night to show my appreciation to them for having me stay in their home. Although we had all been vaccinated, Lizzy still wasn't comfortable eating out.

After Joel parked the car, we walked a little bit together and organized a time to meet again, then went our separate ways. I walked Mimi for about 15 minutes before finding a bench to make my call to Stephen. I checked my watch to figure out what Stephen might be doing, as he was a very scheduled and routine person, so I knew by 3 o'clock on a Saturday he would be done with the gym, cleaning, and food shopping. Perhaps now he was playing his guitar, working on a new painting, or taking a nap. I took a few minutes to just breathe before placing the call.

There was no doubt that I loved Stephen, but I felt misunderstood and a bit fearful because of his display of anger on the last night we were together. I could not allow myself to hold back my thoughts and feelings worrying about how someone, especially my partner, would react. I had spent too many years living with Iden, holding back things that were in my heart because I was fearful of his reaction. I did not want to live like that anymore.

When my thoughts were clear and I was calm I called him and he quickly answered the phone with an indifferent, "Hello, Patty."

We exchanged a few words before I expressed my reason for calling. I explained that I'd decided to rent an apartment because

I felt I needed to be near my family at this time since I was finding it difficult to maintain our relationship while addressing the needs of my family. I went on to say that his reaction that night also made me feel unable to trust exposing what I was feeling, making me feel unsafe. I felt there was a limit to what he was able to tolerate as well as a limit to my own ability to withhold my feelings.

I further explained to Stephen that I thought he was being somewhat disingenuous about his concern for my family, and when my attention to my family affected his time with me, he was not able to deal with it. Stephen remained silent the whole time I had been speaking and then asked if I was finished so he could explain. First, he apologized for losing his temper because he thought I was abandoning our relationship to move in with Claudia. He also said that we are two different people and the way he handles things is very different. If moving into the apartment was what I needed to do, then he suggested I do it. He further said that he would not want me living with him when I was feeling that it was not the best place for me to be.

Stephen also asked me about our future together. He said that he loved me and still wanted me in his life, but he could never just have me as a friend. So if we couldn't continue to be in a romantic relationship, he wasn't sure that was something he could handle. I took a minute to digest all he said, and then I responded with a thank you, and that I also loved him, but I felt I needed some time to get myself situated, and to figure some things out before I could answer him. We then talked about moving details and arrangements since he would need to get some new furniture and items after I moved my things out.

We made a time when I could be at the apartment to pack, and I told him once I signed my lease, I would give him my moving date. Before hanging up we tried to make some small talk to lighten the mood. It was a very difficult conversation, since just six months ago I felt joy and excitement about living with and entering into a real commitment with Stephen. I know that trusting a person fully is difficult.

"Trust can be threatened in small and large ways and needs to be reinforced on a daily basis"-Jay Shetty (*Think Like a Monk*).

At this moment I felt my trust in Stephen was threatened by my need to be involved in my family's life. If I did not address their needs because I felt it was threatening my relationship with Stephen, it would be difficult to be the best person I could be, and that was my dilemma. After our talk I knew Stephen would continue to stand by me, even when I was not in my best place with him and that gave me hope that we would be okay. I believed he had my back no matter what my decision was, even though it was not exactly what he wanted. I had to be more thoughtful about my own needs so I could do what was most important without spending my time and energy worrying about meeting other people's expectations.

My conversation lasted longer than I had thought because I saw Joel waving to me from afar just a few minutes after I had hung up the phone. I took Mimi to Joel, and we headed back to the car. Joel asked if everything was okay since he knew I was talking to Stephen.

"Yes." I said. "Everything will be just fine!"

As we drove home, I looked forward to having dinner because all of a sudden, I felt very hungry.

When we arrived home, Lizzy asked how I was feeling. I said I'd had a good talk with Stephen and that I would be renting the apartment.

"Stephen and I are still talking, but things are a little delicate right now."

Although I had a lot to take care of in the next few weeks, I felt calmer because of the talk with Stephen. I did not know what my future was going to be, but I knew I felt good about stepping into it.

Lizzy and Joel were like two little angels helping me with the lease and sending over documents to the real estate agent, and they also helped me find movers. Joel took me to the apartment in Battery Park City to start packing on the days that I had arranged with Stephen. While there, I felt as if I could not pack my things up fast enough, and then I remembered when I had moved in, I had wanted to unpack slowly, making sure everything was placed in a perfect spot.

The last time I came to the apartment to finish my packing, Stephen asked if I could wait to see him and perhaps we could grab a bite to eat before I left. I had mixed feelings about doing this because I knew once I saw him and talked to him certain emotions would flare up, and I didn't want to start second- guessing my next move.

I decided to stay until he came home but asked if we could go out to a restaurant to talk. I did not trust being in the apartment and having a conversation that might get emotional, which perhaps might lead to a physical encounter.

When Stephen walked in, he was a bit surprised at how I had managed to get everything packed up so quickly. He suggested that we could order some food in, but I used the excuse that I could really use a drink, knowing that he did not have alcohol in the apartment. We went across the street to our go-to restaurant. I had a martini, and he had an ice tea and we shared some fried calamari and oysters. He asked about my family, so I gave him a brief update and inquired about his family and job.

We did not have any involved conversation, but rather just needed to end this encounter in a friendly manner.

"Well at least we did it and we tried," he said.

I agreed, adding that I was sorry He said it was okay and that as long as we were still in each other's lives he was good.

I could tell Stephen wanted me to respond to what he had said, but I did not have an answer how we would be in each other lives at this time. Not knowing exactly what lay ahead in the future was troublesome for him, and I understood that, but I really wasn't sure. We kissed and hugged goodbye and it did feel good to hold him, but it also felt good to let go and get back to Queens.

As moving day arrived, Joel drove me to the city to meet the movers. Stephen would be at work, and he was going to be spending a few nights at a hotel until his new furniture was delivered since all those pieces were mine and I was taking them with me. Once again, I took one last look before closing the door on yet another apartment and life I had lived.

I took an Uber to meet the movers back at my new place. The move went well and all the furniture was in place. All the boxes were neatly arranged in each room so I could start unpacking them one by one. Mimi was staying at Lizzy's for a few days until I was able to get the apartment in order.

The last place I had lived alone was a studio apartment, so now having a very large one-bedroom, offered me much more space to hang my clothes and store my kitchen items. By 6 o'clock I had unpacked almost 20 boxes and still had about 20 more to unpack. I took a short break and went out to grab some pizza. While I was eating my pizza, Stephen called and said he went home to grab some things he needed and that it felt very strange to see such a bare apartment. Although I was hungry before his call, I immediately lost my appetite upon hearing those words and felt guilty.

Stephen said he was looking forward to decorating the place his way and enjoying his stay at a five-star hotel downtown. He then jokingly said if I would like to join him for dinner at 7, to please take an Uber on over. His treat. Knowing that he was joking, I said it sounded inviting, but I was eating a slice and was a bit of a mess, but thanks anyway.

After the call, I got back to work, and Joel and Lizzy came by to see how I was doing. They brought over some groceries so I could have coffee and some things for breakfast the next day. I will always be grateful for all the help they provided me during those days.

I continued to unpack until about 10 o'clock and before going to sleep I made sure the bathroom was set up and that my bed had fresh sheets. I was very pleased with all that I had accomplished on the first day of my move into my new apartment. Although I was very tired, I needed to take a shower. While I was showering that odd sense of newness that happens when you adapt to a new home came over me. I happily got into bed and once again I was aware of the newness of the sounds and the absence of light in my bedroom. As I lay there, I very much wanted to pick up my phone to call Stephen and tell him about my day and to hear about how his first night in the hotel was going, but I resisted. I was so used to talking to him several times a day. He was the first person I spoke to in the morning and the last person I spoke to at night.

Life was surely complicated but beautiful as well, offering us many experiences and lessons to learn. Initially I was angry with Stephen, but I no longer held that inside me. I was grateful for all that he had given me over the years, and I really was not sure of what lay ahead for us. All was okay at this very moment and with that thought I drifted off to sleep.

The next thing I heard was my phone ringing at 6:30 in the morning, waking me from a very deep sleep. It was Stephen and he said he needed to have our morning chat if that was okay with me. I had just woken up so I did not sound that enthusiastic, so he apologized for calling. I quickly corrected him and explained that I was happy that he called, and explained I was very tired because the night before I had worked until late unpacking. He asked how the first night in my new apartment was, and I also asked him how his first night in the hotel went.

We talked for about five minutes and then said our goodbyes. I went to the kitchen and was grateful for the coffee and muffins Lizzy had brought over the night before. She even brought my favorite strawberry jelly. While I was having breakfast Claudia called and asked if she could come over to talk to me. She was going into work a little later and I agreed. I had not asked her about her plans, but I made it known to her that she was welcome to live with me if she needed to.

When she arrived, I could tell by the sadness in her eyes that she was not happy. She told me she had been having a difficult time with Martin, mainly because he refused to commit to their relationship. She felt that he didn't want the same things that she wanted, and whenever she brought up the issue they would have a bad fight. I said I was sorry and asked what could I do to help her. She said she had been staying at a friend's house for the last week because their last fight made her very upset and she did not feel comfortable being in his presence. I totally understood. She then asked if she could stay with me until she could figure things out. I agreed saying she could stay as long as she needed and that we would figure things out as we went along.

Claudia hugged me and apologized for any problems she may have caused between Stephen and me. I told her that whatever happened between Stephen and me was between us and not because of her. She said she'd go to gather some of her things at her apartment while Martin was at work since he was working nights. I sat with her and talked a little more and she ate some breakfast. When she left for work her face seemed a little brighter than when she first came.

I continued to work in the apartment putting away all my dishes, glasses, organizing my linen closet, and wardrobe. By the end of the day I was even hanging up some pictures and decorating some built-in bookcases and nooks with my knick-knacks. Claudia arrived around 8 o'clock and I had done a small food shop with just enough items to have something for dinner and lunch for the next few days.

When Claudia walked in, she immediately said she smelled something good and was happy to have dinner waiting for her after work. I was not sure how long she would be with me, but in the time that we had together I would try my best to provide some comfort and support. I offered to let her sleep with me in my bed, but since I had a large sofa, she said she preferred to sleep there because she was a restless sleeper. She took a shower after dinner, and I made some space in one of my dressers for her clothes and gave her space in one of the closets as well. While she showered, I got out some extra pillows and sheets and a light cotton blanket to make up her bed.

Spring was slowly changing into summer and the nights were still a bit chilly. I said good night to Claudia, then before I retired, I decided to give Iden a call since I had not spoken to him in a while. When Iden answered he apparently knew what had happened and he said that he hoped I was doing okay. His voice sounded stronger and brighter than it had in a long time. He told me he was doing a little better, attending his Zoom meetings regularly, and taking his medicines as prescribed and that he had now been sober for six months. I was very proud of him and told him so. I also encouraged him that his hard work was paying off and that perhaps we could meet for a coffee sometime. Iden liked that idea.

Iden and I still loved one another despite all the hurt we may have gone through over the years, but as they say love is a gift and we should be grateful for it, although its strength may change over time. The past few years were very difficult with Iden and finding the love for him at times was equally difficult. He was, and always will be someone present in my life; however, our roles may have changed but the love remained. I was grateful for all the good he gave me and chose not to focus on the things that he did that hurt my family and me, for it served no purpose.

I would have liked to discuss Claudia with him, but after a few minutes on the phone I could tell he had no more patience to talk and needed to hang up. I opened my phone to check on some deliveries I was waiting on. I was not tired yet, so I started to page through a new fashion magazine Lizzy gave me. I wanted to call Stephen to share my day with him but wasn't sure if it was the right thing to do at this time.

I was a bit restless, so I got up and went into the living room to see how Claudia was doing. She was already fast asleep. I sat on the edge of my bed realizing how much I missed Mimi and could not wait until Lizzy brought her home. I knew having her warm little body snoring next to me would be very soothing. In a whim I dialed Stephen, even though I knew he might already be in bed. He picked up the phone on the second ring, so I assumed he was not in bed yet. He answered with a "Hey," and I said, "I hope I didn't wake you." He said he was still up doing some reading.

I told Stephen that Claudia was now sleeping on my couch, and I was not sure what was ahead. I also told him that I had spoken to Iden, and he seemed to be doing a little better. I couldn't believe I unloaded all that information so quickly. I also said that I had finished unpacking and did some decorating, making my apartment feel like a home. He asked when he could come see the place and

I said that I wanted to get it a little more organized but would set something up soon. His furniture was being delivered the next day and he was excited about returning to his apartment. Again I was having feelings of guilt, but also finding it a bit comical at the same time. I laughed a little, and then he did too and said, "It is a strange situation!"

We said goodnight and I wished him good luck with his new furniture.

The summer had arrived in New York City. Within a year the city and its inhabitants had gone from feeling despair to feeling hopeful. Although tens of thousands of people had moved out of the city and thousands of restaurants had closed as well as many hotels and retail stores, yet people still had hope that the city would make a comeback. It may not be the same as it was prior to the pandemic, however, a "new" New York was emerging, bringing much optimism. Along with the warm temperatures, blue skies and sunshine, and the positivity in the air, many people were smiling more, including Iden and Claudia.

Claudia lived with me for almost a month while continuing to see Martin and slowly working out their relationship issues. She started a new job and seemed very enthusiastic about it and was even considering going back to school.

After about a month or so, Claudia and Martin got back together full time and she decided to move back in with him. Although I enjoyed my time with her, I was looking forward to having my place to myself.

Stephen and I had been able to resume our relationship as well and I was now spending some days in Battery Park City at his place, and he would occasionally spend a weekend in Queens. Our relationship also had gone through changes during the past few months. When I first moved into my apartment, I felt a real sense of loneliness and I was experiencing pain from moving away from Stephen, even though it was something I felt I needed to do; however, it still hurt.

Yet with time and perhaps having the company of Claudia and creating a closer bond with her than I'd had, I slowly started to feel better. After she left, the loneliness was replaced with solitude. A philosopher by the name of Paul Tillich once said, "Our language has wisely sensed these two sides of man's being alone. It has created the word 'solitude' to express the glory of being alone."

I was now living alone, but actually celebrating my time to help develop my self-awareness and to figure out how to make myself happy. I needed to become that person first for myself. I had spent most of my life thinking if I could make others happy that was all I needed for me to be happy. It was very important to me that my family and friends were all in a good place, but if they were not, it shouldn't jeopardize my happiness.

Stephen had tried to instill that idea in me, but I was not ready to accept it. I needed to learn to listen to myself, to trust that what I was feeling and thinking was actually okay, regardless of if others thought differently. Remaining open to new ideas is essential, but not without examination. During the months at home writing, I had the opportunity to reexamine my past actions and allow myself to feel gratitude for all that had happened and to forgive myself and others for all the things we may have done to each other to cause us unhappiness.

Iden continued to do what was necessary to stay in midrange without having episodes of depression and mania. He finally was committed to putting in the effort in maintaining his wellness. Lizzy and Joel adopted a puppy and he brought much love and healing to them. Dogs have a way of making every day better by giving their unconditional love and affection.

At any given moment I know what is present can change, but for now that's all we have. I am grateful for being in a good place myself as well as with the people in my family and with my relationship with Stephen. We can forget that the best place we are currently in is actually magical.

A few months after I had moved into my apartment, Stephen and I were having dinner in the city when he said that he was actually grateful for my moving out. At first, I thought the statement was a bit rude, but then he explained. He started by saying that living with me was and will always be something he totally loved and would love very much for it to happen again, but my moving out made him change. He examined some of his behavior and because of all his journaling and reading self-improvement books, he worked on becoming a better listener. He learned to really listen to the emotions behind the words when people were speaking and to withhold reacting based on personal reasons. He also said that he was painting more and writing more songs since I had moved out. He further stated that when I was living with him all his attention went into our relationship. As I listened to his words, I knew he was being sincere, and I felt a closeness that I had not felt in a long time. We were both in a good place with who we were and with each other.

I had held off finishing my book because I did not have an ending, and although I am still not sure what lies ahead, I have an end to my story and that is to celebrate endings for they precede new beginnings. I may not have the answers to solve many problems, but I have managed over the past year to not try and balance the seesaw of anyone else's existence other than my own, which has enough difficulties.

With my book completed, I made a date to meet my brother Ron for lunch to hand over my writing to him. I mentioned in an earlier chapter that Ron is a professor of philosophy as well as a published writer of several books, so I was very appreciative of his critique of my work.

I met with Ron on a very warm day in July at our usual meeting spot. As usual, I arrived a bit earlier and I sat at the bar waiting for him and ordered a glass of white wine. I never did that before, but I just wanted to do something outside of my comfort zone. Ron showed up around 15 minutes later and we greeted each other with a big hug and a kiss. It had been many months since I'd last seen him. A hostess escorted us to his usual table on the second floor. I loved eating at this restaurant because the atmosphere was very light and joyful, the staff very attentive, and the food quite delicious.

My brother ordered a bottle of champagne in honor of the completion of my book. I told him that maybe he should read it before we celebrate, but he said the very fact that I wrote a book is celebratory. We made a toast and sipped away while talking and waiting for our meal. I took out my manuscript and handed it over to him. It was well over 500, so he read the dedication page and the first few pages. He said it has a great start and that he would read it and give me his review. I looked forward to hearing his thoughts. We then talked about my family and Stephen.

Ron was well aware of my journey and always said that it was necessary to do what I needed to do. I let him know that I was living a purposeful and driven life now, meaning my intention was to be the best I could be for myself first and then for my family, friends, and ultimately the whole human family. He asked if I was making plans to move back in with Stephen and I reported that it had been brought up many times in our discussions, but things were good the way they were for now.

Ron asked about Iden and my girls as well. I said that Iden was taking better care of himself and that was all we could ask for at this time. I would hope that he would be able to have more social contact and get involved in some group activities now after the implementation of vaccines. I informed him next about Claudia stating that she was enjoying her job, but still struggling at times with her anxiety and relationships, which hopefully she would figure out how to maintain emotional and physical wellness in her own time.

Lastly, I talked about Lizzy and Joel. I told him about how supportive and helpful she was in helping Iden get stabilized after a very difficult few years, how she was able to run a school virtually over the past year and be very involved in her father's mental care. Joel was teaching a few law classes at Columbia, while also working his full-time job as a women's advocate lawyer. Joel had been so patient, understanding, and helpful with Lizzy during the crisis with Iden.

When I'd finished updating him about the people and things in my life, Ron gave me a quick update about his work, his wife, Meryl, their new pup, Willow, and their plans for the summer. He walked me to the train station, and we said our goodbyes and he said that he would be in touch with me real soon and that he was very proud of me in many ways, and that meant so much to me. I didn't feel like getting on the subway right away, so I strolled through the Union Square Market for a bit and walked for another 30 minutes heading uptown. My heart was overwhelmingly joyful, and I wanted to look at everything through the eyes of happiness.

"I am waking up to my godself!" (Rupi Kaur).

EPILOGUE

It has only been a little over a year since I have finished writing *See-Saw*, and by the very nature of living we are presented with challenges. Writing *See- Saw* has given me insight in how I used to deal with difficulty. I tried to fix each and every problem and crisis that arose. I have worked hard to understand why I felt compelled to do so and have come a long way in changing that thought and hence the behaviour attached to those thoughts.

Everyone needs a little help along the way, but it is not necessary to soar up or crash down with anyone. We can view the problems from afar while still being present. It is up to the individual to finally commit to taking the path of their own responsibility to a healthy and joyful life, regardless of the bumps along the way.

I am proud of Iden who celebrated a year of sobriety in October 2021. He continues to attend AA meetings, to keep his scheduled doctor's appointments, and to take his prescribed medicine daily. He still has bouts of depression but has not had any severe mania periods. Our relationship and his relationship with his daughters are in a good place now. He and I talk on a regular basis, and we try to keep a scheduled appointment for dinner at least once a month. It's good to have my friend back in my life.

Lizzy still plays a big role in her father's recovery. She visits him weekly delivering meals she has prepared and goes along with him to his psychiatrist appointments. She is working on getting out of the mindset that she can prevent a depression or maniac episode from happening.

Claudia has finally landed a job as a teaching assistant and for the first time seems to have found her niche. She told me that she finally understood the reason why I enjoyed teaching. She said, "It is a wonderful feeling to be around young children because they are so loving. The job allows me to feel like I can make a difference in their lives."

She is no longer dating Martin, but they still remain friends. Forming and maintaining meaningful relationships are still difficult for her to achieve. She is currently single and sees a therapist to work on her anxiety.

As for me I am also living alone while maintaining my relationship with Stephen. I am forever grateful for all the gifts he has given me. It took me a very long time to find my voice again. Expressing what I need and what I can allow in my life has given me much peace. Our family throughout the years has been on both sides of the seesaw, but we never let anyone fall off or come crashing down alone. Our love is strong, and we all know we will always be present in one another's lives, helping the best way we can to give support and understanding.

Patricia and Mimi, ©2021

ACKNOWLEDGEMENTS

With much appreciation and gratitude for all the following people who were each in their own way responsible for the publication of *See-Saw*.

To Iden — who had the courage to let me tell our story through my own words. I am so proud of you.

To Lizzy and Claudia — for their encouragement when I thought I couldn't continue.

To Joel — who is a wonderful partner to Lizzy, and who gives much love and support to help her find a balance between living her life and caring for her family.

To my brothers Mark and Ron – Ron for giving me confidence and believing my story had a voice that should be heard. To Mark for always being there and listening.

To Stephen — for our journey of healing, learning, and loving together. It has been a hell of a trip, but all so worth it! I would not have been able to go through the past years without you holding me up when I felt that I could no longer stand.

To Debbie — for all the walks, talks, and the sincere loving advice given, even when I didn't want to hear or accept it. You were always right! You are an amazing person and our friendship is a true gift.

To Yazmine — my patient neighbor, who taught me much-needed computer skills and helped me send my first drafted manuscript to my publisher.

To Hybrid Global Publishing — which gave me the opportunity to share my story. Thank you to Karen, Sara, and Jonathan and a special thanks to my editor, Dea, who spent countless hours and much love getting my book into print and teaching me valuable editing skills. I am forever grateful and wish you didn't live in Australia!

To the many doctors and nurses and psychiatric support team at Beth Israel Hospital, Elmhurst Hospital, Long Island Jewish Hospital, and to AA and NAMI. It takes hard work and the collaboration of all to start a person on the road to recovery and to continue on every day.

To my parents for giving me their all. I miss them every day.

And last but not least to my best friend, Mimi, who sat by my feet during countless hours of writing and editing while forgoing many daily walks and trips to the dog park to see her friends. She keeps hanging on because she knows I need her in my life.

I Love You All!

CPSIA information can be obtained
at www.ICGtesting.com
Printed in the USA
LVHW081755290322
714729LV00013BA/422

9 781957 013060

CPSIA information can be obtained
at www.ICGtesting.com
Printed in the USA
LVHW081755290322
714729LV00013BA/422